# *Glorious* DEFIANCE

# *Glorious* DEFIANCE

## DENNIS KARL

PARAGON HOUSE
*New York*

First edition, 1990

Published in the United States by

Paragon House
90 Fifth Avenue
New York, N.Y. 10011

Library of Congress Cataloging-in-Publication data

Karl, Dennis.
Glorious defiance : last stands throughout history / Dennis Karl.— 1st ed.
p.   cm.
ISBN 1-55778-029-3 : $22.95
1. Battles—History.   I. Title.
D25.K37   1990
904'.7—dc20                                                      90-31872
                                                                      CIP

Manufactured in the United States of America

10  9  8  7  6  5  4  3  2  1

The paper used in this publication meets the minimum requirements of
American National Standard for Information Sciences—
Permanence of Paper for Printed Library Materials, ANS1 Z39.48-1984.

*For Dorothy and my Mother and Father.*

# ACKNOWLEDGMENTS

INVALUABLE AID was extended to me by the New York Public Library and particularly through the use of the Frederic Lewis Allen Memorial Writers Room.

My wife Dorothy gave editorial assistance along with her unlimited forbearance and moral support. My friend William Schaefer provided essential research and cogent military arguments. Finally, my agent and friend Susan Lee Cohen gave the book its chance.

# CONTENTS

# INTRODUCTION

THE LAST STAND, in which an elite unit of soldiers with little chance of victory fights to the last man, is a much glorified yet little understood theme in military history. A last stand is a time and a place where an end is made. Whether made badly or well, fought intelligently or in ignorance, the last stand has the finality of death for those who stay the course. In military engagements there are always those who run, or are ordered to leave, or arrive too late, but the story of soldiers who fight a hopeless battle to the end continues to enflame the human spirit, and intrigue the student of history.

An elite unit or unique group fighting for their lives, but more importantly for a leader, a symbol, a cause—this is the essential definition of a last stand. Those who fight and die may be few or many, but all are united by determination and desperation.

Last stands have occurred throughout man's history of warfare, and this book will analyze last stands in battles from ancient Greece to Vietnam. A last stand may involve as few as several hundred men on one side versus a few thousand, or hundreds of thousands of men on both sides. The leaders involved could be relative unknowns (save for their part in these battles), or some of the most historically important figures ever to command. Though these battles vary greatly in scale, all have historical importance. Battles, by their nature, involve the exchange of power, the meetings of units of human force which result in victory, defeat and death. Yet often much more is at stake than a patch of ground, a narrow mountain pass or a single citadel. In fact, a seemingly futile and thus scarcely pre-planned event can nonetheless strategically affect the outcome of efforts by great imperial powers to either expand, consolidate, or simply retain their empires.

Strategically, a last stand might buy time for a subsequent, decisive battle to be fought elsewhere or for larger forces to gather to ensure victory. Tactically, it could hold down large forces that could be employed by the enemy in other areas, on other battlefields. And though soldiers cannot know for certain the symbolic effect a last stand might have, the glory of their actions cannot be ignored—it can often be so powerful that the myth of the stand can bring the final victory to the cause of those who died.

To understand the deaths of these men, one has to look carefully at the history of the period: why a campaign was undertaken and why those men came to be in that position at a given time. Only then can we fully appreciate their place in history.

At Chaeronea in 338 B.C., Philip II of Macedonia and his son Alexander (later "the Great") fought the last armies representing independent city-states in Greece. Athens, spurred on by the exhortations of the orator Demosthenes, opposed Philip, as did Thebes, led by their elite shock battalion, the "Sacred Band" of three hundred.

After the Athenians misread Macedonian intentions and committed themselves disastrously early, the allied line broke. Only the Sacred Band held their positions. The eighteen-year-old Alexander, leading his first major command, asked them to surrender. Valuing honor above life, the Sacred Band died under the hooves of Alexander's cavalry. The Macedonian Empire now included Greece and was free to attack the Persian Empire.

Nearly 150 years earlier Persia had attempted to conquer Greece. The Great King Xerxes ostensibly attacked Greece to punish Athens for its earlier support of a Greek colonists' rebellion on the coast of Asia Minor. But expanding his empire was also a major motivation.

The pass of Thermopylae on the northern coast of mainland Greece was garrisoned at first by 5,500 men from over ten city-states. Against this meager force Xerxes threw at least 300,000 and perhaps 500,000 men from over thirty-five nations of his empire. After five days a local shepherd betrayed a secret path around the pass. King Leonidas of Sparta dismissed most of the Greek force, remaining with his bodyguard in the pass while local Thespian soldiers manned the mountainside.

Attacked from both sides Leonidas and his three hundred men fought to the death, killing two brothers of the Great King in their fury. Time gained by the Spartans aided Themistocles of Athens, allowing him to gather an allied fleet that ultimately triumphed over the Persians at Salamis. Xerxes returned home, leaving his general Mardonius (who would lose the decisive battle at Plataea the following year) in charge. The Persian threat was over.

Within Greece itself, Athens and Sparta fought a thirty-year war for supremacy. In an attempt to break the deadlock and starve Sparta into submission, Athens mounted a massive expedition against Sicily, at that time (432–403 B.C.,) the breadbasket for Sparta and its allies. Failing to take the major city of Syracuse, Athens sent a second major army as reinforcement. Both armies were annihilated on the retreat from Syracuse. This disastrous defeat in the Sicilian Expedition ended Athenian designs of imperial expansion and led to Athens's final defeat.

Even the most formidable military empires have experienced last stands, and imperial Rome suffered important setbacks in the forests of northern Europe. Though a minor battle in 52 B.C., Aduatuca proved that native tribes could destroy a legion whose supreme commander was Julius Caesar. He, of course, would become in all but name the first Roman emperor. His successor, Augustus, became the first to bear the title. In 9 A.D., three of his legions (of a total of twenty-eight for the entire Empire) became entrapped through treachery in the wilds of the Teutoberger Forest in western Germany. The complete annihilation of these legions forced Emperor Augustus to halt all further plans for expansion into Germany, a decision that has affected history to this day.

The revolt of the Jewish people in 66 A.D. came at a time of political turmoil in Rome. Two years later, in 68 A.D., the Emperor Nero was compelled to commit suicide and was succeeded the next year by four generals—Galba, Otho, Vitellius, and the final victor, Vespasian. Emperor Vespasian, with his son Titus, reduced Jerusalem and destroyed the Zealots, leading to the "Diaspora" of the Jews. The hilltop citadel of Masada held out with a small garrison. Titus committed a legion in the desert for two years to secure the fortress. The law had to be forcefully reiterated: Rome could not tolerate rebellion anywhere; it would always be crushed as long as the Empire stood.

In 1066 A.D., William of Normandy sought to add the kingdom of England to his substantial holdings in northwestern France. English King Harold had other plans, but first he had to deal with the last great Viking invasion of England, in the north of the island. He scored a major victory and gave Harald Hardraada, the Viking leader, "six feet of earth and more"; the King then force-marched south to fight William and his coalition of knights. After a day-long battle Harold, his brothers and housecarles (men of his house) died in a shieldwall. England was thus joined to continental Europe and the foundation of the great modern state was laid.

The era of modern warfare began in the nineteenth century with the advent of revolutionary France and its awesome human product, Napoleon Bonaparte. Having fought six European coalitions and been exiled to the island of Elba, Napoleon returned in 1815 and formed a new army around his nucleus of veterans, the Guard. At Waterloo, British and allied troops managed to survive eight hours of intense pressure until reinforcements—the Prussian army—arrived. The Emperor was compelled to flee, but his Guard remained to cover the retreat. Offered a chance to surrender, the Guard's commander replied "Merde!" and the British artillery opened up at point-blank range. The First Empire, the Guard, and Napoleon's power disintegrated.

In 1836, one hundred eighty-three men gathered to fight for a chance at a fresh start in life. They and their families would have land of their own in an independent Texas, then affiliated with the United States. But the President of Mexico, General Santa Anna, would not countenance any affront to either the dignity or integrity of his country. The force garrisoned at The Alamo, bravely tying down the stubborn Santa Anna and his main army, gained thirteen days for Sam Houston to mastermind and position himself for a decisive victory at San Jacinto.

The year 1876 marked the centennial of the American Revolution. Ten days prior to July 4, two hundred and ten men of the U.S. Seventh Cavalry died fighting the Sioux and other Great Plains Indians at the battle of the Little Big Horn. Lt. Col. George Armstrong Custer, the youngest brevetted general (at the age of twenty-three) in the Civil War, employed what had proven a successful strategy many times before. At the battle of the Washita River, Custer divided his column into four parts, intending to converge from all sides. The strategy succeeded. (At the Little Big Horn there were also four columns, including pack train.) Tragically outnumbered and outgunned, the last stand (and subsequent annihilation) of ten companies of the Seventh Cavalry caused such a ferment in public opinion that the government committed full resources to the pacification and settlement on reservations—forcibly if necessary—of all native American Indian tribes.

Less than half a century ago, the greatest war in history ended. In Adolf Hitler's Germany, the capital city of Berlin was thought unreachable and invulnerable. Thus provisions to defend the capital of the "Thousand Year Reich" were deemed unnecessary. Waffen SS units from various countries, especially those of Scandinavia, Holland, France, and the Baltic states, held the city, along with teenagers and elderly Volkssturm (Home Guardsmen). Perhaps 200,000 able fighters attempted to defend Berlin from an onslaught of over a million and a half Red Army soldiers from the Soviet Union. The fall of the city simultaneously signalled the end of the Third Reich, Nazism and Hitler. The year was 1945.

At Dien Bien Phu the French colonial empire began to dissolve in 1954. Endeavoring to lure Ho Chi Minh's troops into a trap of French making, the high command sealed fifteen thousand of its own troops into a cul-de-sac from which there would be no escape. The French Foreign Legion and Paratroopers fought valiantly—and in vain—for fifty-five days, but no significant reinforcements ever came to their rescue. Each hill and bunker was contested to the end. When the smoke cleared and fighting ceased, France had retained only an obstreperous Algeria in its empire; it would lose that within a decade.

The events and historical significance of these eleven battles will be related in detail in the chapters that follow. And in a concluding essay I will analyze the similarities and contrasts that mark these engagements, as well as the various forms of loyalty that motivated legions of soldiers to make the ultimate sacrifice.

By necessity many battles have been omitted, but I have chosen representative battles, ancient and modern, with a variety of combatants, weaponry, and strategic and tactical situations, all of which are joined by the common theme of the last stand.

For documented citation, consult Selected Bibliographies.

*"Who the hell should care about saving his soul when it is a man's duty to lose it intelligently, the way you would sell a position you were defending, if you could not hold it, as expensively as possible, trying to make it the most expensive position that was ever sold. It isn't hard to die."*

—Ernest Hemingway

# 1

## THERMOPYLAE, 480 B.C.

*"Here fought and fell Megistias, hero brave,*
*Slain by the Medes, who crossed Spercheius' wave;*
*Well knew the seer his doom, but scorned to fly,*
*And rather chose with Sparta's king to die."*

*"Go stranger, and to Lacedaemon tell,*
*That here obeying her bequests, we fell."*

IN THE LATE SUMMER of 490 B.C., a fleet carried over fifty thousand Persian and allied soldiers to a beachhead in a bay northeast of Athens. The Great King of the Persian Empire, Darius, had decided that Athens must be punished for aiding the Greek colonies on the coast of Asia Minor which had dared to revolt against the "King of Kings."

Eretria, the small city-state which had provided just five ships to the colonists, was razed for its folly. Darius's punitive mission then turned toward his main objective, Athens. She had provided twenty ships to the colonists' fleet, and the Great King ordained she must also die. Athens sent the runner Phidippides to Sparta to seek aid. He delivered this message to the rulers of Sparta: "Lacedaemonians, the Athenians entreat you to send them help and not suffer a most ancient city of Hellas to be brought into bondage by foreigners; for even now Eretria has been enslaved, and Hellas is the weaker by the loss of a notable city." Citing religious custom the Spartans said they could not march until after the moon was full. Athens was effectively on its own.

Athens' army was recruited from the various demes, or precincts, of the city and its outlying suburbs. A general from each deme comprised its war council,

1

with each general commanding in rotation. When the Persians arrived Miltiades commanded the Athenian forces consisting of nine thousand heavy-armed Athenian hoplites and six hundred Plataeans. They marched to the plain of Marathon with the beach there encompassed by hills on one flank, swampy land on the other.

After several days of waiting in vain for Spartan reinforcements, Miltiades arrayed his forces. He positioned the Plataeans on the left flank and put his Athenians in strength on both the left and right flanks. The Athenian center was left relatively thin thus forming a crescent, with its horns backed by the hills and the sea. The center was unsecured. The Persian commander, Datis, acutely aware that the Athenians were awaiting reinforcements, ordered part of his fleet and army south to destroy Athens. He was confident the 25,000 men deployed at Marathon would defeat the Athenians and prevent their withdrawal to aid the city in time.

His hand forced, Miltiades ordered his men to advance first at a trot commencing a mile distant from the Persian line. The Athenians had the advantage of a slight downward slope which increased their momentum. The light-armed Persians were stunned by the impact of bronze-armored men striking their ranks at the dead run. When about a furlong separated the armies the Athenians came into arrow range. They therefore closed the gap as rapidly as possible to lessen casualties and increase their own momentum. The wings struck savagely and effectively; the center, only a few ranks deep, gave way.

As the horns of the crescent beat back the Persian levies the Greek center was at the point of being overwhelmed. The Persian flanks then broke and the Athenians wheeled in a pincer movement to save their men in the center. The maneuver had a devastating effect—the Persians were crushed. Six thousand four hundred Persians lay dead on the field; the Athenians had but 192 killed. The first Persian threat against the West had been routed by Athens. The playwright Aeschylus had but one thing inscribed on his gravestone: "I fought at Marathon."

The Athenians had won the battle by 9 A.M. Miltiades ordered a forced march in full armor back to Athens, racing the Persian fleet. The infantry won the race and assumed defensive positions. The Persians, seeing the futility of an attack, turned and sailed for Asia.

The Immortals crossed first. The elite of Persian and Median fighting men, their number was a constant ten thousand; if a man fell in battle or became ill he was immediately replaced so that there was no depletion in the ranks. The best-armed division in the Persian Empire, its mission was to guard the person of the Great King and provide his most powerful infantry attack unit in battle.

In 481 B.C., Xerxes, King of Kings, commanded the armies of thirty nations and fifty peoples to march against the city-states of Greece in a massive war of revenge and conquest. He intended to avenge his father Darius's defeat at Marathon nearly a decade ago and conquer Greece to match the deeds of his forebears. The Great King summoned an army so large that it could not be transported by sea and therefore ordered the Hellespont to be bridged. Two bridges were constructed by lashing hundreds of boats side by side. Over the boats earthen and wood roadways were laid. In the spring of 480 B.C., the infantry and cavalry crossed the northern bridge, near the Black Sea. Pack animals, the supply train, and servants and camp followers used the southern bridge.

The leading contingent of the ten thousand Immortals arrayed themselves in full panoply. Each man wore a long flowing robe sashed at the waist. The main weaponry was a seven-foot spear of very hard cornel wood, silver-bladed with the butt end formed of silver in the shape of a pomegranate. Of the ten thousand there was yet a most select group, the "One Thousand." Each had gilt-tipped spears with gilt pomegranates on the spike end and all were additionally armed with bow and arrow and short sword.

The Persian "Order of Battle" gives an idea of the extent of the imperial forces arrayed against Greece. The regular Persian division followed the Immortals. The men wore armor of fish-like iron scales approaching the protective quality of Greek armor. Over the mail came an embroidered tunic, baggy trousers beneath, with a soft felt cap. They bore light wicker shields, and fought with powerful bows and arrows of cane, short spears and daggers.

The Medes, second in importance of the nations of the Empire, were accoutered in the same fashion as the Persians. In fact, it had been the Median style first, for their people had originally ruled the imperial dominions until Cyrus the Great and his Persians had supplanted them in the previous century.

The Cissian division had marched from the head of the Persian Gulf, and was armed much the same as the Persian. The Hyrcanians, also in Persian style, came from the shores of the Caspian Sea. The Assyrians, whose empire not long before reigned supreme, wore bronze helmets and linen corselets. They carried shields, spears, daggers and wooden clubs studded with iron. Chaldeans, the ancient people, marched with the Assyrians.

From the Empire's eastern frontier came Bactrians bearing short spears and cane bows. The Sacae, a tribe of the Scythians, were from the extreme northeast. They wielded battle-axes, along with the bow and dagger. From the southeast edge of the Empire marched Indians dressed in cotton; their cane arrows were tipped with iron. The heart of the Empire sent Arian bowmen, along with Parthians, Chorasmians, Sogdians from the frontier, Gandarians and Dadicae.

The Caspian contingent wore leather jackets and fought with bow and sword. The Sarangians, in bright clothes and knee-high boots, carried bow and spear. The Utians and Myci, the Paricanians and the Pactyans, wore leather jackets and bore bow and dagger. The southwest of the Empire sent Arabians in flowing robes armed with the long bow. The warriors of the Ethiopian division came dressed in lion and leopard skins. They carried bows up to six feet in length and fired arrows tipped with finely-honed stone. Their spears had heads of antelope horn and they carried knotted wooden clubs. To prepare for battle the Ethiopians smeared their bodies half with chalk, half with vermilion.

Eastern Ethiopians fought as part of the Indian division. These warriors wore headdresses of horses' scalps with ears up and manes flowing. The Libyans wore leather clothing and used fire-hardened spears. Paphlagonians from the shores of the Black Sea had wicker helmets buttressed by small shields, short spears, javelins, and daggers. Similarly equipped were the Ligyans, Matieni, Mariandynians and Syrians. The Phrygians and Armenians followed, equipped in the same fashion.

The Lydians, being from the east coast of the Mediterranean, were accoutered in the Greek way. The Mysians had fire-hardened spears and small shields. Thracians from northeast Greece, the furthest point west where Xerxes held sway, wore fox skin headdresses and high fawn skin boots. They fought with javelin, shield and dagger.

The Milyans had spears, bows and leather helmets. The contingents of the Moschians, Tibareni, Macrones and the Mossynoeci all carried long-headed spears and shields. Marians wore plaited helmets and bore javelins; Colchians, short spears and swords, as did the Alarodians and the Saspires. Various exiles from the mainland who lived on islands in the Persian Gulf also sent a unit armed like the Medes.

The actual size of each division has long been a matter of dispute. Herodotus, the first true historian in Western history and the narrator of the history of the Persian Wars, placed the total Persian numbers at an impossibly high 1.7 million:

> The numbering was on this wise: Ten thousand men were collected in one place, and when they were packed together as closely as might be a line was drawn around them; this being drawn, the ten thousand were sent away, and a wall of stones built on the line reaching up to a man's middle; which done, others were brought into the walled space, till in this way all were numbered.

However, since the Immortals numbered ten thousand in their division, that figure seems reasonable and viable for a militarily flexible unit (approximately the size of light modern divisions). There were twenty-nine other divisions, some composed of a single nation's troops, others a combination of several. The Persian Empire used the decimal system, and if each division numbered ten thousand, the entire infantry force mustered for the invasion of Europe totaled 300,000. Considering that Xerxes' Empire stretched from the Mediterranean in the west to the Indus in the east, Libya and Egypt in the southwest to the mountains of the Hindu Kush in the northeast, the size of his land force is reasonable.

Accompanying the infantry were cavalry contingents from ten nations including chariot and camel units. The Persian squadrons were again preeminent, armed as was their infantry with bow, spear and short sword. Scale armor and sometimes bronze or iron helmets were worn. A Persian-speaking nomadic tribe called the Sagartians provided eight thousand men as part of the regular Persian cavalry division. The Sagartians fought with lasso and dagger; having snared an enemy they dispatched him with the dagger.

Most of the cavalry divisions were equipped similarly to their infantry. The Median and Cissian divisions were armed as the Persians were. The Indians, armed like their footmen, rode horseback or in chariots drawn by either horses or wild asses.

The Libyans drove chariots, and the Bactrians, Caspians and Paricanians rode horseback. The Arabians were mounted on camels, equal in speed to horses. The Arabians brought up the rear because horses could not endure the presence of camels. The total number of cavalry was put at eighty thousand.

The total Persian fleet including troop and horse transports numbered several thousand vessels. Of these, 1,207 were warships of the trireme class. Each carried a complement of at least two hundred, of which one-half to three-quarters were rowers aligned on three decks manning three banks of oars.

The Phoenicians and Syrians of Palestine contributed three hundred ships. Phoenician triremes differed from the classic Greek galley by having a slightly raised central deck that helped serve as a fighting platform for their marines, who were more numerous than the Greek on similar-sized ships. The marines were armed with bronze Greek-style helmets, plaited linen corselets, rimless shields and javelins.

Egypt sent a squadron of two hundred ships with marines wielding boarding-spears, heavy axes, and short swords. The Cyprians contributed 150 ships, the Pamphylians thirty, Dorian Greeks from Asia thirty, and the Ionian Greeks one hundred. All were equipped with Greek-type arm and armor.

The Cilicians sent one hundred ships; their men carried two javelins, short swords and rawhide shields. The Lycians, with bows of cornel wood, cane arrows and javelins, provided fifty ships. The Carians, also with fifty ships, fought with riphooks and daggers. The Aeolians sent sixty ships, the coastal islanders seventeen ships, and cities along the Hellespont and Bosphorus one hundred ships. The entire fleet carried Persian, Median, or Sacae marines in addition to their own complements. The fastest squadron, and thus the most powerful for ramming and maneuver, was the Phoenician. The city of Sidon produced its best unit.

One of the most famous commanders in the Persian fleet was a woman, Artemisia, ruler of Halicarnassus on the western coast of Asia Minor. She brought a small squad of five ships to the fleet—it being the most famous contingent after the Sidonese—and Xerxes held her strategic advice in high esteem. Counting transports and supply boats the entire fleet numbered around three thousand vessels. The land and sea forces gathered by Xerxes were greater than any previously unleashed against the West.

The Persian crusade arose out of the revolt by the Ionian colonies on the western coast of Asia Minor in 499 B.C. The cities were all Greek colonies founded over several preceding centuries by settlers from mainland Greece. In the latter half of the sixth century B.C., the colonies had been brought under the suzerainty of the Persian Empire. It had been founded in 550 B.C., when the Persian Cyrus the Great overthrew the ruling Medes and began to build the greatest empire of the time upon the ruins of Mesopotamia, Sumeria, Chaldea and Assyria.

After elevating himself to Great King, Cyrus advanced toward the Mediterranean intending to first reduce the kingdom of Lydia and its ruler Croesus. Croesus had been able to resist the Medes, but fell to Cyrus. Since the Greek colonies had been under the dominion of Lydia, they were now prey for Persia. Though its overlordship was not unbearable, for the colonies it was much less acceptable than that of Lydia. By October 539 B.C., Cyrus had subjugated Babylon and its own domains. Cyrus was now acknowledged "King of the world, legitimate king, king of Babylon, king of Sumer and Akkad, king of the four rims (of the world)."

Cambyses succeeded Cyrus as "King of Kings" in 530 B.C. He, too, pursued imperial acquisition adding Egypt (ancient even then) to the Persian Empire. In 522 B.C., Darius acceded to the throne. A decade later, he made the first major incursion into Europe from the East by bridging the Hellespont and bringing Thrace under Persian hegemony. A bridgehead in the West had been secured. The consequences of that foothold would, in an unforeseen way, help to set the foundations of Western civilization.*

Commencing in 500 B.C., the Ionian cities rose in revolt. Even with the marshalling of all their own forces the Greek cities of coastal Asia still had no hope of throwing off the Persian yoke. The colonists decided to appeal to their mother cities in Greece.

Only Athens and Eretria answered the request for aid. Athens sent twenty

---

* The invasions by Darius, and especially by Xerxes, helped to unify Greece in the long span. Though Athens, Sparta and then Thebes contested for Greek hegemony, it was Macedon under Alexander the Great which would finally prevail. The spread of Hellenic and thus Western civilization laid the groundwork for the Roman Empire and all of Western Europe.

triremes and crews, Eretria five to aid the Ionians. Even so, the colonists fought off the forces of Persia for six years, finally surrendering in 494 B.C. Four years later the first Persian attempt at vengeance ended at Marathon. Planning and implementating a second invasion of Greece were interrupted by two events. Darius the Great died in 486 B.C., having failed to destroy Athens. His son Xerxes became King of Kings and planned to complete his father's mission against Athens and Greece. In 484 B.C., however, Egypt rebelled against the Empire and diverted Xerxes' attention. It took two years to pacify the province. By 482–481 B.C., Xerxes was ready to mobilize his Empire. He set as his first task the destruction of Athens.

Other impulses also drove Xerxes. Addressing his counselors (the following quotes are from Herodotus) he first expressed his duty to his father, saying, "I therefore on his behalf, and for the benefit of all my subjects, will not rest until I have taken Athens and burnt it to the ground in revenge for the injury which the Athenians without provocation once did to me and my father." Xerxes was doubtless aware, too, of the deeds of his predecessors who, beginning with Cyrus the Great, had formed a huge empire in only seventy years. Xerxes yearned to match, and exceed, their conquests.

"If we crush the Athenians and their neighbors in the Peloponnese, we shall so extend the empire of Persia that its boundaries will be God's own sky, so that the sun will not look down upon any land beyond the boundary of what is ours. With your help I shall pass through Europe from end to end and make it all one country," he proclaimed.

Of all his counselors the chief non-Persian was the exiled Spartan King Demaratus. Sparta traditionally had two kings ruling at one time. One would administer at home with the advice of the ephors, or elders; the second led the army in the field in time of war, a frequent occurrence for Sparta.

King Demaratus lost his throne after being deposed in an internal political struggle following the crushing of the Ionian revolt in 494 B.C. He later took refuge at the Persian court, acting first as adviser to Darius, and then to Xerxes on matters concerning the Greeks. As he mustered his vast army, Xerxes questioned Demaratus as to whether the Greeks would offer him battle, for "My own belief is that all the Greeks and all the other western peoples gathered together would be insufficient to withstand the attack of my army— and still more so if they are not united."

Demaratus replied that the Spartans "will not under any circumstances accept terms from you which would mean slavery for Greece; secondly, they will fight you even if the rest of Greece submits. Moreover, there is no use in asking if their numbers are adequate to enable them to do this; suppose a thousand of them take the field—then that thousand will fight you; and so will any number, greater than this or less."

Xerxes doubtless disliked the Spartan's answer, and continued to reject their will to oppose his power. Demaratus reiterated that, "fighting singly, they are as good as any, but fighting together they are the best soldiers in the world.

"They are free—yes—but not entirely free; for they have a master, and the master is Law, which they fear much more than your subjects fear you. Whatever this master commands, they do, and his command never varies: it is never to retreat in battle, however great the odds, but always to stand firm, and to conquer or die."

The Great King laughed at Demaratus's suggestion of Spartan defiance and continued his preparations. The size of the Persian army and its everyday need for vast amounts of supplies made close cooperation with the fleet essential. It would hug the coastline, sailing not far offshore. The army, meanwhile, would march down the coast. Aside from the necessity of receiving seaborne supplies, the broken and mountainous countryside of Greece made it practically impossible to march such a large force south by any way other than the coastal route.

Xerxes' grand strategy was to proceed south through the sparsely-settled lands of Thrace and Macedonia. Passing by Mt. Olympus the Persian army would descend into the plains of Thessaly and conquer the cities there. The major objective, Athens, would then be open to destruction. If all went as planned in taking Athens the conquest of mainland Greece would, in essence, be complete. Sparta, Corinth, and the rest of the Peloponnesus could then be cut off and taken by storm, from land and sea. The remainder of the West would follow if resources, circumstances and will allowed. Xerxes would have far surpassed his great-grandfather Cyrus in empire-building.

As the massive expedition began its march south the envoys which the Great King had sent to the city-states of Greece returned. The emissaries had demanded "earth and water" from the Greeks, the giving of which would symbolize their submission to Xerxes.

At least ten states sent tokens. "Against all of these the Greeks who declared war with the foreigner entered into a sworn agreement, which was this: that if they should be victorious they would offer to the god of Delphi a tenth of the possessions of all Greeks who had of free will surrendered themselves to the Persians."

Xerxes did not send envoys to Athens and Sparta. He omitted them because his father Darius had sent the same demand before his failed invasion of 490 B.C. The Athenians "had given earth" to the Persian emissaries by throwing them into the 'Pit' where criminals condemned to death were put. The Spartans had tossed theirs into a well. Xerxes decided not to bother to ask again.

The Greeks realized upon first knowledge of Xerxes' expedition that the Persian advance would perforce be along the coast with the fleet in cooperation. Accordingly, a conference of all the Greek city-states that had not given earth and water met at the Isthmus of Corinth while Xerxes was still mustering his armies.

Three major defensive positions in Greece could be held by numerically inferior forces. The Vale of Tempe was south of Mt. Olympus. A rocky defile which fed into the plains of Thessaly, Tempe was a position thought defensible for some time given a solid force of hoplites to defend it. Further to the south of Tempe was the Pass of Thermopylae, an extremely narrow gorge between high rocky cliffs and the sea. At its center the pass was fifty feet across. Thermopylae presented the last position at which greatly outnumbered forces could hold out in an ultimate defense of Athens, the main Persian target, and the free remnant of mainland Greece.

The third and best defensive zone was the Isthmus of Corinth, the narrow neck of land which joined the Peloponnese to the mainland. With sufficient naval support to prevent encirclement, the Isthmus could be held even against overwhelming Persian numbers. The major drawback with the Isthmus as the Greek defensive point, of course, was that Athens would be burnt and all of northern Greece enslaved before the Persians reached it.

The chief strategist was Themistocles, leader of the Athenian force at Tempe and a commander ten years before at Marathon. He, and others, saw that the defile at Tempe could be bypassed by two passes further west. If the position was turned it would mean the loss of ten thousand heavy-armed men, and an equal number of light-armed infantry, with no real tactical gain.

Themistocles instead heeded the words of the oracle at Delphi, to which Athens had sent petitioners. They hoped to find the answer to the city's crisis. The priestess gave this oracle:

> *Yet shall a wood-built wall by Zeus all-seeing be granted*
> *Unto the Trito-born, a stronghold for thee and thy children*
> *Bide not still in thy place for the host that cometh from landward,*
> *Cometh with horsemen and foot; but withdraw at his coming,*
> *Turning thy back to the foe;*
> *    thou shalt yet meet him in battle.*
> *Salamis, isle divine!* . . . .

Though many took the "wooden wall" to mean the ramparts around the Acropolis of Athens, Themistocles believed it meant the Greek fleet, with the Athenian contingent being the strongest by far.

After only a few days at the Vale of Tempe, the Greek army abandoned the site. The chief commanders belatedly realized that with two parallel passes unguarded, Tempe was untenable.

Thermopylae now became the center of the Greek defense. The pass lay sheltered in a bay across from the island of Euboea, which stretches one hundred miles on a line roughly parallel to that which could be drawn from Thermopylae to Athens. The waters were narrow between the mainland and Euboea, and it was Themistocles' hope and intention to draw the huge Persian fleet into the channel where its numbers would be ineffective, even detrimental.

Opposing upwards of one thousand galleys the Persians could throw into a fight the Greeks could counter with three hundred ships at best, half of which were Athenian. Themistocles' strategy proved sound: the Persian fleet, sailing in the narrows, could not bring its numbers to bear, just as the land army could not do at first at Thermopylae.

When the decision was made to confront the Persians at Thermopylae, the leaders of the Greek city-states turned to Sparta. While the Athenians alone had been able to crush a relatively small Persian army at Marathon a decade earlier, more than ten times their number were marching south toward Athens, and eventually on to Sparta in the Peloponnese.

The conference designated King Leonidas of Sparta to command the Greek garrison that would be placed at Thermopylae. Once again the Spartans cited their religious piety for not sending all their forces north. They had to celebrate the feast of the Carneia, which fell in early September, a month hence.

Themistocles and other Greek leaders suspected that the Spartans planned to hold back their main force to defend the Isthmus of Corinth, essentially leaving the mainland to fend for itself. But Leonidas was a man of honor, according to family tradition the descendant of Hercules, and he would not allow his or Sparta's loyalty to the freedom of Greece to be questioned. He therefore determined to display Sparta's commitment by marching north with his royal bodyguard of three hundred men.

The King and his three hundred men were joined by 2,800 other hoplites from the Peloponnese. Five hundred men each came from Mantinea and Tegea. Arcadia, long a state that had produced mercenaries, sent 1,120 troops. The trading capital of Corinth sent four hundred men, Phlius two hundred, and Mycenae, the ancient citadel of Agamemnon, eighty men.

On the mainland Athens had its fighting men either in the fleet on its 150 ships, or manning the walls of the city itself. Seven hundred Thespians joined the force, along with four hundred Thebans. A thousand Phocians, in whose region Thermopylae lay, also came. In all, Leonidas could count somewhat over six thousand heavy-armed hoplites to hold his pass. The odds at that point were only fifty to one; it would get much worse.

The Phocians and Locrians were most in danger of reprisals for joining the allied force. Other Greeks sought to reassure them by saying their force was the advance guard, with full reinforcements to come, and that the fleet led by the Athenians would hold the flank in the Euboean channel.

According to the oracle at Delphi, "There was nought for them to fear; for the invader of Hellas was no god, but a mortal man, and there was no mortal, nor ever would be, to whom at birth some admixture of misfortune was not allotted; the greater the man, the greater the misfortune; most surely then he that marched against them, being but mortal, would be disappointed of his hope."

The Spartans had also sought counsel from the Oracle at Delphi concerning the war. The Pythian priestess predicted an unfortunate outcome:

*Fated it is for you, ye dwellers in wide-wayed Sparta,*
*Either your city must fall, that now is mighty and famous,*
*Wasted by Persian men, or the watcher of fair Lacedaemon.*
*Mourn for a king that is dead, from Heracles' line descended.*
*Yea, for the foe thou hast nor bulls nor lions can conquer;*
*Mighty he cometh as Zeus, and shall not be stayed in his coming;*
*One of the two will he take, and rend his quarry asunder.*

King Leonidas knew of the prophecy before he marched: that either a Spartan king or Sparta herself must fall. His men presumably knew it also; it did not matter to them.

Upon reaching the pass of Thermopylae, Leonidas began to make his dispositions. The Spartans would take the foremost position in the pass, and would be the first to receive the Persian army's attacks.

Not even battalion strength in numbers, Leonidas's men nevertheless would atone for Sparta's failure to help at Marathon, and for sending only a token force against this second Persian invasion. A token, but Leonidas was determined that their token would leave an example for all who would ever fight for freedom.

The Spartans fought in platoon-sized units, called enomotia. In combat phalanx formation, each enomotia would form six files wide, six ranks deep. Every man wore a heavy bronze cuirass over his chest and back, and bronze greaves to protect his lower legs. A full bronze helmet shielded his head. Each man carried an eight-foot hardwood spear, short thrusting sword, and bronze-faced shield.

With a fifty-foot front to hold at the center of the pass, three enomotias could form up, shield-to-shield, with a yard of front per man. A man killed or wounded seriously enough to leave the line could be easily replaced from the rear.

The Spartan and Greek allies arrived at Thermopylae in the second week of August, 480 B.C. The main body of the Persian army camped within striking distance of the Greeks by August 12. For the next three days the Persians remained inactive whereupon a scout was dispatched to observe the Spartans. He found "some of the men at exercise, and others combing their hair (the

Spartans wore their hair shoulder-length). Marvelling at the sight, and taking exact note of their numbers, he rode back unmolested, none pursuing nor at all regarding him."

Herodotus continued on to say of the Greeks, "Yet the bravest of them all was Dieneces, a Spartan, of whom a certain saying is reported: before they joined battle with the Medes, it was told Dieneces by a certain Trachinian that the enemies were so many, that when they shot with their bows the sun was hidden by the multitude of arrows; whereby being no whit dismayed, but making light of the multitude of the Medes, 'Our friend from Trachis brings us right good news, for if the Medes hide the sun we shall fight them in the shade and not in the sunshine.' "

The fifth day after the Persians arrived the Great King decided to act. Xerxes ordered the divisions of the Medes and Cissians to assault the pass with an added exhortation to take the Greeks alive to be brought before him. The Medes attacked ferociously for hours attempting to force the pass. However, "they made it plain to all and chiefly to the king himself that for all their number of human creatures there were few men among them."

Xerxes now dispatched the imperial guard. All thought that "they at least would make short and easy work of the Greeks." The Immortals, in their first attack, fared no better than the Medes. The toll of Persian casualties was many times that of the Greeks. Such was Xerxes' fear that the repulsion of his crack troops would cause his subject nations to panic that, "During these onsets the king thrice sprang up in fear for his army from his throne where he sat to view them."

On the second day of fighting each Greek city-state present took its turn in the pass to spell the Spartans. After each onslaught was repulsed another city's men took the post of honor. For a second day six thousand Greeks had held off over 300,000 troops of the Persian Empire. But as often happened in Greek tragedy a traitor appeared.

A native of the area, Epialtes, gave the King of Kings his "winning opportunity." He went to the king seeking a reward for disclosing the location of a mountain path which circumvented Thermopylae and could be used to place a force to the rear of the Greek army.

The Persian incursion over the saddle of the mountains had one Greek contingent to contend with. Since the Phocians were from the area, Leonidas had them posted on the highest approach road. The Immortals approached at dawn; their commander Hydarnes feared that "the Phocians might be Lacedaemonians, and asked Epialtes of what country they were." Having discovered their identity Hydarnes prepared his men to attack with arrows. The Phocians, meanwhile, believed that they were the focus of the Persian elite's attack, and they "fled away up to the top of the mountain and prepared there to perish." Hydarnes, advised by Epialtes, ignored the Phocians and descended the path leading to the rear of the Greek army.

"The Greeks at Thermopylae were warned first by Megistias the seer, who, having examined the offerings, advised them of the death that awaited them in the morning." The Greek leaders then held council with opinion divided between holding to their post, no matter what the outcome, or heading back to their various city-states to prepare for their defense, or the defense of the Peloponnese at the Isthmus of Corinth. Athens, of course, would die.

Leonidas decided to keep only the soldiers from nearby Thespia and Thebes as part of his doomed garrison. The Thespians "remained with great goodwill. They refused to depart and leave Leonidas and his comrades, but remained there and died with him." The Persians, including the Immortals, were ready to attack between 10–11 A.M.

"The Greeks with Leonidas, knowing that they went to their death, advanced now much farther than before into the wider part of the strait. For ere now it was the wall of defense that they had guarded, and all the former days they had withdrawn themselves into the narrow way and fought there.

"But now they met their enemies outside the narrows, and many of the foreigners were there slain; for their captains came behind the companies with scourges and drove all the men forward with lashes. Many of them were thrust into the sea and there drowned, and more by far were trodden down bodily by each other, none regarding who it was that perished; for inasmuch as the Greeks knew that they must die by the hands of those who came around the mountain, they put forth the very utmost of their strength against the foreigners, in their recklessness and frenzy."

The Spartans were now fighting with swords, their spears having broken. They fought with their short swords, and Leonidas fell. Two brothers of Xerxes died fighting over the body of Leonidas. "There was a great struggle between the Persians and Lacedaemonians over Leonidas's body, till the Greeks of their valour dragged it away and four times put their enemies to flight."

The Spartans carried the body of their king to a hillock in the mouth of the pass. "In that place they defended themselves with their swords, as many as yet had such, ay and with fists and teeth; till the foreigners overwhelmed them with missile weapons, some attacking them in front and throwing down the wall of defense, and others standing around them in a ring."

---

King Leonidas and his royal bodyguard of three hundred men had fulfilled their appointed task. At the cost of every life they had held the pass at Thermopylae for seven days, and took twenty Persians for every one of their own dead including two brothers of the Great King Xerxes.

Themistocles, both general and admiral of Athens, had put those seven days to particularly good tactical use. He had argued that if the Persian army could be held in one of the northern passes of Greece, enough time could be gained thereby to prepare the Athenian-led fleet to attack and cripple the Persian support armada in the waters off Attica, the home state of Athens.

Under Themistocles' leadership a strong fleet of over 370 triremes had been gathered. Against this force the Persians would deploy over one thousand ships. To turn the enemy's own numerical superiority against him, Themistocles drew the enemy into a relatively narrow cul-de-sac off the coast of Athens. Forced to fight in such waters the Persian numbers proved useless. Outmaneuvered and outfought, the Persian fleet's losses were in the hundreds of ships; the Greeks lost only twenty galleys.

Following this naval disaster Xerxes decided he must retreat to his Asian strongholds before the bridges he had constructed across the Hellespont were destroyed by the Greeks, trapping all of his armies in Europe. He left behind his chief general, Mardonius, with 200,000 men.

Scarcely one year after Thermopylae and Salamis, Mardonius was brought to bay by a finally-united Greek army. Inspired by the examples of the three hundred Spartans, and emboldened by the ensuing naval victory at Salamis, the city-states raised an army of 100,000 men. In late September of 479 B.C., King Pausanias of Sparta crushed Mardonius and the Persians at Plataea, a plain northwest of Athens. The Greeks gave no quarter: only three thousand of the Persians escaped.

The freedom of the West had been saved, but if Leonidas and his three hundred men had not stood until the end in that small pass at Thermopylae, outnumbered one thousand to one, Eastern tyranny might well have submerged the embryonic democracy developing in the West.

Greek unity defeated the Persian Empire's thrust at the West and led to a fifty-year period during which Athens led the way to the modern western world in the fields of philosophy, science, architecture, the arts, and political science. Leonidas and his guard helped make it possible.

# 2

# THE SICILIAN EXPEDITION, 415–413 B.C.

### PROLOGUE:

On the night of June 6, 415 B.C., a band of vandals attacked and desecrated the Hermae, the statues of the household gods of Athens. This act was tantamount to burning the crosses of Rome before the First Crusade set out, for the Athenian Empire was on the verge of the greatest, and most disastrous, expedition it was ever to undertake, the Sicilian. The magnificent and absolute failure of this campaign was to help determine the course of Western history in the succeeding centuries.

IT WAS THE seventeenth year of the great war between Athens and Sparta for the hegemony of Greece. Alarmed by the growth of the power of the Athenian Empire, Sparta and her allies in the Peloponnesian League in 431 B.C., had renewed in earnest a conflict which had proceeded spasmodically. It was due to victory by the Greeks, albeit in their one moment of unity, over the mighty Persian Empire in 479 B.C., a triumph effected by the combination of Athenian naval power and Spartan land power, each of which was vastly superior to the other in its chosen arm.

The marked preeminence of the rivals in their martial specializations led directly to the basic strategies employed in the first decade of their war. Each year in late spring at the beginning of the campaigning season, Sparta and her allies marched north across the Isthmus of Corinth and invaded Attica, the farming region around Athens. The invading force always had two objectives

15

in mind: luring the Athenians into a pitched battle and almost certain defeat, and ravaging the country estates while burning crops.

In response, the strategy of Athens (initiated by Pericles in 431 B.C.) was to withdraw behind the Long Walls of the city and avoid any major land confrontation with the superior Peloponnesian forces. At the same time naval expeditions were mounted which sailed to various points on the Spartan homeland of the Peloponnese, landing the heavily-armed hoplites who ravaged that countryside in turn. The result of these exchanges (besides the necessity of increased grain imports for both sides) was a virtual stalemate.

In 421 B.C., the Peace of Nicias was negotiated which provided much needed respite to the war-weary parties. The truce was nominally still in effect in 415 B.C. although the intervening years had resulted in reciprocal testing of each other's weak spots through the use of surrogates, their respective allies. Clearly a major new strategy was needed to break the deadlock, and it was now provided by the brilliant and arrogant Alcibiades, a former pupil of Socrates and one of Athens's chief generals. He was a man of overweening ambition who gloried in thinking on a grand strategic scale. The plan which he envisioned involved nothing less than the conquest of the entire west Mediterranean basin.

Alcibiades planned to sail first to Sicily and conquer it, then to proceed north up the Italian peninsula, subduing all in his path (including a minor city-state named Rome), and finally sail to Carthage and reduce that empire. Those grand designs were merely a prologue, however, for in the event of all or most of this scheme succeeding, Alcibiades planned to form a great new army using manpower provided by the Greek city-states he had subdued in Sicily and Magna Graecia (the boot of Italy). Planning to pay them with his newly-won resources while hiring the best barbarian fighters as mercenaries, he would transport them in the vast fleet to be constructed from the timber found in Italy.

The ultimate purpose of this enormous army and armada would be the subjugation of Sparta and the Peloponnesus through a blockade by sea and the investment and assault of the cities on land, culminating in the rule of the entire Hellenic name (and most of the Mediterranean) by Athens—and Alcibiades. He believed wholeheartedly that if they stopped ruling others, they would be in danger of being ruled.

Sicily, the primary objective of the expedition, was the food basket for the Dorian city-states of the Peloponnese. Elimination of this source would cause great hardship for several of Sparta's allies, though she herself would suffer less given her possession of the fertile plains of Laconia and Messenia (worked by her serf helots).

The Athenians, for the most part, were ignorant of the size and population of Sicily and that the campaign they were planning to undertake there was not much inferior to the war already underway against the Peloponnesians. Syracuse, Sicily's dominant city, was comparable to Athens in size and resources. At the time of the siege she could send eight thousand heavy-armed hoplites into battle along with 1,200 horse and an appropriate number of lightly-armed men. The number of cavalry she possessed were to be of great advantage, for though her hoplites were inferior to the Athenians and their allies from Argos, in battle retreating foot-soldiers can almost always be covered by superior cavalry. This would prove to be true.

The whole Sicilian fleet numbered eighty ships, second in number and quality to Athens. The Syracusan economy was strong, with a brisk trade existing with the commercial giant (and mother city) Corinth. The distance from Syracuse to Athens aided the defenders because of the time delay involved in bringing to bear Athenian reserves of both men and money, while the physical location of Syracuse was itself advantageous: the "old city" was situated on a nearly impregnable island in the harbor while the mainland sections had been built to gain security from the local cliffs and swampy areas. The Syracusans were at first incredulous about the rumored Athenian expedition, but after an initial panic realized the truth. Henceforth, a determination grew in them to resist Athenian domination. Their leader was Hermocrates, a nobleman and a very able statesman and orator who would become the savior of his city and the island.

The Athenians, on the other hand, were to be crippled in their decision-making by their utilization of three generals in joint command of the Sicilian Expedition. In 416 B.C., ambassadors from the Hellenized city of Egesta in Sicily arrived in Athens to seek help against the Dorian city of Selinus. The Egestaens pointed out to the Athenian Assembly that if they were themselves defeated and the Syracusans remained unpunished after vanquishing Athenian allies, then their power would grow to consume the whole island.

Alcibiades immediately took advantage of the situation to propose a great expedition to subdue Sicily completely, but kept the rest of his grand strategic plan of conquering the Mediterranean to himself. The senior general, Nicias, concerned himself with more immediate matters, namely that Sicily was so far away that if taken, it would be too hard to hold on to, and that the sheer numbers of the Sicels might be too great to handle anyway. The distance also provided misgivings about his supply lines, as did the severe shortage of cavalry.

All of Nicias's objections received short shrift, however, from Alcibiades. The rivalry between the two generals went back to the younger Alcibiades' earliest political days, and reflected the juxtaposed forces arrayed on the Athenian domestic political scene over the Sicilian issue. Nicias represented Athens's older generation—a defensive strategist at heart who was over-cautious and slow to take the initiative. His supporters included the wealthy

large landholders and small farmers and other refugees from Attica who
wanted peace to restore their farms, a peace he had given them in 421 B.C.
Others who opposed the expedition at first were many of the priests of the
temples, whom Alcibiades countered with his own priests. Socrates, and the
playwrights Aristophanes and Euripides also objected to the expedition on
moral grounds.

Alcibiades's peculiar blend of brilliant statesmanship, boundless ambition,
and reckless courage in his public life combined with his ostentatious and
insolent life-style to attract many by his magnetism who didn't particularly like
his policies. Nonetheless, he had a naturally large constituency, for the younger generation tended to support his adventurous gambles. His main bloc of
votes, however, came from the thetes, or lower class citizens. They universally
supported foreign expeditions because of the pay they would receive laboring
as rowers in the fleet (and perhaps as marines), and the future prosperity
promised by the extension of the Empire. Demagogues like Demostratus
helped engender support for Alcibiades's policies with the middle class craftsmen, artisans (especially armorers) and merchants all supporting the expedition for business reasons.

The great majority of the Assembly clamored for the expedition; the dis-
senting minority kept silent lest they appear unpatriotic. Three commanders
were voted for the expedition: Alcibiades, Nicias and Lamachus. Everyone in
the Assembly thought it wise to limit Alcibiades's complete freedom by
tempering it with Nicias's caution, while balancing them both with the forthright old soldier Lamachus. Nicias made one more attempt to stop the expedition. With the Assembly having voted sixty ships, Nicias demurred, stating
that Athens itself should supply one hundred ships, plus allies, and a large land
force. To his surprise, the Assembly agreed with him and authorized the
generals to ask for everything they deemed necessary.

Athens by 415 B.C., had recovered from the great plague of 430–429 B.C.
(which had taken nearly one-third the population, including Pericles), and
from the first decade of fighting, by means of the Peace of Nicias. A large
number of young men had grown up to fill out the rolls and a store of capital
had been accumulated. The annual income of the Athenian Empire amounted
to 1,200 talents (approximately $200 million today) for a city-state of
250,000 people. (One talent = 36,000 obols; subsistence level in Attica at this
time was three obols a day). The total treasury might have been as high as
seven thousand talents; it was at least five thousand talents, however, for three
thousand talents were allotted for the expedition outright, with one thousand
in reserve; another one thousand would be needed for government operating
expenses.

Even though large numbers of troops were needed to defend the Long
Walls and garrison the outposts of the Athenian Empire, 1,500 hoplites were

produced from the enlistment rolls, along with seven hundred thetes, members of the lower class shipped along as marines. There were 2,900 allied hoplites, along with five hundred Argives, serving only because Alcibiades was commanding. The best mercenaries of the period were represented by 250 Mantineans who likewise deemed it a privilege to serve with him. The lightly-armed men were all specialty soldiers, 480 archers (eighty Cretan) and seven hundred Rhodians—the best of slingers (using leather thongs and lead 'bullets', a slinger could kill a man at a hundred yards). There were also 120 lightly-armed exiles from Megara.

All in all, the foot soldiers were crack troops, easily a match for the Sicilian forces at the outset. The only serious deficiency was in the mounted force—Athens could send but one horse transport with thirty horses, the upshot being a cavalry mismatch of forty to one in favor of the Syracusans and the reason why early Athenian victories couldn't be capitalized on.

The Peloponnesian War brought with it the introduction of a 'mixed-arms' concept to Greek warfare. The standard Greek army prior to that war consisted of a solid hoplite line, each man heavily armed in a bronze helmet, cuirass (chestplate), and greaves (leggings). Hoplites carried a bronze, wood and leathern shield, and wielded a two-foot short sword and eight-foot thrusting spear. The inexorable rush of a hoplite line could be devastating to a lighter-armed or less-disciplined enemy, as was the case with the Athenians versus the Persians at Marathon.

Each hoplite's shield overlapped his neighbor's unprotected spear side, as his other neighbor's did in turn. Thus, the post of honor was traditionally on the right flank, and occasionally if cavalry were available they would be stationed on each flank to harass the enemy and prevent encirclement. A third arm now began to be utilized, the lightly-armed footman. These troops were originally almost all mercenaries but their ranks soon were to include citizen-soldiers.

There were no shortcomings in the fleet. It consisted of 134 galleys in all—one hundred Athenian ships, and thirty-four from the island of Chios and allied Ionian cities on the coast of Asia Minor. Each galley carried a complement of 170 rowers and thirty well-armed fighting marines. The Syracusan fleet was clearly the inferior in this arm. To provision the Greek armada there were thirty large supply ships carrying grain, weapons, and siege equipment, along with one hundred smaller supply boats, and a number of merchant trading vessels. This fleet was the largest to sail the Mediterranean Sea since the great attempt upon the West by Xerxes in 480 B.C.

The unchallengeable supremacy of their navy enabled the Athenians to overlook the physical distance between Syracuse and Athens, making it seem less of a disadvantage to them than the Syracusans would think. The campaign was planned to begin just before the height of the fighting season, in midsummer, so that if a quick decision was sought it could be had in good weather. Should none be gained there would still be time to firmly establish a fortified base of operations before winter set in. The fact that Nicias was a skilled engineer also aided Athenian prospects in a campaign that might well be decided by siege.

On June 7, 415 B.C., Athens awoke to find the sacrilege of the Hermae. To a people whose daily life, political and social, was closely intertwined with their belief in gods the ominous nature of the event was evident. Nevertheless it was ignored, and all physical preparations were soon complete for the armada. Assigning blame for the crime was not ignored, however, and soon the city was rife with rumor spread by Alcibiades's enemies that Athens preeminent general, along with his arrogant and drunken young entourage, were responsible.

Alcibiades demanded an immediate trial to clear his name before the expedition sailed. His conservative enemies led by Theramenes had most likely rigged these charges yet were successful in outmaneuvering him in his demand for vindication before sailing. They hoped to recall him later and execute him while fifty thousand of his supporters were engaged in Sicily.

And so, with capital charges of profanation of the Mysteries hanging over the chief general of the commanding triumvirate the vast Athenian armada sailed for Sicily in late June, 415 B.C. Aside from the perverse intent of some Athenians in attempting to remove the catalyst behind the expedition (Alcibiades) just as it was getting underway, the main obstacle to the success of the campaign was in the allocation of responsibility for the implementation of the plan: the appointing of the generals. Each of the three had his own strategic plan, differing significantly from the others: Lamachus wanted to sail forthwith to Syracuse and fight for a decision immediately; Alcibiades wanted to gain more allies in the other cities and then proceed with increased strength to reduce Syracuse; Nicias wanted to settle matters for the Egestaeans, then sail about Sicily showing the flag and return home. The result was confusion and muddled purpose.

Though the Lamachus plan was the most forthright, and possibly the soundest of the three, he eventually sided with Alcibiades and together the two outvoted Nicias. In consequence the campaigning season of the summer and fall of 415 B.C., was spent sailing up and down the coast of Sicily, seeking allies and especially a good port to use as a base of operations.

Rhegium, a city on the toe of the Italian peninsula, had allowed Athens to operate from there at the time of a smaller expedition during the 420's B.C., but this time remained neutral. Many other Greek city-states on the island of Sicily followed suit, and the opportunity to land a decisive blow in 415 B.C., with troops fresh, well-supplied and high-spirited passed.

Meanwhile, Alcibiades's enemies among the oligarchy had been active in

Athens. With a large number of the middle and lower classes serving in the army and navy in Sicily, wealthy conservatives had been able to pass a motion to recall Alcibiades to stand trial on charges attested to by paid informers. The state galley, the Salaminia, was therefore dispatched (by vote of the Assembly) to retrieve Alcibiades.

Fearing a mutiny among the great armada, the crew of the Salaminia had been ordered to proceed carefully but Alcibiades offered no resistance, nor did he try to incite any. Instead he promised to follow the state galley in his own. Somewhere off the coast of southern Italy Alcibiades gave them the slip. He next appeared publicly in Sparta. With most of his supporters in Sicily and facing almost certain conviction and execution in Athens, Alcibiades had defected. The greatest Athenian general of his age had been ousted politically from the greatest Greek military expedition in history.

Nicias, as the stronger of the remaining two generals, was now in command. A military conservative and expert in siege warfare, Nicias realized that the expedition must finally achieve a beachhead within striking range of the principal city Syracuse. Through a ruse utilizing an agent, Nicias convinced the Syracusans that the Athenians could be caught off-guard by a forced march north to the coastal city of Catana, where the Athenians had forcefully set up camp as their base of operations.

The plan worked. The Syracusan army left the city garrisoned by their Sicilian allies and headed for Catana, forty miles north. The next day the Athenians sailed into the Great Harbor of Syracuse and secured a beachhead. The Syracusans soon realized they had been tricked, however, and marched back to force the issue in open battle.

But Nicias, meanwhile, had drawn up the fleet, built a stockade and camp, and aligned his troops in order of battle. Arrayed on the south bank of the Anapus River, southwest of Syracuse, the Athenians held the center in a standard phalanx, or dense shield-to-shield formation, eight ranks deep. The Argives and the Mantineans held the right flank and the other allies the left. Nicias used only half of his troops in these dispositions, keeping the other half behind the line arranged three deep in a hollow square with civilians and supplies inside.

Opposing the Athenians, the Syracusans deployed their entire force in a phalanx sixteen deep. In fighting where the weight of a charge by bronze-armored men often carried the battle, the Syracusans had a two-to-one advantage. On each flank they posted a formidable cavalry force totalling 1,200; the Athenians had none. To compensate for this serious deficit Nicias had the right wing resting on swampy land and the left on a sharply rising incline leading to a temple of Zeus.

The battle began with some minor skirmishing by light-armed infantry. Sacrifices were then made to the Olympian gods and trumpets sounded in preparation for the charge of the phalanxes. The Athenians crossed the Anapus and advanced at the run. The Syracusans met the attack, and though they enjoyed an advantage in numbers, the superior discipline and experience of the Athenians and their allies carried the field. The Argives first broke the Syracusan left flank and the Athenians followed suit by driving back the center, effectively cutting the Sicilians in two. Throwing away their shields, the infantry fled toward the protection of the city walls.

This was the crucial moment, but unfortunately for the Athenians, one which they could not take advantage of, for the Syracusan cavalry now charged from both wings to guard the retreat of their foot-soldiers. Even Athenian hoplites could not hope to engage heavy cavalry successfully. The lack of cavalry was to trouble the Athenians later in the campaign as well.

There were 260 Syracusans dead on the field. The Athenians and their allies, who had lost fifty men, returned the bodies on the following day, set up a victory trophy, gathered their spoils and sailed for Catana. Nicias believed he could not decisively defeat the Syracusans without cavalry and more money for an extended siege, and so he chose not to follow up his victory, preferring instead to winter at Catana.

Whether acting with sensible caution or foolish vacillation, the commander of the Sicilian Expedition had thrown away the first opportunity to force the issue and avoid a war of attrition. A tactical victory in the initial battle was thus left unexploited, resulting in a strategic failure for the campaign. Though the veteran general Nicias had erred in not requesting cavalry from the Athenian Assembly in the original appropriation, possibly because of his disinclination for the expedition, he now was forced to send a galley to Athens to ask for additional horses and money.

Syracuse, meanwhile, used the winter of 415–414 B.C. to strengthen its defenses. Recovering from the depression caused by the rout at the Anapus, the Syracusans lengthened the walls of the city, adding to the area the Athenians would have to surround, and reorganized their army's command, appointing three generals (including Hermocrates) with supreme powers to replace the fifteen who commanded at the Anapus.

While both the Athenians and the Syracusans continued preparations for renewed hostilities, Alcibiades became an active participant once more by offering to divulge the Athenian strategic plan to the Spartan leadership. Though the Spartans distrusted Alcibiades both as a democrat and traitor to his city-state, they recognized his value as both general and statesman and gave him a hearing. Stressing that if Syracuse and Sicily fell Athens would use the new and vast resources in men, money and ships to defeat Sparta, Alcibiades impressed his audience of Spartan elders with the necessity of sending a Spartan general to take command of the defense of Syracuse. Alcibiades reasoned that a Spartan general would provide the necessary discipline and organizational skills while also giving proof of Spartan commitment to the city. The Spartan command agreed and chose a skilled and resolute general, Gylippus, to go to Syracuse.

While preparations were being made at Sparta to send Gylippus and a small flotilla, the spring of 414 B.C. came to the Mediterranean bringing with it the start of a new campaigning season. Having received 250 horsemen and three hundred talents in silver (enough to supply the army for a year), Nicias decided to move on Syracuse. Bolstered also by the arrival of four hundred allied horsemen, the Athenians now had 650 cavalrymen to ward off the Syracusan horse from the engineers, masons and laborers who would build the walls necessary for the siege of the city.

Through spies Nicias had learned that the entire Syracusan army would be drawn up for a review on the banks of the Anapus in early April of 414 B.C. In a great tactical maneuver the whole Athenian force sailed the night before the review and landed at Leon, a small town near the plateau of Epipolae which towered over Syracuse to the northwest. The purpose of the Syracusan review had been, in part, to secure that plateau. It was now too late; the Athenians had secured the heights overlooking Syracuse. The Syracusans struck anyway in a futile attempt to dislodge the Athenians. They lost three hundred men. The shaken Syracusan army then retreated within the city walls, and the Athenians set themselves to the monumental task of circumvallating the city.

With Nicias the chief engineer and expert in siegecraft the Athenian masons soon had constructed two forts on the plateau of Epipolae, the Labdalum on the northeast and the "Round Fort" on the southwest. A wall was begun at the stockade on the beach of the Great Harbor (which protected the fleet), and it circumvented the marshes and proceeded up the foothills to the Round Fort on Epipolae. Before the wall was completed the Syracusans constructed a counter-wall at right angles to the Athenian, hoping to cut it in two. Nicias and Lamachus agreed upon an immediate counterattack to negate this threat. Nicias had become increasingly ill with a kidney ailment that he had suffered from for years, so Lamachus led the attack. It was a complete success, and the Athenians dismantled the wall and continued work on their own, aiming to reach the Great Harbor on the southeast side of the city.

Undaunted the Syracusans attempted to construct a second counter-wall, this time across the marshes near the Anapus. The Athenians again counterattacked and were gaining the advantage when their right wing was pincered by a combined force of Syracusan cavalry and hoplites. Lamachus, commanding the left flank, rushed to the right's aid, but was caught isolated with a few men on the enemy's side of a ditch and died in the fighting. The Athenians had defeated the Syracusans once again yet had lost another general.

Nicias now became overconfident; having defeated the Syracusans in every land engagement he did not press the completion of the circumvallation as aggressively as he should have. This procrastination would ultimately prove fatal to the Sicilian Expedition, for Gylippus now arrived with a force of three thousand hoplites and two hundred cavalry, crossing into Syracuse through the unfinished section of the wall on the plateau. Gylippus immediately began a counteroffensive. Sending a diversionary force to threaten the main Athenian wall at the base of Epipolae, the Spartan general also dispatched a force to attack the fort at Labdalum. The fort was stormed and all the defending Athenians killed. The spoils included an important supply and treasury depot, and Gylippus followed this victory with a decisive repulse of another Athenian attempt to blunt the counter-wall erected by the Spartans and targeted to stretch from the shores of the Great Harbor to the fort at Labdalum.

The Syracusans and their Sicilian and other allies, under the command of the Spartan Gylippus, had now succeeded in turning the tables: the Athenians had not won a permanently-decisive engagement, the city had not been effectively isolated from the rest of Sicily, and the ability of the Athenian fleet to effectively blockade the harbors of the nearby coast was clearly questionable.

Nicias, never sanguine about the possibilities of success for the expedition, now found himself in the unenviable position of seeking a way of extricating his forces. He therefore decided to propose either a complete withdrawal or substantial reinforcements from Athens. In the winter of 414–413 B.C., the Athenian Assembly, still believing in the divine favor of Pallas Athena, the city's patron goddess of victory and wisdom, voted a vast armada equal in strength to the first in order to ensure the conquest of Syracuse and Sicily.

While the second Athenian armada was gearing for battle, Gylippus ordered a twofold attack on the Athenians. His ruse—feigning a major naval attack in the Great Harbor which successfully drew all Athenian land forces to watch it—worked while Gylippus attacked overland, capturing the forts that served as guardians and supply depots for the fleet. Now both the land and sea forces of the Athenians were on the defensive; the besiegers had become the besieged. The relief force was on the way, however, bearing five thousand heavily-armed hoplites and large numbers of less-equipped javelin throwers, slingers and archers. Its commander, Demosthenes, had been critical of Nicias's hesitancy in pursuing the enemy after the victory at the Anapus, and now felt that an immediate all-out attack would decide the issue.

Attacking at night with ten thousand hoplites and as many light infantry, the Athenians gained ground again on Epipolae. But numerous counterattacks from all sides soon caused a stunning reversal: the battle became a large-scale rout. The Athenians lost over two thousand men and their overall strategic position now became critically untenable.

Demosthenes advocated complete withdrawal in order to salvage as much of the expeditionary forces as possible for redeployment on the Greek mainland. Nicias disagreed however, feeling perhaps that the situation was still militarily salvageable and realizing also that a defeated general was as good as dead when appearing before the Athenian Assembly to answer for such a grave defeat. Nicias chose to fight, the inherent potentialities for failure on a grand scale notwithstanding. Though many of his hoplites and marines were ill from camping in close proximity to the coastal marshes, Nicias still felt some fortuitous event might yet occur to tip the scales of Fate in the Athenians's favor once again.

Nicias was a deeply religious, even superstitious, man and gave great weight to the possibility of intervention by the gods. A cosmic event did occur, in fact, but scarcely the kind he had hoped for. On the night of August 27, 413 B.C., the moon underwent a total eclipse. His soldiers felt that any action taken during it would be unfavorable to the expedition, and the soothsayers whom Nicias consulted agreed that, as religious custom dictated, the army should wait "thrice nine days" before making any attempt to breakout.

Since the Syracusans were in possession of the plateau commanding Syracuse, Nicias looked to the Athenian military arm which had never yet failed— the fleet. Though the actual attempt at a breakout would have to wait upon the advice of the priests, preparations were begun with that aim in mind. The Syracusans, meanwhile, were able to make active use of the military hiatus by manning their ships and practicing naval maneuvers while the Athenians watched from shore, their ships beached. By the time Nicias had made the decision to challenge the enemy fleet barring the Great Harbor's entrance, clear it, and create a viable disengagement route, it was too late. The Syracusans preempted the Athenians again.

The Sicilians by now had achieved the confidence necessary to unhesitantly press the initiative. Accordingly, Gylippus ordered simultaneous attacks, with the army assaulting the Athenian walls and the fleet offering battle. On September 3, 413 B.C., the Syracusans struck with both arms. While the Syracusan hoplites attacked the remaining Athenian positions on Epipolae, the fleet of seventy-six Sicilian galleys was sent against eighty-six Athenian warships. Though essentially equal in numbers, the Athenians were fighting to open up an avenue for either escape or reinforcements. The Syracusans fought not only to protect their homeland but also to completely destroy the enemy army which they felt had originally invaded their island unjustly.

The Syracusan crews were in better physical shape through their daily drills while the Athenian crews were inactive and weakened by illness ashore. Though the Athenian fleet still held a slight numerical advantage, the size of the harbor favored the smaller fleet, as substantial maneuvering room to ram or grapple enemy ships was crucial. The Athenians were thus not able to bring their total resources to bear.

The battle raged all day. By sunset the Athenians had lost nearly half their fleet, the Syracusans more so, but they did not have to rely on their ships for flight. There was now only one option open to Nicias: retreat overland to Catana, there to regroup, recoup losses through the addition of allies and send word to Athens for yet more reinforcements (perhaps more generals), and prepare for the next campaigning season (412 B.C.).

The standard order of march through hostile territory at the time was to proceed in a hollow square. Two brigades marching in columns formed the left and right flanks of the square while two other brigades arrayed in the phalanx shield-to-shield formation held the front and rear of the square. All non-combatants, baggage carriers and camp followers marched in the center. Nicias divided what was left of the great expedition into two such squares. He himself led the remnants of the army which he had first brought to Sicily in 415 B.C. Demosthenes commanded the second division made up of his reinforcements.

Nicias's division led the march, keeping a five- to six-mile distance between the squares. Demosthenes's square bore the brunt of the continued and unrelenting Syracusan attacks. Since the Syracusans feared the losses they would incur in fighting heavily-armed desperate men in open battle, they instead employed cavalry, plus lightly-armed slingers and javelin throwers to cut down the Athenians on the march. The losses for Demosthenes's division finally became so severe that he chose to surrender, throwing himself and his men on the uncertain mercy of Gylippus and the Syracusans. He was summarily executed.

Ill as he was, Nicias refused to surrender, reminding his men that they were still a formidable force and that "the thought of each man must be that the spot on which he may be forced to fight must be conquered and held as his country and stronghold." Those brave words could not shield the Athenians from the incessant rain of arrows, javelins, and bullets from the slingers, and the burning heat of the Sicilian summer took its toll on the bronze-armored infantry. Diverted from their original course toward the relative safety of Catana by the overwhelming numbers of the Syracusans, the remnants of the great Athenian Sicilian Expedition found themselves trapped in the gorge of the Assinarus River, dying under the unremitting rain of missiles from the Sicilians. The Syracusan cavalry slaughtered the few who managed to cross the river.

The Syracusans marked their victory by decorating "the tallest and finest trees by the riverside with the Athenians's arms." The Athenian Empire had lost two armies and two fleets: fifty thousand men and two hundred ships.

Thucydides said of the Sicilian Expedition:

> They were beaten at all points and altogether; all that they suffered was great; they were destroyed, as the saying is, with a total destruction, their fleet, their army—everything was destroyed, and few out of many returned home.

Athens fought on for ten more years.

The annihilation of two major Athenian armies had both immediate and great long-range effects on the political fortunes of the most powerful city-state in Greece at that time. The core of the Athenian land forces—the knights of the upper and upper-middle classes—died near Syracuse. The heavily armed hoplites died, and with them Athenian infantry capabilities against the Spartans's centuries-old mastery of warfare on land. At sea, Athens had sustained its first great defeat at the hands of the Peloponnesian allied fleet in the harbor of Syracuse. Absolute supremacy at sea was lost; Athens now had to rely on its Long Walls guarding the harbor of Piraeus while at the same time attempting to replace its losses.

The Spartan/Peloponnesian victory at Syracuse drastically altered the balance of power in the Greek world, and by extension, in the West, too. Athens had no hold on the West, of course, but did seek to extend its influence to the western regions which Alcibiades had sought to conquer. Sparta and its allies no longer had to fear that their grain supply from Sicily would be cut off.

Athens continued the struggle. Its people were forced within the walls. Farmers and their families streamed en masse from the countryside into the city. They brought the reality of a disrupted life on the homesteads of Attica along with their need for food and protection to the keepers of the government in Athens.

The rulers of Athens changed dramatically in the aftermath of defeat in Sicily. Foiled earlier in their efforts to destroy Alcibiades and his democratic party, conservatives now greatly increased in influence. Alcibiades was condemned and the infantry which he could command were now either dead or enslaved in Sicily. He could not at that time return as a force in Athenian military or governmental circles. The inability of Athens and its allies to capture Sicily led to the beginning of the end of the Athenian Empire. The decisive battle of Aegospotami in 405 B.C., destroyed its fleet and sealed Athens's fate. At Aegospotami 170 Athenian galleys were taken while beached, ending Athenian supremacy on the seas forever.

Conservative autocrats, the "Thirty," finally surrendered Athens to Sparta. They also brought about the death of Socrates. Convicted of blasphemy against the gods and corrupting the morals of the young (Alcibiades had been his pupil), he was forced to commit suicide.

Sparta's final victory enabled a culturally stagnant city-state to take control of Greece, slowing the riptide of knowledge and art which had flowed from Athens. It also opened the way for other city-states to seek hegemony in Greece, ending in the triumph of Macedon under Philip II and his son Alexander the Great.

# 3

## CHAERONEA, 338 B.C.

*"Then if any device could be found how a state or an army could be made up only of lovers and beloved, they could not possibly find a better way of living (since they would abstain from all ugly things and be ambitious in beautiful things toward each other) and in battle side by side, such troops although few would conquer almost all the world."*

—*Phaidros, as quoted by Plato in* The Symposium

ATHENS WAS ABLE to continue the struggle with Sparta for another decade after the disastrous Sicilian Expedition through the strength of its fleet and the Long Walls of the city (which both protected it and guaranteed its access to the sea at the port of Piraeus). In 405 B.C., however, the situation changed abruptly and catastrophically for the Athenians. The Spartan admiral Lysander with two hundred triremes surprised the Athenian fleet of 180 galleys at Aegospotami, near the Hellespont.

Caught by surprise, possibly through treachery by the general Adeimantus, the chief Athenian admiral Conon escaped with only twenty ships. More than three thousand Athenians were put to death by the Spartans. The thirty-year war had now reached a fatal turning point for Athens; indeed within two years the city was starved into submission by the combination of Lysander's navy, and the land forces under Spartan kings Agis and Pausanias.

Having subjugated her main Greek enemy, Sparta had to govern a newly-won empire and decide what foreign policy to pursue next. It was not a task the city-state was well-suited to. Sparta had accepted subsidies from Persia to aid in waging her war against the Athenian Empire. In return she had agreed to hand over all the land in Asia which had once belonged to the Great King—namely all the Greek cities of Asia Minor that she had "liberated" from Athens. To return these cities to the Persian yoke would be dishonorable in Greek eyes, while refusal could result in a new war with Persia. For three years after the conclusion of the Peloponnesian War (twelve years after the Sicilian Expedition), Sparta pursued neither course, but instead waited upon events.

The campaign of Cyrus, rebellious younger brother of Artaxerxes II, with the "Ten Thousand" Greek mercenaries whom he had hired to depose his brother decided the issue. After the death of Cyrus in battle, Tissaphernes, the Persian satrap of the region, advanced on the cities of Ionia, which appealed to Sparta through envoys. Considering the recent reaffirmation of the superiority of Greek arms over Persian (the Ten Thousand had marched and fought their way through the Persian Empire to reach safety at the Black Sea), Sparta decided to reopen hostilities with Persia.

An expedition was mounted in 399 B.C., with Thibron in command, and he arrived in Asia Minor at Ephesus with a force of one thousand neodamodes, newly enfranchised helots (former serfs) who served as hoplites, and four thousand auxiliaries. He enlisted two thousand Ionians and began his campaigning by capturing Magnesia. By sending two Spartan envoys to Thrace, Thibron was able to hire the approximately five thousand mercenaries left from Cyrus's original ten thousand. Neither Thibron nor his successor Dercylidas achieved any great success.

King Agesilaus of Sparta assumed command in 396 B.C. The following year Pharnabazus, Tissaphernes' colleague, dispatched a Rhodian, Timocrates, to Greece with fifty talents in gold along with orders to stir up anti-Spartan sentiment. He distributed the money to the appropriate parties in Thebes, Corinth and Argos and within the year sufficient animosity was generated to form an anti-Spartan confederacy among these three cities, in league with ever-ready Athens. Thus began the Corinthian War.

By 394 B.C., the Spartan ephors (elders) had decided the situation was serious enough to warrant using all of their forces at home, and so Agesilaus was recalled. Forced to leave behind only a few garrisons, Agesilaus virtually sacrificed the Ionian cities to Persia. The Spartan king proceeded to march rapidly through Macedonia and Thessaly and met the forces of the confederacy at Coronea in Boeotia. This was the first pitched battle on the Greek mainland in which Greek mercenaries played a prominent role. The Thebans began the engagement with a stiff charge that broke the Spartan left while mercenaries and another Spartan contingent did likewise to the Argives on the confederacy's left wing. The result was inconclusive, though it did hinder Agesilaus's previously victorious march to the Peloponnesus.

By 392 B.C., the Corinthian War had become a war of attrition. Xenophon, a commander of the "March Up Country" through the Persian Empire by

Cyrus's mercenaries, stated that, "After this (the battle of Coronea) the great armaments of both belligerents had ceased to exist. The states merely furnished garrisons—the one set at Corinth, the other set at Sicyon—and were content to guard the walls. Though even so, a vigorous war was carried on by the dint of mercenary troops with which both sides were furnished."

The walls at Corinth were blocking the Isthmus for the confederacy, defending the north, mainland Greece. The ones at Sicyon were the Spartan League's counterpoise to those. The commander of the mercenaries at Corinth, all peltasts (soldiers with light armor who threw spears and used slings), was Iphicrates of Athens, the prototype for the fourth century mercenary commander. It was the momentous advent of the mercenary, and with it the nearly simultaneous introduction of the "mixed-arms" concept to Greek warfare, which most contributed to the decline of the standard classical city-state hoplite armies.

Iphicrates often led his peltasts on raids deep into the Peloponnesus, ravaging the countryside in Sicyon, Phlius, and Arcadia, where even their hoplites feared him. Iphicrates won his reputation as a great general at the battle of Amyclae in the summer of 390 B.C. There his peltasts' quickness and efficiency destroyed most of a Spartan mora, one of six hoplite divisions Sparta possessed.

The peltasts became a standard arm of all Greek armies through the example of Iphicrates's success with his light-armed mercenaries. In the fifth century light-armed troops had been considered inferior, barbarous, and undisciplined. They were used to open battles with unimportant skirmishing, to harass the enemy on the march, and to attack the baggage train. Iphicrates changed all this by demanding high-level training and the esprit de corps he was able to instill in his men.

This training was so effective that, "at Corinth he commanded the army with so much strictness, that no troops in Greece were ever better disciplined, or more obedient to the orders of their leader; and he brought them to such a habit, that when the signal for battle was given them by their general, they would stand so regularly drawn up, that they seemed to have been severally posted by the most skillful captain." Iphicrates had an advantage in the methods available to him for use in professionalizing his army as opposed to those available to an Athenian general of the citizen-hoplite army, for a mercenary command at this time offered a much freer field for the exercise of authority.

For example, the Roman Sextus Frontinus recorded in his *Strategems* that, "When Iphicrates, the Athenian general, was holding Corinth with a garrison and on one occasion personally made the rounds of the sentries as the enemy were approaching, he found one of the guards asleep at his post and stabbed him with his spear. When certain ones rebuked this procedure as cruel, he answered, 'I left him as I found him.' " The citizen hoplite was not considered to be under martial law; generals would wait to the end of a campaign and try offenders in a civil court. An Athenian general was an officer elected by his citizen-subordinates and therefore could not be as strict, if he valued his position. Even in the march of the Ten Thousand, "It was further resolved that the generals themselves should undergo a judicial examination in reference to their conduct in past time."

Besides greater emphasis on discipline to improve his peltasts, Iphicrates also made innovations in their weaponry. He increased the length of their short spears by half, to twelve feet, and nearly doubled the length of their swords, to more than three feet. According to Nepos, he also "changed the character of their cuirasses, and gave them linen ones instead of those of chainmail and brass; a change by which he rendered the soldiers more active for, diminishing the weight, he provided what would equally protect the body, and be light." Diodorus Siculus states that, "The actual use of these arms confirmed the initial test and from the success of the experiment won great fame for the inventive genius of that general." These changes helped strengthen the esprit de corps of the peltasts, for they were now almost on an equal footing with hoplites. Indeed, their technical skill and discipline were such that, under a commander who understood their limitations, they could match the best Hellenic hoplites.

Iphicrates and his mercenary peltasts proved this conclusively. They captured all of the Spartan-garrisoned towns in Corinthian territory except for Lechaeum by the end of 390 B.C. In 388 B.C. a new Spartan harmost or military governor, Anaxibius, was sent to Abydos with enough money for one thousand mercenaries to be used to stir up trouble against Athens. Iphicrates transferred to nearby Sestos with eight ships and 1,200 peltasts. Iphicrates ambushed the unsuspecting Anaxibius during the latter's return from a neighboring town. Caught in a pass by a surprise attack, the harmost died, along with twelve other Spartan governors, fifty of the Abydene vanguard, and two hundred mercenaries. After the signing of the ignominious King's Peace ending the war in 386 B.C., by which the Greek cities of Asia were ceded to a descendant of the man who put Athens to the torch, Iphicrates continued warring in Thrace, valuing his independence.

Iphicrates' successor at Corinth was Chabrias, the other great Athenian mercenary commander of the age. He also did not return to Athens on conclusion of the Peace, but continued to ply his trade. Both Athenian generals abroad in command of mercenaries, then, preferred to continue their profession apart from the service of their city, yet not opposed to it. This had not occurred before and it reflected the increased independence of the now highly professionalized Greek mercenary armies and their commanders.

Chabrias, according to Demosthenes, had an unblemished record of victories for Athens: "To sum up, he alone of all our generals never lost a city, a fort, a ship, or a man, as long as he led you; and none of your enemies can boast a single trophy won from many enemies while he was your general." He was successful on both land and sea. In a naval battle off Naxos in 376 B.C. he captured forty-nine Lacedaemonian warships and Athens suitably honored him with a gold crown, a bronze statue in the forum, and freedom from taxation. He liked to spend his war earnings lavishly, "as he was accustomed to live splendidly, and to indulge himself too freely to be able to escape the envy of the populace."

In 379–378 B.C., Chabrias commanded the Athenian mercenary peltasts on the Attic border when Cleombrotus of Sparta invaded Athens's ally, Boeotia, to the north. King Agesilaus took over command in the summer of 378 B.C. and encountered Chabrias and his Theban allies near Thespiae: ". . . he (Agesilaus) led the whole army against them closely arrayed to strike them with terror. Chabrias the Athenian, however, leading his mercenary troops, ordered his men to receive the enemy with a show of contempt, maintaining all the while their battle lines, and, leaning their shields against their knees to wait with upraised spear. Since they did what they were ordered as at a single word of command, Agesilaus, marvelling at the fine discipline of the enemy and their posture of contempt, judged it inadvisable to force a way against the higher ground . . ." This constituted a moral victory over the much vaunted Spartan hoplite and illustrates clearly the respect which the newly professionalized and highly disciplined Greek mercenary now commanded, even from the elite of Greek hoplites.

Sparta began in 383 B.C. "to allow any state, so wishing, to give money instead of men, at the rate of three Aeginetan obols a day per man; or where the contingent consisted of cavalry, the pay given for one horseman was to be equivalent to that of four hoplites"; later, in 378 B.C., this was amended to include peltasts, reckoning the contribution for one as equivalent to half of that for a hoplite.

Thus, just as Athens in the fifth century, by having her allied states send money instead of ships and crews to the league, helped cripple the rest of Greek seapower through atrophy, Sparta in the fourth century encouraged the decline of her allies' citizen-hoplite armies through neglect and the substitution of money for men. This helped to lay open the city-states of Greece for Philip II and Alexander of Macedon.

Meanwhile, Sparta was continually unsuccessful in her use of mercenaries, particularly peltasts. In 382 B.C., an outbreak of war with the Chalcidic League occurred in which Teleutias, a Spartan general, ordered his peltasts to pursue Olynthian cavalry across a river. This they attempted, though at an obvious disadvantage, and were routed with heavy losses. In a similar way the Spartan Phoebidas allowed his peltasts to be defeated by Theban cavalry in

378 B.C. A Lacedaemonian invasion of Corcyra in 373 B.C. met with failure through the Spartan commander Mnasippus's mishandling of his mercenaries. "He began to try experiments on his mercenaries. Some of them he had already paid off; others still in his service had as much as two months' pay owing to them by the general, who, if report spoke true, had no lack of money, since the majority of states, not caring for a campaign across the seas, sent him hard cash instead of men." This caused his mercenaries to be deprived of the necessities and when grumbling broke out he punished some of the men. As a result morale broke, Mnasippus was killed in battle, and the expedition ended a total failure.

The incompetence manifested by Spartan commanders especially with regard to hired peltasts, as contrasted to the great success enjoyed by Athenians Iphicrates and Chabrias, can doubtless be traced to the narrowness of the Spartan mind. Having conquered an empire, they had no idea what to do with it. Faced with a new kind of warfare made possible by a new brand of soldier, they obstinately held to the citizen hoplite as the only true means of making war. It was not by mere chance that Sparta had undergone no constitutional changes from the time of Lycurgus (circa 700 B.C.) onward. Sparta had become a stagnant society and her traditional method of making war in a period of flux for military strategy made her vulnerable to a brilliant innovator.

Such a man was Epaminondas of Thebes. The city-state of Thebes had begun her meteoric rise to a brief period of hegemony in Greece when along with her allies in Boeotia she joined with Chabrias of Athens in repulsing the much vaunted Spartans near Thespiae in the summer of 378 B.C. Gorgidas, the Theban lochagos or captain, had that year formed an elite battalion of picked troops, the "Sacred Band."

The Band, which might have originally been formed as a guard for the sacred precincts of the city, consisted of three hundred men, 150 pairs of the closest of friends, most likely lovers, for as Plutarch wrote, "a band cemented by friendship grounded upon love, is never to be broken, and invincible; since the lovers, ashamed to be base in sight of their beloved, and the beloved before their lovers, willingly rush into danger for the relief of one another. It is likely, therefore, that this band was called sacred on this account; as Plato calls a lover a divine friend."

Gorgidas apparently deployed the Sacred Band throughout the length of the front line of the Theban phalanx, in order to strengthen it. This utilization of the Band actually diluted its overall power. With Gorgidas having been killed in battle sometime between 378 B.C. and 376 B.C., his successor Pelopidas overcame the problem by arraying the corps d'elite en masse, thus turning the Sacred Band into a true shock battalion.

Under Pelopidas's command the immense value of the battalion was proven near Tegyra, a town northwest of Thebes. In 375 B.C. an invading force of

Lacedaemonians was confronted by the Sacred Band. Though outnumbered three-to-one, the Band routed the enemy, inflicting six hundred casualties and killing both Spartan generals. This marked the first land victory over a superior-in-numbers Spartan army by another city-state in Greek history.

The triumph of the Sacred Band was but a prelude to the battle of Leuctra, one of the most decisive struggles in Greek history. Pelopidas's own companion was Epaminondas, commander-in chief of the Theban army. In 371 B.C., King Cleombrotus of Sparta and his Peloponnesian forces met the army of Thebes and the Boeotian League on the Theban plain of Leuctra. In the center the King placed 1,500 Phocian hoplites, along with 6,500 other allied hoplites in left-center and on the left flank. All were deployed in standard depth. Cleombrotus had ten thousand hoplites and arrayed his men with the right wing twelve ranks deep, all two thousand Spartans holding the position of honor.

Using a radical tactic, Epaminondas therefore formed his left wing into a very deep formation of fifty ranks directly opposite the Spartans. The Theban infantry advanced with the select Sacred Band of three hundred at its head. The Spartan foot held their line for awhile but were finally overcome by superior Theban numbers. When the Spartan ranks broke the rest of the line followed suit, not even having come into contact with the Theban allies, for Epaminondas had the line advance in echelon from left to right. The thrusting weight of the Theban flank led by the shock troops of the Sacred Band carried the day.

Though the numbers actively involved on both sides were small, amounting to less than ten thousand altogether, one thousand Spartans were left dead on the field including their king, as well as the myth of Spartan invincibility. Thebes had gained ascendancy and nine years later, in 362 B.C. a combined force of Arcadians and Thebans defeated the Spartans, Athenians, and Mantineans at Mantinea in Arcadia.

Epaminondas again used the tactics of heavily weighting his left flank to the depth of fifty ranks and broke the right held by the Mantineans; the rest of the line was rolled up from right to left. Epaminondas died there, however, and with him Theban hopes. This battle marked the beginning of the end of city-state politics for soon after the Greek political scene was dominated by a cunning military and political figure, Philip II of Macedon.

The precursor of Philip II and model of an autocratic mercenary leader of the time was the dynast Jason of Pherae in Thessaly. In the year 374 B.C. he emerged full-blown in Xenophon's *Hellenica*, when Polydamas of Pharsalus, in Thessaly, appealed to the Lacedaemonian assembly for aid against him. At that time Jason had six thousand mercenaries in his service and he believed that "citizen armies have this defect—they include men who are already advanced in years, with others whose beards are scarcely grown. Again it is only a fraction of the citizens who attend to bodily training in a state, whereas with me no one takes mercenary service who is not as capable of endurance as myself."

Jason resembled Iphicrates in his actions as a martinet: "He is always at their head, whether on a field day under arms, or in the gymnasium, or on some military expedition. The weak members of the corps he weeds out, but those whom he sees bear themselves stout-heartedly in the face of war, like true lovers of danger and of toil, he honours with double, treble, and quadruple pay or with other gifts." Through his mercenaries Jason became war chief of Thessaly, a title not held for the preceding century. Using his position he drew up a quota for each state to furnish, "with the result that his calvary, inclusive of allies, numbered more than eight thousand, while his infantry force was computed at not less than twenty thousand; and his light troops would have been a match for those of the whole world."

Jason proved the value of a well-trained professional standing army in 371 B.C., when he received an appeal for help from the Thebans concerning Cleombrotus's invasion. He immediately gathered together his mercenaries and personal cavalry and rushed through hostile Phocis "appearing like a vision to many states before his approach was even announced—at any rate before levies could be mustered from a dozen different points." The battle of Leuctra had already been won but his example of a lightning campaign with picked troops from a professional standing army was not lost on Philip (nor on his son). Jason was assassinated in 370 B.C., and the power of Thessaly ended with him.

Athens, Sparta and Thebes had all coveted leadership of the Greek world, and each had succeeded in its goal for a period of time. It remained for a state far to the north of "classical" Greece to produce two men who would not only unite Greece (by force), but also conquer most of the known world and set the pattern for Western history in the two following centuries.

Most of the Greek city-states by the accession of Philip in 358 B.C., had become accustomed to hiring professional peltasts to supplement, or supplant entirely, their citizen-hoplites. Athens in particular found it increasingly more difficult to persuade its citizens to fight for their polis. Athenian citizens instead expected the state to spend for replacements thereby eliminating the possibility of going abroad on campaign themselves.

Philip accomplished in Macedon what the short-lived Jason had begun in Thessaly for he began with a standing army awaiting his reforms. He conceived the Macedonian phalanx and brought it into being through change both in formational tactics and weaponry. He remodeled the hoplite line for greater mobility, making it a less dense body and no longer dependent on sheer mass for success.

Philip II put into use both a lighter shield and a much longer spear (the sarissa of sixteen feet) giving his phalanx the advantage of speedier attack and maneuver, along with the ability to land the first blow of an engagement. His innovations in Macedonian warfare were akin to those of Iphicrates and his peltasts in mercenary warfare. Philip even began a special light-armed force known as the hypaspists, or shield-bearers, who were used in tandem with the phalanx just as the peltasts were used with the hoplite line.

By this utilization of "mixed-arms" Philip went farther than any before him. Aside from the heavily-armed phalanx and the javelin-throwing hypaspists there was also a superb cavalry force, the hetairoi or Companions of the King. Archers, darters and slingers were also included in the mobile elements by which Philip could support the phalanx.

The flexibility of this system with regard to the enemy, terrain, and conditions on any given day was enormous, especially compared to the rigid hoplite line. The discipline he commanded as king and the national spirit he embodied, added to the great tactical superiority of the phalanx and its support elements, made the Macedonian army virtually invincible against any other army of the time.

Athens provoked Philip in the very first year of his reign by sending a hired force of three thousand hoplites under the strategos, or general, Mantias to support Argaeus, pretender to the throne of Macedon. This was the first time Athens had hired such a large body of hoplites. Philip surprised Argaeus and captured or killed the entire force. Peace brought a short respite but hostilities resumed in 356 B.C. By 352 B.C. Philip II was engaged in taking possession of Phocis and Thessaly and Athens became alarmed enough to raise a citizen-hoplite army of five thousand, along with four hundred cavalry, under the command of Nausicles. This force was sent to hold the pass at Thermopylae, the northern gate of Greece proper and a breach for invading armies from the Persians to the Germans in World War II. Philip advanced to Thermopylae but finding the pass held retired to Macedonia.

Philip II then turned his attention to Thrace and the Chalcidice. Demosthenes in his *First Philippic* proposed an expedition to counter Philip's moves. But Demosthenes insisted that this force should not just consist of mercenaries and an Athenian general for he realized that the Athenian army, except for the expedition that forestalled Philip at Thermopylae, no longer possessed an Athenian character. The lack of even Athenian subalterns to the strategos he attacked particularly. "Now have you not all along been electing from among your own countrymen ten captains and generals, and cavalry officers, and two masters-of-the-horse? And what are they doing? Except the one single individual whom you happen to send to the seat of war, they are all marshalling your processions for you with the commissioners of festivals. Your captains and your cavalry officers are elected to be displayed in the streets, not to be sent to the war," Demosthenes said. But Demosthenes was not heeded. In 349 B.C. an army of two thousand mercenary peltasts under Chares was dispatched. Peltasts now could form a complete expedition without citizen-soldiers as part of the complement.

By the spring of 346 B.C., Philip II had expelled all of the Athenian garrisons in Thrace and posed a threat to the Chersonese. Because of its strategic position controlling the entrance to the crucial Black Sea grain producing region, Chersonese was one of Athens' most valued possessions. Accordingly, the mercenary captain Diopeithes was given free rein to try and ameliorate the situation there. Since Athens was nearly bankrupt from incessant warmaking and the constant hiring of mercenaries, Diopeithes had to fend for himself and his army. He extorted money from passing ships, sacked some of Philip's towns in Thrace, and even held one of his envoys for ransom. Needless to say, Philip was not pleased, and he expressed this displeasure in a letter to Athens in 341 B.C.

Demosthenes was quite content that Athens now had a standing army abroad attacking Philip II—despite the methods Diopeithes was employing—and he defended the mercenary successfully in his speech *On the Chersonese* before the Athenian Assembly. In 339 B.C., Athens and Thebes became allies against Philip, supported by Euboea, Achaea, Corinth, Megara, and several smaller states. Most of the states of the Peloponnesus had prior alliances with both Philip and Athens and thus remained neutral.

Demosthenes instituted a money contribution to the alliance, over and above the troop levy required of each state. Though his plans had also included a fleet he did raise a land force of fifteen thousand mercenary foot and two thousand horse, apart from the citizen soldiers. The mercenaries were used to block the two most likely routes into Boeotia which was Theban territory and Athens's immediate neighbor to the north. Chares of Athens and Proxenus of Thebes commanded one force of ten thousand mercenaries near Chaeronea in Boeotia. After eight months of inactivity, Philip purposely allowed a letter announcing his return to Thrace to put down a "revolt" there to be captured, and the allies relaxed their vigil. Philip immediately launched a night attack, swept away the mercenaries, and took the pass.

The combatants met again on a Boeotian plain near the town of Chaeronea, northwest of Thebes, in 338 B.C. The phalanx Philip II employed at Chaeronea was sixteen ranks in depth, twice that of the normal classical Greek phalanx, but only one-third the depth of the Epaminondan phalanxes at Leuctra and Mantinea. Philip had been a hostage at Thebes at the age of fifteen and had learned much of their military tactics. Nevertheless, he did not employ the Macedonian phalanx in such great depth as Epaminondas had for he wished to retain and utilize both the power and maneuverability of the division.

Accordingly, the Macedonian infantry formed up sixteen-deep, with the first rank holding its sixteen-foot sarissas two-handed, level to the enemy, the next rank elevating its pikes slightly higher, and so on back to create the effect of a hedgehog of spears. In support of the roughly twenty-four thousand men forming his phalanx, Philip placed two thousand cavalry under the command of his son Alexander, and five–six thousand mercenary hoplites.

The Athenians, Thebans and allies, on the other hand, had approximately thirty thousand hoplite infantry and five thousand mercenaries, most of whom were light-armed peltasts. They had no cavalry, though, which would prove a fatal deficiency. The Theban contingent numbered twelve thousand led by the Sacred Band.

Instead of the Sacred Band and the rest of the Theban contingent being on the left flank as in previous engagements, it now assumed the position of honor on the right wing in a strong defensive emplacement resting on the banks of the river Cephisus. Allied contingents were assigned to the center of the line, while the Athenians under the generals Chares, Lysicles and Stratocles secured the left wing on some low foothills anchored to the acropolis of the town of Chaeronea. The total length of the line was approximately three- to three-and-a-half miles.

The battle began at dawn with the Macedonian line advancing at an oblique angle to the Athenian-Theban line. Alexander and his Companion heavy cavalry were opposite the Sacred Band, the Macedonian phalanx was in the center, and Philip and his hypaspists opposed the Athenians. Philip, seeking to obtain more favorable ground on which to fight, feigned retreat on his flank and the inexperienced Athenian hoplites, sensing victory, abandoned their solid defensive positions and advanced gradually to confront the Macedonians on slopes more advantageous to Philip.

At the same time the Thebans held to their assigned positions permitting a fatal gap to grow in the allied line. Into this gap broke the first major charge by Alexander the Great. While his heavy cavalry struck the Sacred Band on its left flank, a body of Macedonian light cavalry hit its right. The Sacred Band was now inextricably caught in a pincer movement yet it did not attempt to abandon its post of honor.

Meanwhile the Athenian general Stratocles, believing victory to be with the allied army, exhorted his Athenians forward with shouts of, "On to Macedonia." Philip, moreover, continued to contract his phalanx until he felt that the slope favored the Macedonian infantry charge.

At that point, remarking that, "the Athenians don't know how to win," the King reversed field and swept downhill with the full weight of his phalanx, routing the Athenians. Over one thousand Athenians died and two thousand were taken prisoner. Their Boeotian allies fared no better.

The Sacred Band fought on to the very end, each man falling in his rank. It is said that Alexander asked them to surrender for he knew the value of their bravery and loyalty to one another; his own boyhood friend, and later second-in-command, Hephaestion, was with him in the charge of the Companions. When Philip came to inspect the slain of the Band, "he shed tears and said, 'Perish any man who suspects that these men either did or suffered anything that was base.' "

All of mainland Greece was now Philip's. The King called off the cavalry pursuit, raised a victory trophy on the field, made sacrifice to the gods, and decorated his men for conspicuous gallantry. The ashes of the Athenian dead were returned to the city without ransom, as were its prisoners.

Philip guaranteed Athens's borders and permitted her to retain part of her island empire on the condition that she abandon all other territorial claims and become a Macedonian ally. Athens, one time leader of the Greek world, acquiesced.

Thebes did not fare as well. Though allowed to raise a monument to the Sacred Band's dead at Chaeronea, politically the city was rendered impotent through the loss of her lesser allies in Boeotia (as they were granted independence by the King). Chaeronea marked a major turning point in Greek history, for there the citizen army of the fifth century which had withstood the multitudes of the Great King and thirty years of internecine warfare, fell before a professional army commanded by a non-Greek semi-barbarian (to Greek eyes)—Philip. And just as the citizen-hoplite army had made its last stand at Chaeronea, so also did city-state politics meet their end on a Boeotian plain.

The orator Isocrates of Athens had long wished for a war of vengeance against the Great King to punish the Persians for the invasion of Hellas and the burning of the Acropolis during the Persian Wars, and to enrich a resource-depleted Greece from the storehouse of Asia.

Though he had at first opposed Philip, Isocrates now envisioned him as the leader of this crusade against the "barbarians." The exhortation did not reach unreceptive ears, for Philip "was ambitious to be designated general of Hellas in supreme command and as such to prosecute the war against the Persians."

Philip opened the campaign in 336 B.C., by sending an advance force of 10,000 men under his generals Attalus and Parmenion to the Asian side of the Hellespont to secure a beachhead. Shortly thereafter Philip was assassinated by a member of his bodyguard, and the crusade against the barbarians passed to his son Alexander as the most fateful part of his legacy.

Having begun by breaking the Sacred Band of Thebes at the age of eighteen, Alexander the Great went on to conquer half the world and die at the age of thirty-three.

The traveller Pausanias in the second century A.D., wrote of Chaeronea that, "As you approach the city you see the general grave of the Thebans who died in battle against Philip II. They have no inscription, but a Lion stands on their monument, as a symbol of their courage. I suppose nothing was inscribed because the fortune that rewarded them was so much worse than their courage deserved." Beneath that Lion were found 254 of the dead, arrayed in seven ranks.

―――

The passing of Athens and Sparta as the major imperial antagonists for the hegemony of Greece led to the disruption which brought all Greek city-states to a new age under the aegis of Macedonia. Through a combination of skillful diplomacy and Machiavellian maneuvering, Philip II had incited a war which gave him the opportunity to mold Greece into a unified state under one ruler.

With the virtual elimination of the military power of Thebes and Athens, Philip freed his hand to extend his course of conquest to the East: the Persian Empire. Ever since Persia had attempted to conquer the Greek city-states in 480 B.C., the desire to reciprocate had been growing in the minds and wills of the statesmen and generals of Greece. But the Peloponnesian War had lasted for thirty years during which plans to invade Persia were put on hold.

Alexander had grown up with the vision of subjugating the East. As a boy his tutor was Aristotle, who had written "that some men rule, while others are to be ruled." Greeks, Aristotle thought, should rule; barbarians should be ruled.

In the letter To Philip, in 346 B.C., Isocrates asserted, "it is incumbent upon you to work for the good of the Hellenes . . . and extend your power over the greatest possible number of the barbarians."

The victory at Chaeronea had permitted Philip II to prepare his massive crusade against the Persian Empire, and for his son and successor Alexander to ultimately carry out the conquest of Persia and the creation of the greatest empire the world had known to that time.

Though the Sacred Band of Thebes and Athenian hoplites died fighting to preserve the independence of Greek city-states their defeat ultimately led to the spread of Greek power, influence and culture over vast territories. The security of Greece itself was to last for several centuries until the rise of Rome.

# 4

# THE FORESTS
# OF THE NORTH:

## Aduatuca, 52 B.C., and
## Teutoberger Wald, 9 A.D.

"GALLIA EST OMNIA divisa in partes tres." So begins one of the most famous war memoirs in history, Julius Caesar's *Commentaries on the Gallic Wars*. At the beginning of Caesar's rise to the military and later the political apex of Rome, however, the Republic held only the southernmost third of Gaul in strength, Transalpine-Gaul, the province nearest the Italian homeland and Rome. In 61 B.C., a Gallic tribe, the Sequani, who lived between the Jura Mountains (at the western edge of present-day Switzerland) and the Vosges Mountains in France, were at war with a neighboring tribe called the Aedui. The Sequani appealed for aid to a major German chieftain, Ariovistus, and with his leadership and forces the Aedui were defeated. For their aid to a Roman ally Ariovistus and his people were given land in the Upper Alsace, the first established Germanic foothold in Gaul—considered to be Roman territory.

The political leadership of the Roman Republic in 60 B.C., was essentially in the hands of three men, the First Triumvirate. These men had important political power bases and a shared mutual interest toward increasing the power of Rome and themselves. The men were Julius Caesar, who enjoyed the idolatry of the masses; Gnaeus Pompeius, known as Pompey, who had the loyalty of the legionary veterans; and Marcus Licinius Crassus, who had great wealth.

Ariovistus was "king" of his tribe, and "friend of the Roman people." With formal recognition, Ariovistus began to exhort other German tribes to cross the Rhine and settle in Gaul, requesting of Rome both friendship and land grants. In the same year, Julius Caesar was made Governor-General of Trans-alpine Gaul, and he immediately saw the threat to Rome. Caesar wrote in his *Commentaries on the Gallic Wars*, "I saw too that the Germans were gradually getting used to the idea of crossing the Rhine, and I realized that it would be very dangerous for us to have great numbers of them coming into Gaul. One could not imagine that these wild savages would be content with the conquest of the whole of Gaul; instead they would, as the Cimbri and Teutons did in the past, break out into our Province and go on from there into Italy."

The German tribes whom Julius Caesar and his successors would have to face were composed of many tribes, nomadically roaming from the North and Baltic Seas to the Rhine and Danube rivers. The eventual goal of the Roman Empire was to contain them within those boundaries but first Rome had to prove her strength there.

The Roman historian Tacitus, around the year 100 A.D., wrote, "I accept the view that the peoples of Germany have never contaminated themselves by intermarriage with foreigners but remain of pure blood, distinct and unlike any other nation. One result of this is that their physical characteristics, in so far as one can generalize about such a large population, are always the same: fierce-looking blue eyes, reddish hair, and big frames—which, however, can exert their strength only by means of violent effort."

The numerical fighting force of the German tribes was enormous; their equipment and tactics minimal.

Even iron is not plentiful; this has been inferred from the sort of weapons they have. Only a few of them use swords or large lances: they carry spears with short and narrow blades, but so sharp and easy to handle that they can be used as required, either at close quarters or in long-range fighting. Their horsemen are content with a shield and a spear; but the foot-soldiers also rain javelins on their foes: each of them carries several.

Generally speaking, their strength lies in infantry rather than cavalry. So foot-soldiers accompany the cavalry into action, . . . The best men are chosen from the whole body of young warriors and placed with the cavalry in front of the main battle-line. The number of these is precisely fixed: a hundred are drawn from each district, and 'The Hundred' is the name they bear among their fellow-countrymen . . . a title of distinction. The battle-line is made up of wedge-shaped formations. To give ground, provided that you return to the attack, is considered good tactics rather than cowardice.

Political and military power was much more dichotomous than in Rome at this period. "They choose their kings for their noble birth, their commanders for their valour. The power even of the kings is not absolute or arbitrary. The commanders rely on example rather than on the authority of their rank—on the admiration they win by showing conspicuous energy and courage and by pressing forward in front of their own troops." The Germans believed the gods to be present on the field of battle and, "They actually carry with them into the fight certain figures and emblems taken from their sacred groves. An especially powerful incitement to valour is that the squadrons and divisions are not made up at random by the mustering of chance-comers, but are each composed of men of one family or clan."

For the military chiefs, "both prestige and power depend on being continually attended by a large train of picked young warriors, which is a distinction in peace and a protection in war . . . On the field of battle it is a disgrace to a chief to be surpassed in courage by his followers, and to the followers not to equal the courage of their chief. And to leave a battle alive after their chief has fallen means lifelong infamy and shame. To defend and protect him, and to let him get the credit for their own acts of heroism, are the most solemn obligations of their allegiance. The chiefs fight for victory, the followers for their chief. For the Germans have no taste for peace; renown is more easily won among perils, and a large body of retainers cannot be kept together except by means of violence and war."

Caesar soon had to deal with this Germanic trait. The Helvetii, Gauls living in Switzerland, had begun to migrate westward on a large scale under the pressure of the Suebi, a German tribe. Having gathered an army of five legions (roughly twenty-one thousand men) in north Italy, Caesar routed the clan which formed the Helvetian rearguard, and after a two-week trek brought the main body to battle. The ensuing victory brought resettlement for the Helvetii in their Swiss homeland. Caesar could have sold them as slaves, but he was prescient enough to realize that they, as a buffer to the Germans, were necessary to Roman security.

Ariovistus, king of the Suebi, had continued to encourage more German tribes to cross the Rhine. Caesar accordingly decided to eliminate the menace and fuel his political ascendancy at the same time. He first attempted a diplomatic initiative, offering to meet in conference with Ariovistus. When the king replied in an arrogant manner, Caesar marched against him with six legions and four thousand Gallic cavalry.

A Roman legion, the fighting equivalent of the modern-day division, consisted of approximately 4,800 men organized in ten cohorts. A cohort consisted of three maniples of 160 men each; the maniple was divided into two centuries of eighty men. The legion could be arrayed in one, two, three or even four lines, but three, the "triplex acies," was standard. The breakdown to the level of an eighty-man unit gave great flexibility to a commander in battle. When this organizational asset was combined with Roman discipline and drill the result was a superlative fighting machine.

In triplex acies formation the legion would be deployed with the first lines consisting of nine maniples each, with a heavier third "strategic reserve" line of twelve maniples. By grouping the maniples in threes, a legion commander would have three "battalions" of 480 men each in the first and second lines with four in the third line. The legionary was armed with two heavy pila, or javelins, which were used mainly for throwing at a distance. The pilum was seven feet long, approximately one-third of which was the iron head with a slender soft iron neck, the remainder a wooden shaft. The purpose of the soft iron was twofold: if the soldier did not hit an enemy with his cast, the neck bent on hitting the ground in most cases and could not be thrown back by the enemy; if it hit the enemy's shield only, it would bend and its weight would drag both downward.

The Roman foot soldier utilized his pila within an effective distance of approximately one hundred feet, and closed with his main weapon, the gladius. This was a short two-foot cut-and-thrust sword, heavy enough to shatter armor or shield and sharp enough to penetrate the same. The soldier also carried a large oval shield, the scutum, about four feet in length, made of wood covered by hide with an iron rim and boss. The legionary wore a chain-mail cuirass of either solid or open linking rings, providing a good defense against both cuts and thrusts.

The Germans fought in large wedge-shaped formations of infantry, while cavalry units had their own foot soldiers interspersed within their ranks. The average German infantryman wore trousers or a loincloth with a tight-fitting tunic above, or fought bare-chested. He carried a framea, a weapon half-way between a spear and sword, which could be used for both throwing and thrusting. His shield was similar to that of the Romans but flatter. The wealthier Germanic nobles often carried a long twelve-foot spear and a type of sword modeled on the gladius.

Upon the failure of negotiations with Ariovistus, Caesar decided to offer battle. With the opposing armies encamped two miles apart on the plain of Alsace, Caesar marched his legions out in battle order for five consecutive days. Each day the king declined to engage the Romans. To prevent the enemy from cutting his supply lines Caesar marched his entire force out in triplex acies formation to a spot six hundred yards from the Germans. There, with the first two lines giving protection, the third line's legionaries constructed a second camp. This was garrisoned with two legions.

Ariovistus finally attacked the smaller camp at noon but his forces were repulsed by sunset. On the following day, Caesar led all six legions up to the

German line. The king arrayed his own warriors by tribe: the Harudes, Marcomanni, Triboces, Vagiones, Nemetes, Sedusii and Suebi. In all the Germans fielded approximately twenty-five thousand foot-soldiers, of whom six thousand were paired with an equal number of cavalry. Per their usual practice the Germans placed their carts and baggage train in the rear of the line with their women, who, as Caesar puts it, "stood there with hands out-stretched and tears streaming from their eyes, imploring the men, as they marched out to battle, not to deliver them into Roman slavery."

Upon Caesar's command, a fierce charge ensued, so rapid that the legionaries had no time to hurl their javelins. They were tossed aside, and the infantry closed with the sword. The Germans were in such close shield-to-shield formation to avoid the sword thrusts that many Romans leapt onto the shields to strike from above. The German left soon staggered under the Roman right, led by Caesar himself.

At the same time, however, the Roman left was pressed hard by the weight of the German right. Publius Crassus, commanding the cavalry, recognized the problem and ordered the third line, held in reserve, to charge the German right. The onslaught broke that wing and the entire army fled toward the Rhine, fifteen miles away. Survivors were few. Though Ariovistus was one, his two wives were killed in the rout and subsequently he never troubled Rome again.

Following Ariovistus's defeat, Caesar returned to his administrative duties in Cisalpine Gaul, leaving his legions encamped west of the Jura Mountains for the winter of 58–57 B.C. During that winter and the following spring a major conspiracy of Belgic Gauls, numbering over fifty thousand warriors, was formed. These Belgic tribes were mainly Germanic in origin though some were of Celtic blood. Together, fifteen of these tribes held the northernmost third of Gaul. Caesar decided to alter the balance of power.

Having raised two new legions in Cisalpine Gaul, Caesar marched rapidly north and routed elements of the Belgian army near the Aisne River between Laon and Reims. The tribes elected to disperse and reunite only if attacked. The Nervii tribe, however, refused to relent. Utilizing good intelligence information about the standard Roman line of march, the Nervii ambushed the Roman cavalry vanguard, sweeping them away and crossing the river Sambre in expectation of catching the Romans in the process of encampment. The Nervii expected each legion to have marched separately with its own baggage. Instead, Caesar had his first six legions en masse followed by the baggage train guarded by two rear legions. Even so, the Nervii had caught the Romans by surprise, and a fierce fight broke out down the length of the haphazardly formed Roman line (each legionary had fallen in where he stood, regardless of his century or maniple's position).

Seeing that his troops needed steadying, Caesar snatched a shield from a soldier in the rear and rushed to the fore. His other senior officers were likewise engaged, and the situation soon reversed itself with the arrival of two legions of the rearguard. With new troops arriving and those in the line emboldened, the Romans forced the enemy into a fighting retreat. Caesar wrote that "these were people of absolutely outstanding courage. Their daring had carried them across a very broad river, up the steep banks on the other side, and then forward against a strong defensive position. Certainly their spirit must have been great to make light of such difficulties as these." Nevertheless, the Nervii were virtually wiped out. Caesar then had to find new enemies for Rome and himself, but this was not a difficult task.

After Crassus repressed a revolt of the coastal tribes led by the Veneti, Caesar, Crassus and Pompey (who had been very active as an imperator in the East) renewed their Triumvirate in 56 B.C. The following year, Caesar again was forced to action by the Suebi. Two German tribes, the Usipetes and the Tencteri, had crossed the Rhine under pressure from the Suebi. The Suebi at this time were estimated by Caesar to number one hundred clans, each of which would put into the field one thousand men, rotating on a yearly basis. Thus the Suebi could field an army of 100,000 in any given year.

Caesar saw this as yet another opportunity to further his military and political ambitions. The Germans were a distinct threat when they attempted invasion of the Roman homeland, as the Cimbri, Teutoni and Ambroni had done when they were destroyed in 102–101 B.C., by the imperator Marius. Caesar now had his chance.

The first encounter between Caesar and the Germans took place with the imperator at the head of over 35,000 legionaries (eight legions), along with five thousand cavalry. The total of the Germanic tribes was 430,000 with a fighting force of well over 100,000.

Caesar advanced in three parallel columns and covered ground so rapidly in the eight miles that separated the two armies that the Germans were completely surprised. As Caesar writes, "Great numbers were killed and the rest hurled themselves into the river and perished there, overcome by panic, exhaustion, and the force of the current." On that day Caesar also recorded that several hundred thousand Germans died in the slaughter.

The Ubii were the only German tribe across the Rhine which had sent deputies and hostages to Caesar after the defeats of Ariovistus and (later) the Nervii. They were at that time hard pressed by the Suebi themselves, and asked if military action were not taken, would not Rome cross the Rhine and show the Eagles? To further both his political and military ambitions along with those of Rome, Caesar in 55 B.C., bridged the Rhine for the first time in history (for the West). A bridge was constructed in only ten days near Coblenz covering a distance of approximately four hundred yards, with trestles sunk down from five- to twenty-five feet.

Having left a strong guard at both ends of the bridge, Caesar now determined to teach the Germans a lesson. To show the length of the Roman Republic's reach, he therefore made only an excursionary intervention of eighteen days. During this interval he burnt the villages and crops of the Sugambri (who had agitated against Rome), released the Ubii from blockade by the Suebi, promising them assistance from Rome in case of future trouble, and proved, above all, that Rome could strike at will across the Rhine against the Germans. He then turned his, and Rome's attention, across the seas to Britain.

He understood that in almost all the Gallic campaigns help had been furnished to Rome's enemy from that quarter, and Caesar intended to undertake another "reconnaissance in force" before the campaigning season ended in autumn. With the news of his successes in Gaul and against the Germans preceding him, Caesar had already received conciliatory embassies from some British tribes.

Since the island's size and inhabitants were mostly unknown, except to traders, the incursion would be in large part exploratory. He dispatched a lieutenant, Gaius Volusenus, with one warship to reconnoiter the coastline, particularly for a landing area, and report back immediately. Caesar then proceeded to the territory of the Morini, closest to Britain, which contained Portus Itius (Boulogne)—the post of concentration.

Caesar's first expedition to Britain was very limited consisting of two legions (ten thousand men) conveyed via eighty transports escorted by warships. Since Caesar had sent a Gallic ally, Commius, ahead to negotiate with the coastal tribes, the British were under arms awaiting the fleet's arrival. The first landing place proved unsuitable; steep cliffs were guarded by tribesmen. Proceeding north for eight miles the Romans forced a landing, fighting their way through the surf in full armor led by the standard bearer of the Tenth Legion (Caesar's most trusted). He overcame the men's hesitation at the depth of the water by leaping in with the Eagle of the Legion, shouting that "he would do his duty to his country and his general." Boat by boat, the legion followed fearing the disgrace of losing the Eagle, and defeat.

Once ashore and formed in ranks the Romans drove back the Britons, who fought both from chariots and on foot. But pursuit was impossible because the horse transports were delayed by inclement weather. British chieftains soon sued for peace. However, after the Romans had fortified a camp, a storm swamped most of their ships, destroying some entirely. Caesar ordered salvage materials used to repair the basically sound galleys while sending out troops to forage the surrounding countryside for all available grains. Once again, Caesar's foresight was proven for after the storm the British resolved to fight again, reasoning that the loss of ships and lack of grain would weaken the Romans. If they could hold them in the beachhead until winter, and then defeat them in battle, the chieftains believed that no one would invade Britain again.

Caesar recognized the situation, and since his army was too small and lacked the horses for the necessary mobility to effectively conquer large amounts of territory, he withdrew to the continent (Gaul) before winter set in. Only two of the British tribes from which Caesar had demanded hostages delivered them; the rest did not.

The following year, 54 B.C., Caesar attempted an invasion on a much larger scale, crossing in over six hundred ships he had specially ordered. These custom-built ships were lower in draught for easier landing and broader to accommodate more baggage and animals. With him were five legions (twenty-five thousand men) and two thousand cavalry, a formidable force under Caesar. However, always pragmatic, he realized several prevailing limitations: the lack of in-depth, accurate intelligence as to the territory and its numerous inhabitants, and more importantly the tenuous communications link to the home base, Gaul, which itself could rise up in revolt at any time or be threatened once more by the Germans.

Once disembarked, the Romans secured their ships and fortified a camp. Caesar posted ten cohorts, the equivalent of one legion, and three hundred cavalry to guard the ships. After a night march of twelve miles, the Romans spied the British army. A battle quickly ensued and a combined British cavalry and chariot attack was repulsed by the Roman cavalry, which drove the tribesmen back into a previously fortified position. The Seventh Legion then advanced with their shields locked over their heads in the "tortoise" formation and captured the position.

The next day Caesar divided the infantry and cavalry into three "flying columns" to pursue the enemy. Soon thereafter he learned that a violent Channel storm had completely destroyed forty ships of the fleet, and badly damaged many more. All ships were ordered beached; craftsmen from the legions were sent to commence repair work and more transports ordered from the continent.

Caesar then advanced again on the same route with four legions. During the ten days that had elapsed in repair work on the fleet, the British had called in all available forces, placing them under the command of Cassivellaunus, a chieftain whose tribe's territory began about seventy-five miles inland from the sea. These tribes were (normally) at war continually among themselves; the arrival of the Roman army caused a coalition to form.

British tribal tactics soon proved a source of consternation for the Romans. The British often would feign retreat by their cavalry and chariots, drawing the Roman cavalry away from the support of the legions. When clear of the legions, the British leaped from their chariots and fought on foot, odds now numerically in their favor. They also fought in scattered groups with reserves at various strategic points, both of which were troublesome to Roman formation and drill.

The Britons failed to hold consistently to their tactics, however. In need of forage, Caesar sent out three legions and all the cavalry from the Roman encampment. The British attacked from all sides, pressing the attack up to the legions who were arrayed in battle order.

In response, the Roman cavalry charged, supported in close order by the legions. With the infantry nearby the cavalry redoubled their attack, driving the tribesmen ahead of them and not allowing them to stand, nor fight or jump from their chariots. A great rout and slaughter ensued. With the defeat the coalition's forces began to disperse. The whole army was not to appear again in the field against Caesar.

Cassivellaunus now gave up any idea of pitched battle and instead disbanded most of his army retaining four thousand charioteers. Keeping in contact with the Roman line of march, he ordered the territory in front of the advance to be stripped of people, cattle and grain. When Roman cavalry ranged wide to forage, the Britons attacked from chariots, hampering Roman operations and limiting their geographical extent. Nevertheless, the Roman army reached the river Thames at the frontier of Cassivellaunus's country. The opposite bank of the Thames was fortified with sharpened stakes and prisoners had reported that stakes were also fixed in the riverbed. Regardless, Caesar ordered an immediate fording. Led by the cavalry, the legions followed in full armor with only their heads above water. Keeping to close order, the combined attack of the cavalry and infantry routed the Britons.

At this stage, deputations arrived from six tribes offering their surrender and hostages. Intelligence concerning the location of Cassivellaunus's stronghold was also given to Caesar. Confidently the legions marched on the encampment, for as Caesar wrote, "the Britons call it a stronghold when they have fortified a thick-set woodland with rampart and trench."

An assault from two sides by the infantry soon drove the Britons out the other side of the stronghold. A large number of cattle were seized and many tribesmen were caught in the act of fleeing and put to death. Cassivellaunus meanwhile had sent to Kent for aid. The kings of the four districts of Kent proceeded to attack the naval camp. In reply, the Roman sortie from the camp killed many and forced a general retreat by the Kent tribesmen.

After news of this latest lost engagement reached Cassivellaunus he decided to treat for peace. Caesar was quite willing to accommodate him, for the general had already decided to winter on the continent. The time for campaigning was now short with fall fast approaching. At the same time, there were ever-increasing rumors of unrest among the Gallic tribes, rumors that could not be ignored while encamped in enemy—and largely unconquered—territory, separated from Rome by a stretch of open sea and a continent full of often hostile tribes.

Caesar therefore demanded and received hostages of Cassivellaunus; the taking of well- or high-born hostages to secure the loyalty and/or cooperation of subject peoples was standard Roman practice. He then determined the amount of annual tribute the Britons would pay to Rome. Having settled these affairs for the territories he had secured (temporarily, at least) Caesar returned to the naval camp. The storm-damaged ships had been repaired or replaced but the large numbers of British prisoners, to be sold as slaves, necessitated two trips.

Once in Gaul a council of the tribes was held at which Caesar dictated the positioning of the legions in their winter quarters. Due to droughts in Gaul the previous summer, wheat was scarce and the legions were dispersed more than usual, one legion and its auxiliaries being sent to each of seven tribes for quartering. Caesar felt that in this way the grain shortage problem could best be met. Of course it meant at the same time that only one legion would be immediately available to confront a whole tribe should an uprising occur. Caesar also had administrative duties to attend to in the south, but he elected to remain in Gaul until word arrived that all legions were safely encamped for the winter.

A comparatively new legion raised from Italy north of the Po River, was sent to Aduatuca in the territory of the Eburones, a tribe which lived mainly in the lands west of Cologne between the Rhine and the Meuse. This legion had dual commanders, the legates (lieutenant-generals) Quintus Titurius Sabinus and Lucius Aurunculeius Cotta. However, two weeks after the legions had moved into their winter quarters, but before Caesar had departed for the south, a revolt began among the Eburones.

Incited by Indutiomarus, chief of the Treveri, a neighboring tribe and long-time enemy of Rome, the Eburones attacked a wood-gathering party and proceeded to assault the camp. The legionaries manned the wooden ramparts and a counter-attack by Spanish auxiliary cavalry repulsed the tribesmen. The Eburones next requested a parley, "affirming that they had something to say for the interest of both parties, whereby they trusted to be able to reduce the matters in dispute." A Roman knight, Gaius Arpineius, and the Spanish officer Quintus Junius, who had previously been an envoy of Caesar's to this tribe, were sent to the parley.

The Eburone chieftain Ambiorix, who with his co-ruler Catovulcus had met the legion at the border and provided grain, now attempted to convince the envoys of his tribe's good intentions. He said that he personally was indebted to Caesar for relieving the Eburones of tribute and hostage-giving to another neighbor, the Aduatuci, and by this his son and a nephew had been freed and returned to him.

Ambiorix stated that he had been forced to attack by his own people, who in turn had been compelled to do so by a great overall conspiracy of the Gauls. Each tribe would attack its garrison legion on this appointed day so that no legion could march to support one of the others. Since he could now claim he had satisfied the other Gauls by the assault, he baited his trap by saying "he had regard to his duty in response to the good offices of Caesar," and must warn them concerning the soldiers' safety.

Caesar wrote: "A great company of Germans had been hired, and had crossed the Rhine; in two days it would be at hand. It was for the Romans themselves to consider whether they would choose to bring the troops out of cantonments before neighbors could know of it, and to march them either to Cicero or to Labienus, one of whom was about fifty miles from them, the other a little farther." Under oath, Ambiorix offered safe passage to his borders.

After the envoys reported Ambiorix's story a sharp debate arose between the two generals and their respective staffs. Both sides agreed the story should be taken seriously, mainly because they believed that since the Eburones were not a great tribe like the Suebi or the Nervii, they would never dare challenge Rome alone. Therefore the possibilities of a general uprising could not be summarily dismissed.

Cotta and several of the senior tribunes and centurions felt that no departure from winter quarters should be considered without Caesar's order. Cotta and these officers believed that a well-defended Roman fortified camp could withstand any Gallic or German attack. Moreover, since the legion's grain supplies were sufficient they could afford to wait for reinforcements from the nearest forts and from Caesar. "After all," Cotta said, "what was more senseless or more discreditable than to take the advice of an enemy in deciding supreme issues?"

Sabinus answered that, "it would be too late to act when larger bodies of the enemy, with Germans in addition, had come up, or when some disaster had been experienced in the cantonments next their own." He believed Caesar had left for Italy because the enemy would not have dared act so recklessly otherwise.

Sabinus was not heeding the enemy but rather the facts: that the Rhine was nearby, the Germans were angry over the defeat of Ariovistus and other losses, and the Gauls hateful of their subjugation to the authority of Rome. On the one hand, if nothing serious happened, they would reach the next camp safely; on the other, if all Gaul had risen with the Germans, safety would lie in swiftness. Hesitation would lead ultimately to famine.

Cotta and his supporters remonstrated vehemently, but Sabinus replied loudly for many of the recruits to hear: "If you would allow them, they would by the day after tomorrow have joined forces with the nearest cantonments, and would abide the event of war along with the rest, instead of perishing by sword or famine, far removed and isolated from their comrades."

The debate continued until midnight. Unfortunately, Cotta finally yielded and issued orders to march at dawn. After a sleepless night of preparation, a very long and heavily-laden column set out for the nearest Roman camp. The Eburones waited until they were certain of Roman intentions, then positioned a double ambush in the woods two miles ahead of the march.

When most of the legion had entered a large ravine simultaneous attacks occurred on all sides; the flanks of the column were engaged from the sides of the ravine while the vanguard was checked from ascending and the rearguard harassed. "Then indeed, as he had anticipated nothing, Titurnius (Sabinus) was alarmed: he ran hither and thither posting cohorts, yet even this he did in timid fashion and with all judgment evidently gone, as generally happens when men are forced to decide in the moment of action." Cotta, however, thinking an ambush probable, had deployed his men as well as possible and fought heroically in the line alongside them.

Because of the length of the column and the resultant inability to transmit orders effectively, the two generals ordered the baggage abandoned and the troops arrayed in a circle. Though reasonable for defensive purposes, it ceded the offensive entirely to the Eburones. Whereas some of the Romans broke ranks to retrieve their baggage, the tribesmen held their places. "Their leaders passed the word around among their whole army that no one was to leave the ranks; all the plunder was theirs and everything left by the Romans was reserved for them alone; meanwhile they were told to make up their minds that everything depended on winning the battle."

Roman courage was not lacking, however. Cohorts launched attacks in turn on the enemy inflicting large numbers of casualties. Ambiorix accordingly ordered his men to give way when the Romans charged, to discharge their missiles at a distance from the legion, and to pursue only when the enemy retired on their standards. Each attack by a cohort leaving the ring brought missiles on to its exposed flanks, and if it wished to stand and fight the density of the formation made an even better target for the Eburones. With all these disadvantages and a large number of wounded the legion fought from dawn until 2 P.M. At that point several senior centurions fell, one of whom, Quintus Lucanius, died trying to rescue his son who had been surrounded. The legate Cotta was severely injured when he received a sling-bullet full in the face while exhorting the troops.

Sabinus, through a messenger, now asked for a parley. Ambiorix guaranteed the general his personal safety, and would try to do the same for his men. After Cotta had refused to meet an enemy still in-arms, Sabinus ordered all the nearby tribunes and senior centurions to accompany him to the parley. Having been disarmed, Sabinus and his party were surrounded and killed.

The Eburones immediately charged and threw the Roman ranks into confusion. Cotta died in the line along with the greater part of the legion. The rest made a fighting retreat to the camp. The standard-bearer of the legion, Lucius

Petrosidius, found himself hard pressed outside the ramparts by a large number of the enemy. He flung the Eagle over the wall to protect it, and died fighting. The remaining legionaries held off the assaults until nightfall; despairing of relief all committed suicide. A few soldiers who had escaped the battle through the forest brought news of the disaster to the lieutenant-general Titus Labienus.

Ambiorix meanwhile raised the neighboring Aduatuci, and then the Nervii, convincing them that each legion in Gaul could be destroyed consecutively. The next legion targeted was that of Quintus Tullius Cicero, quartered among the Nervii for the winter. The Gallic cavalry again caught a Roman wood-gathering detachment away from the camp and cut it off. The combined mass of the Eburones, the Nervii and the Aduatuci, numbering sixty thousand men, now assaulted the walls.

The Romans, perhaps five thousand legionaries and auxiliaries, barely held on to nightfall under the relentless attack which was pressed the harder because of the tribes' determination for victory through speed and surprise. That night Cicero dispatched messengers to Caesar but all roads had been blocked. At the same time the entire legion worked furiously to construct wooden towers to reinforce the ditch and ramparts already there. One hundred twenty towers were constructed from the wood stockpiled in the camp.

The following day the tribesmen attacked en masse and were repulsed. This occurred day after day. Night after night the Roman soldiers repaired the damage of that day's fighting and prepared for the next. Stakes were sharpened and strengthened with fire, pikes for wall-fighting readied and towers reinforced.

The leaders of the Nervii, following Ambiorix's example, used his arguments with Cicero. He wisely replied that, "if they would lay down their arms, they might use his good offices and send deputies to Caesar." Having failed at treachery, the Nervii built a counterwall around the camp using methods they had learned in fighting Rome and from prisoners (held in secret) they had captured.

On the seventh day of the siege the Gauls took advantage of the strong winds to attempt to fire storm the camp. The legionaries fought the most violently, though their huts and possessions were ablaze. When the Nervii moved a tower up to touch the rampart the centurions of the third cohort there withdrew their men a space and invited the enemy in. The Nervii did not enter as they were dislodged by stones and the tower was set afire.

Among all the messengers sent for aid a Gallic slave finally managed to get to Caesar, who immediately dispatched orders to three legions to converge, if practicable under the circumstances, on his line of march to the relief of Cicero.

Labienus wrote to Caesar of the loss of Sabinus and Cotta and that the

Treveri were under arms three miles from his camp. Caesar therefore had three legions. He delegated a legion to Crassus to guard the baggage, hostages and grain, and advanced rapidly with seven thousand men. A letter announcing the relief column, written in Greek in case of capture, was sent with a Gallic trooper to Cicero. Soon after he had received and read it to the legion the smoke of burning villages was seen in the distance. Caesar had arrived.

The Gauls now raised the siege and regrouped to face him. Since Cicero had replied to him Caesar knew he would face the Gauls. He ordered a much smaller camp to be built to deceive the enemy and an illusion of fear and confusion to be presented. When the Gallic horse attacked, Caesar ordered the Romans to retire to camp. After Gallic heralds asked for surrender, tribesmen began filling the ditch and attacking the walls. "Then Caesar caused a sally to be made from all the gates, and sending out the cavalry put the enemy speedily to flight, so effectually that never a man stood to fight. He slew a great number of them and stripped all of their arms."

At Cicero's camp, Caesar praised the commander and his legion and found that only one-tenth of them had come through unwounded. On the following day a parade of the legions was held at which Caesar spoke about the disaster of Sabinus and Cotta. "The loss incurred through the fault and foolhardiness of a general, inasmuch as by the goodness of the immortal gods and by their own valour the misfortune had been made good, leaving to the enemy no lasting joy, to themselves no long-enduring grief," he said.

Upon hearing of Caesar's victory the Treveri under Indutiomarus, who had begun the insurrection, abandoned their planned assault on Labienus. Instead the Treveri sought aid from the Germans. They refused in light of their past defeats. Indutiomarus then decided to attack the legion anyway. At the same time Labienus called for all available cavalry to be gathered from allied tribes at his camp on a set day. Under cover of night a large force entered the camp secretly, greatly strengthening the legion.

The following day Indutiomarus and the Treveri, as per custom, rode to the camp, discharging missiles and challenging the Romans to fight. Finally, near sunset, the Treveri began to disperse in disorder. At this, Labienus ordered the gates opened and all the Roman and allied cavalry to charge with cohorts following in support.

The orders were clear: "they should all make for Indutiomarus alone, and no one was to wound any until he saw the chieftain slain." Rewards had been offered and the chief was summarily caught during the ford of the river, slain, and his head brought back to camp.

After another punitive campaign against the Nervii in the spring of 53 B.C., Caesar laid waste the land of the Eburones. Using volunteers from nearby tribes enticed by the plunder offered, everything standing was burned to the ground and all crops and cattle taken. Ambiorix escaped with a few horsemen.

About two thousand German Sugambri had crossed the Rhine to take part in the incursion on the Eburones. They seized an opportunity to attack the newly-recruited XIVth legion guarding the baggage train at the ill-fated camp at Aduatuca, and slaughtered two cohorts caught outside the walls. Caesar again made a brief foray across the Rhine but soon had to return for lack of corn.

The last great revolt of the Gauls in the final century of the Republic now took place. It followed hard upon the news of a catastrophic disaster for Roman arms in the East: Marcus Crassus and his son Publius (who had fought under Caesar in Gaul) were destroyed at Carrhae by Parthian mounted archers; an army of thirty thousand was lost. This meant an end to the First Triumvirate, for Crassus had been a centering balance to the weights of Caesar and Pompey.

The Gallic revolt began with a massacre of Roman citizen-traders at Cenabum (Orleans). Caesar was in Italy but quickly sped north at receipt of the news. A young prince of the Arverni tribe in central Gaul named Vercingetorix had helped plan the rebellion and was now named its leader. Vercingetorix's ability as a military leader worried Caesar for two reasons: he was able to field a united force of many Gallic tribes quickly, and he knew enough of Roman tactics and strategy to fight them effectively. Vercingetorix chose to give battle as the Romans often did, from strongly fortified positions; in this case, cities. He also employed horsemen supported by large numbers of missile-equipped infantry, archers, slingers and darters.

The rebellion was reduced through three brutal sieges, the first at Avaricum (Bourges) in 52 B.C. Vercingetorix's scorched-earth strategy left Caesar and his eight legions barely enough to eat. The picked garrison of ten thousand and city population of thirty thousand also suffered. A month-long siege ensued in which the Gauls used iron-miners from the ranks to tunnel under the Roman ramp and siege towers and set fire to them.

An all-out assault stormed the city, and only eight hundred of forty thousand escaped the revenge the legions took for the massacre at Cenabum. Vercingetorix was not caught up in the defeat, however, because he was encamped outside the city within a fortified marshy area.

The Gallic leader now retreated to the town of Gergovia in his own Arvernian territory. The siege of Gergovia proved to be the most serious setback Caesar suffered in the six years of campaigning in Gaul. Vercingetorix's use of archers and other missile-troops in large numbers had a devastating effect on the legions, who replied with catapult artillery firing large bolts (cross-bow missiles) and stones. An infantry attack breached the town wall, exceeded their orders, and was repulsed. A short time later Caesar raised the siege. At the same time Labienus with four legions routed several Belgian tribes at a battle on the Seine in front of Lutetia (Paris).

Vercingetorix now deployed a vast number of horsemen against Gallic tribes who had given their allegiance to Rome. Caesar meanwhile had enlisted German cavalry from tribes with which he previously had come to terms. The combined Roman and German forces drove Vercingetorix into his strongest hold, Alesia, southeast of Paris. Caesar besieged him with ten legions, or forty thousand men; the cavalry and auxiliaries came to another ten thousand—the largest force under Caesar to fight in one army in the border wars.

The Gallic chief had nearly 100,000 troops; eighty thousand infantry and fifteen thousand cavalry. Caesar prepared a double circumvallation, an inner siege wall of ten miles circumference, and an outer of thirteen miles. The inner wall contained the besieged and the outer repulsed any would-be relief armies. Caesar's walls had seven legionary camps linking them and outer defenses consisting of a double network of ditches, alternating rows of stake pits (lilies) and seven lines of embedded iron spikes (stimuli).

When Vercingetorix realized he could not break the Roman siege with his own forces in Alesia, or hold indefinitely against it for want of food, he sent cavalry contingents out to their own individual tribes to gather troops. The eight thousand cavalry who were dispatched returned with 250,000 infantry for Alesia's relief. Vercingetorix next ordered the expulsion of all non-combatants from the city—not to spare them from the fighting but to burden the Romans with thousands of starving who were unfit to fight. (One Gallic leader, Critognatus, proposed to cannibalize them for the welfare of the garrison but Vercingetorix rejected this.) Caesar, in turn, refused to take the outcasts within his lines.

The final battle for Gaul was decided by cavalry, which was clearly the most inferior Roman arm. Vercingetorix fixed all his hopes and resources on simultaneous attacks by the relief army of 250,000 upon the Roman outer wall and his own attack from within with well over fifty thousand men. The leaders of the relief army hand-picked sixty thousand men to deliver the main external blow aimed at the Roman camp on Mount Rea, the position of which gave the Gauls an advantage in downhill attack.

The battle began nearly simultaneously around the entire besieged city. The great length of the lines left the Roman defense extremely thin in some areas with the camp on Mount Rea the hardest hit. The Gauls had the advantage of the slope and advanced at speed, some hurling javelins, others moving in the "tortoise" formation. Filling in the trenches and traps with earth, the Gauls reached the walls with a great advantage in arms and men. Caesar sent his trusted general Labienus with six cohorts to reinforce the walls.

Vercingetorix attacked the inner wall fiercely in another quarter, his men clearing towers with showers of missiles, filling in trenches with earth and pulling down ramparts and breast-works with grappling-hooks. Twice reinforcements were sent to the endangered position, a third time commanded by

Caesar himself, and it was restored. He next went toward Mount Rea leading four cohorts and part of the cavalry; the rest he sent out around the outer wall to attack the enemy's rear.

Labienus realized that neither trench nor wall would hold the camp. He therefore formed up a total of forty cohorts from the camp and the nearby outposts while informing Caesar of his intentions. When the general arrived at the camp his scarlet cloak of a commander-in-chief betrayed his presence almost immediately. The Gauls sent up a shout, and the Romans on the ramparts answered it. Discarding their spears, the legionaries attacked with the sword, Caesar's on one hand, Labienus' on the other; the cavalry struck the rear.

The elite of the relief force panicked, and a great number were slaughtered by Roman and hired German horsemen in the rout. The entire relief now abandoned the counter-siege; Vercingetorix retreated within his walls. Seventy-four war standards were brought to Caesar. On the following day Vercingetorix surrendered himself to Rome. Keeping aside the Arverni and Aeduan prisoners in order to regain the loyalty of those states, Caesar distributed the rest of the captives as prizes to his legions, one to each soldier. In Rome a public thanksgiving period of twenty days was declared.

The political and military energies of the Republic now turned inward. From the border wars against foreign tribes and states, and the pacification of those already subjugated, the leaders of Rome started on the road from imperial Republic to Empire ruled by an emperor.

In 50 B.C., Caesar, having served two five-year terms as military governor of Gaul, returned to northern Italy a victorious general. The law of the Republic stated that a general could not enter the province of Italy proper with his army. With Pompey and most of the Senate opposing him, Caesar crossed the Rubicon River into Italy saying, "Let the die be cast."

At dawn on January 11, 49 B.C., the greatest civil war the world had yet known began. It would last eighteen years and Caesar would be assassinated less than halfway through it; it would end with one man as master of the Roman world.

The First Triumvirate had died with Crassus at Carrhae in 53 B.C. The clash of Caesar and Pompey, conqueror of Asia Minor for the Republic, became inevitable. At the battle of Pharsalus in northeastern Greece in 48 B.C., Caesar's outnumbered army broke Pompey's left wing through a cavalry attack closely supported by infantry. The commander of that wing was Titus Labienus, who had earlier gone over to Pompey.

The defeated imperator took ship to Egypt where he was treacherously murdered upon arrival. Caesar anchored at Alexandria soon after. The following year, Caesar became intimately involved with Cleopatra (VII) and through a hard-fought campaign—especially for the city of Alexandria—

placed her in sole possession of the throne of Egypt over her brother Ptolemy XIII. Though he had given the many partisans of the Pompeian cause a year in which to raise new armies, still within two years Caesar had defeated or won them over, in campaigns through north Africa and in Spain. In 46 B.C., he was voted "dictator" for ten years by the Senate. The first part of the Civil War had ended.

During the next two years Caesar attended to his legislative reforms and planned what was intended to be his supreme campaign—the conquest of the Parthian Empire, the slayer of Crassus and seven legions, Rome's great rival in the East. Instead, on the Ides of March, 44 B.C., three days before he would set out, Caesar was assassinated by pro-Republican members of the Senate led by Brutus and Cassius, men whom he had forgiven after they had fought and lost to him. He died at the foot of Pompey the Great's statue.

Gaius Octavius, grandnephew of Caesar, had been adopted by him and now became his official heir through the will administered by Marcus Antonius. Endowed with masterful political skills and keen ambition, Octavian soon formed a coalition with Antony (who married Octavian's sister in 40 B.C.) and Marcus Lepidus, the Master of the Horse under Caesar, to initiate the Second Triumvirate. The work of destroying the assassins of Caesar was in large part completed at the battle of Philippi in northwest Greece in late 42 B.C. There the Caesarian army under Antony and Octavian utilized classical hoplite tactics and simply rolled back the army of the conspirators by sheer force. Cassius first, and later Brutus, committed suicide.

The Roman world was divided among the victors: Antony received Gaul and the East, Octavius most of the West, and Lepidus, Africa. Though renewed in 37 B.C., the inherent natures of the two principals of the Triumvirate made it a fragile political arrangement. By 32 B.C., Antony had divorced Octavia and was in Egypt with Cleopatra, whom he had met when the East became his domain in 40 B.C. In 31 B.C., Antony and Cleopatra fell before Octavius in the great sea battle of Actium, off the western coast of Greece. The couple returned to Egypt and death.

Octavian now held the Principate, or "first citizenship." In 27 B.C., he took the title Augustus, or majestic, Caesar. Though keeping to Republican forms of government, Augustus simply and gradually took the most important titles upon himself.

The northern frontier became the most important item on Augustus's foreign policy agenda. Julius Caesar had left the Roman frontier secure at the Rhine. To the east, the river Danube formed the border through central Europe. The major strategic problem arose where the defensive lines along the rivers met. Since the Rhine curved southwestward, a large triangle of land between the rivers lay open to occupation by the Germans giving them the tactical advantage of interior lines. The Roman legions would thus have to march the length of two sides of the triangle to reinforce the outposts on the opposite river.

To eradicate this hostile salient into the Empire, Augustus planned to extend the Rhine frontier first to the Weser River and then on to the Elbe. The emperor believed that this would not only cut off the salient but also ensure the safety of Gaul, which he considered the "Egypt of the West" as a producer of grain for his armies of the Rhine.

It was Augustus's stepson, Drusus Caesar, who first attempted the task of conquering Germany. Using the armies of the Rhine and Gallic levies, Drusus Caesar pushed the frontier to the Elbe River by 9 B.C. He died soon after in an accident. His elder brother Tiberius, who had subdued the Pannonians and Dalmatians whose tribal lands abutted the Danube, took over the campaign and completed it in 7 B.C. He then proceeded to a command in the East.

In 1 B.C., the Cherusci rose; by 4 A.D., the situation in Germany had become such that Tiberius was recalled to deal with it. To avoid the waste of resources and men through protracted warfare, Tiberius decided upon the most ambitious campaign plan yet used against the Germans, a triple offensive using the armies of Germany, Raetia, and Illyrium to cut off and eliminate the German salient. Having taken northern (coastal) Germany in 5 A.D., with an army of twelve legions mobilized (out of twenty-eight for the entire empire), Tiberius had to abort the attack because of insurrections in Pannonia and Dalmatia which had revolted with the garrison legions gone.

Tiberius then had to abandon the German campaign entirely and turn his legions to quashing the rebellion. Employing eight legions with auxiliary infantry and seven thousand cavalry, it took three years to put the insurrection down. Tiberius now commanded upwards of eighty thousand men, enough to trouble his stepfather, Augustus. Accordingly in 7 A.D., Germanicus, son of Drusus and nephew of Tiberius, was sent to join him in the Illyrian command.

Saturninus, military governor of Germany, had joined Tiberius for his campaign, and Publius Quintilius Varus was named to replace him. Varus, as described by Velleius Paterculus, "Was a man of mild character and of a quiet disposition, somewhat slow in mind as he was in body, and more accustomed to the leisure of the camp than actual service in war." He had previously been governor of Syria where he had increased his income considerably through exploitative measures.

Unfortunately for himself and Rome, Varus did not leave his habits of governmental indiscretions behind in Syria. "Besides issuing orders to them as if they were actually slaves of the Romans, he exacted money as he would from subject nations." Germany was not a subject nation and did not respond well to being treated as one. Varus had five legions under his command, with their attendant auxiliaries, over forty thousand men.

The five legions were encamped for the summer of 9 A.D.; two were at

Mogunticum (Mainz) and three near Minden on the upper Weser river. One of Varus's auxiliaries, Arminius, was the son of the chief of the Cherusci and as such a trusted tribal follower. Arminius had long held a grudge against Rome. He aspired to do what Vercingetorix had failed at in the south sixty years before.

Arminius also had a grievance with his uncle, Segestes, a loyal supporter of Varus and Rome, whose daughter, Thusnelda, had been forbidden to Arminius but who had eloped with him anyway. He also had great contempt for Varus, considering him to be more a city administrator than a field commander. In this assessment he was right.

Arminius baited his trap with the rumor of a local insurrection. Since Varus was planning the movement of the three legions on the upper Weser to its winter quarters, Arminius hoped to channel the move into an ambuscade by the Cherusci.

Varus ignored all warnings, including that of Segestes, which he dismissed as being made out of pique over his daughter. Instead of marching directly to his winter quarters, Varus elected to march through the territory where the uprising was taking place. On an early fall morning Varus set out with three legions, the XVIIth, XVIIIth and XIXth, approximately twenty thousand men in all, along with accompanying families and a lengthy baggage train. It was not necessarily a recipe for disaster, and with a commander like Julius Caesar, it would not have been.

Varus, however, suspected nothing and was prepared for no more than a local dispute, not the wrath of the entire Cherusci nation. Arminius and his co-conspirators rode with Varus until well into the woods, then left the column saying that they had to raise their forces to aid the Romans.

Those forces were already in place ahead of the Roman line of march. The area the legions would traverse was mountainous and cut by heavily wooded ravines. The column had to fell trees, clear paths and bridge minor streams. As a result, the troops and their train were spread out over a mile or more. The Roman order of battle was not suited to forest warfare and Arminius took full advantage. The Cherusci struck at the moment of a violent thunderstorm, fierce enough to make the footing unsteady, "a violent rain and wind came up that separated them still further, while the ground, that had become slippery around the roots and logs, made walking very treacherous for them, and the tops of the trees kept breaking off and falling down, causing much confusion." Under cover of the storm the Germans attacked on all sides, hurling javelins into ranks which were already loose and extended.

In response to the attack Varus halted and encamped. On the next day the Romans either burned or abandoned their wagons. Without their wagon train, the legions were able to advance in better order. For a short time they were in open country but soon came into wooded territory again. The Germans continued their attack on the column for the next two days.

On the fourth day a thunderstorm struck again and the greatly outnumbered Romans were trapped without a camp to fall back upon. Caught in narrow quarters where they could not form into fighting units, the cavalry and infantry collided with each other when trying to cooperate in attack. The unending rain made their bows and javelins unwieldy, and their thoroughly soaked shields were weighted down. Under the incessant attacks the legions could not hold. Several cohorts, at least, broke away from the column and attempted to hastily throw up a fortification behind which to make a stand. Reaching a small hillside some legionaries dug a shallow ditch and constructed a partial breastwork while others covered them. "Varus, therefore, and all the more prominent officers, fearing that they should either be captured alive or be killed by their bitterest foes (for they had already been wounded), made bold to do a thing that was terrible yet unavoidable: they took their own lives."

It was the end of an army unmatched in imperial history. "An army unexcelled in bravery, the first of Roman armies in discipline, in energy, and in experience in the field, through the negligence of its general, the perfidy of the enemy, and the unkindness of fortune was surrounded, nor was as much opportunity as they had wished been given to the soldiers either of fighting or extricating themselves, except against heavy odds; nay, some were even heavily chastised for using the arms and showing the spirit of Romans.

"Hemmed in by forests and marshes and ambuscades, it was exterminated almost to a man by the very enemy whom it had always slaughtered like cattle, whose life or death had depended solely upon the wrath or the pity of the Romans. The general had more courage to die than to fight, for, following the example of his father (who died a suicide at Philippi with Brutus and Cassius) and grandfather, he ran himself through with his sword."

In Rome, when Augustus learned of the disaster, he rent his garments and mourned, striking his head against a doorpost and crying out, "Quintilius Varus, give me back my legions." Portents of doom were seen both within and outside the city: "the temple of Mars in the field of the same name was struck by lightning, . . . the peaks of the Alps seemed to collapse upon one another and to send up three columns of fire; the sky in many places seemed ablaze and numerous comets appeared at one and the same time; spears seemed to dart from the north and to fall in the direction of Roman camps; . . . a statue of Victory that was in the province of Germany and faced the enemy's territory turned about to face Italy."

Augustus mourned for his lost legions, but more importantly, feared that Gaul and thence Italy and Rome herself were threatened by the barbarians.

There was no strategic reserve to speak of in Italy at the time and manpower was short. Augustus therefore turned to forced conscription which he had used only once before, in the rebellion of 6 A.D. Again Tiberius led the armies. After reassuring the Gauls and strengthening garrisons along the way, Tiberius crossed the Rhine and took the offensive back to Germany.

On August 29, 14 A.D., Augustus Caesar died at the age of seventy-six; he was succeeded by his stepson, Tiberius. In the following year, Germanicus invaded Germany on a punitive expedition against Arminius, the Cherusci and their allies. At the head of eight legions, Germanicus first stopped to bury the dead of Teutoberger Wald. "Every soldier with him was overcome with pity when he thought of his relations and friends and reflected on the hazards of war and of human life."

"Varus' extensive first camp, with its broad extent and headquarters marked out, testified to the whole army's labours. Then a half-ruined breastwork and shallow ditch showed where the last pathetic remnant had gathered. On the open ground were whitening bones, scattered where men had fled, heaped up where they had stood and fought back. Fragments of spears and of horses' limbs lay there—also human heads, fastened to tree trunks."

In the campaigning season of 16 A.D., Germanicus caught up with Arminius at a place called Idistaviso near the Weser River. With elements of eight legions, roughly thirty thousand men, an equal number of auxiliaries and one thousand of the Praetorian Guard, the Romans met fifty thousand or more German tribesmen. Though the Cherusci broke through the center of the Roman first line made up of auxiliaries, Germanicus repelled the assault with the four legions of the second line and the Praetorians. Meanwhile, the German flanks were thrown back and a general rout occurred. Arminius escaped in the confusion but the slaughter of the enemy continued from noon until dusk. The Germans paid twice over for Varus's legions.

Germanicus Caesar received his triumph in Rome leading Arminius's wife, Thusnelda, and their son, along with other Cherusci nobles in chains. However, all further triumphs for Roman generals over the Germans were hollow victories after the destruction of Varus and his legions. The Roman Empire's northeastern boundary became fixed at the banks of the Rhine. Arminius had proven to both his Germans and the Romans that the legions could be defeated. If done once, it could be done again. Tiberius and the succeeding emperors left Germany alone. The Legions XVII, XVIII and XIX were never raised again.

In 357 A.D., the last great Roman offensive against the Germans was undertaken by the future emperor Julian, the Apostate, so-named because he wished to renounce Christianity and return to the worship of the old gods. Commanding cohorts of three legions and their auxiliaries (approximately 12,500 men), Julian met and crushed a German force of forty thousand at Argentoratum. The king, Chnodomar, was captured and over six thousand Germans were killed. The Romans lost 247 dead. Nevertheless, the time had now come for the offensive tide to turn to those who were yet to come from the North and the East.

---

The major thrust of Roman imperialism had begun in the second century B.C., with the destruction of Carthage, its chief rival in the western Mediterranean. Following Senator Cato's oft-repeated dictum, "Carthage must be destroyed," the legions of Rome did just that in 146 B.C. At the end of the third war with Carthage Scipio Africanus captured the city, razed it to the ground and sowed its soil with salt. With that action Rome signaled its intent: empire without bound save its own will.

With the taking of the Mediterranean basin Rome looked north. In the following century the legions marched to attack Gaul, and eventually, Britain. During the campaigns a young legion of Caesar's was ambushed and destroyed by Belgian tribes at Aduatuca. The loss began to suggest to Rome the possible real costs of its expansionist policies.

More than fifty years later three legions commanded by an inexperienced political appointee were trapped and slaughtered in the Teutoberger Wald. The catastrophic disaster cost Rome three entire legions, plus the equivalent number of men in auxiliaries. Augustus Caesar could only afford, in terms of financial resources and manpower, to field twenty-eight legions to defend the frontiers of the entire empire.

Therefore, in one battle Rome had lost over ten percent of its fighting strength. The lost legions could not be replaced at that time; the depleted army stretched itself even thinner to defend a line running from the North Sea and the English Channel to the Rhine, from Spain in the west through North Africa to Egypt and Syria.

Twenty-five legions with equivalent auxiliaries constituted a field force of approximately 250,000 men at full strength. These legions were expected to hold borders which extended well over ten thousand miles.

The Emperor Augustus, always the supreme pragmatist, realized that after the defeat of Varus and the resultant diminution of military power, Rome would have to halt its northern expansion at the Rhine, leaving Germany unconquered. Accordingly, in his last will and testament to the Senate and people of Rome, Augustus dictated that the Empire should hold to its borders at his death. A campaign of vengeance against the ambushers of Varus was carried out successfully by Germanicus, grandson of Augustus, but no attempt was made to hold German territory, and Roman expansion was never attempted seriously again.

The battle in the Teutoberger Wald, fought as it was in a wilderness far from the centers of Western civilization, nevertheless had a great effect on its future course, very conceivably for the following two millennia, into the twentieth century.

If Roman law, commerce, customs and its binding road networks had penetrated deep into Germany, the wide abyss which opened between Romanized France and Teutonic Germany might not have occurred. And the catastrophic clashes between the two countries and their allies over the last two centuries, which in large part have produced the contemporary world, might not have happened.

# 5

# JERUSALEM, 70 A.D., AND MASADA, 73 A.D.

TWO THOUSAND of the crucified lined the roads leading to the gates of Jerusalem. Left to die of exposure, starvation and wounds suffered in a vain revolt against the Roman Empire, the rebels had been placed upon their crosses on the orders of P. Quintilius Varus, governor-general of the province of Syria. As such, Varus was administrator of Judaea for the Empire. The year was 4 B.C. (thirteen years later Varus, then governor-general of Lower Germany, would die with three legions in the Teutoberger forest). The Judaean uprising came in a period of turmoil following the death of King Herod the Great, ruler of Judaea from 37–4 B.C.

At Herod's death, factions arose on all sides. First, there were those who supported his appointed heirs, sons Archelaus, Antipas and Philip (three of his children who had not been executed by the power-hungry, paranoid monarch). The brothers had traveled to Rome to plead their individual claims before the Emperor Augustus, as all heirs to subject kings had to do to validate their right to rule.

The second party consisted of those Jews of the priestly order and other notables who wished to restore the "Temple Constitution" under which the High Priest retained a fair amount of autonomy, while the people would still accede to Roman rule in the form of a procurator or local governor.

Finally, there were the anarchistic usurpers to the throne who sprang up with the support of bands of brigands throughout the country, fomenting turmoil and rebellion where profitable and possible. Serious rebellion began, however, with the arrival of the imperial finance officer of Syria, Sabinus, who in that post also had tax-collecting power over Judaea.

65

With the death of Herod Sabinus marched toward Judaea, hoping to swell Rome's—and especially his own—coffers with the immense wealth left by the king. Governor Varus stopped him, however, ordering him to wait until the decision arrived from Augustus concerning the future of Judaea. Deferring to Varus, Sabinus promised to take no action.

Nevertheless, after Varus had returned to his capital of Antioch in Syria and Archelaus, the chief designated heir, had left for Rome, Sabinus hastened to Jerusalem. There he took control of the palace and ordered a full accounting from all finance ministers and guardians of the treasuries of Herod's many strongholds. Since it was now Pentecost (or seven weeks after Passover), a very large number of native Judaeans filled the city as happened at every festival time.

Indignant over Sabinus and his avariciousness, the great crowds invested the Roman legion which was garrisoned around the palace precincts. Sabinus, securing himself in a tower, ordered the legion to attack which it did with effect until it in turn was assaulted from above by Jews hurling missiles from the porticoes surrounding the legion. Attacked from above and in front, the legionaries set the porticoes afire killing many and putting others to the sword. With the way now cleared soldiers plundered the Temple treasury of four hundred talents (well over $1 million). Retiring to the palace, the Romans now found themselves besieged by ever larger numbers. Sabinus had been sending messages for aid to Varus from the onset of the crisis; the governor-general now set out in force to save the legion (if not Sabinus).

Mobilizing his two remaining legions of eight thousand men, and their four attack alae (wings) of cavalry, two thousand in all, he headed south. Having ordered the auxiliaries of various client kings and chieftains to assemble ahead on the line of march, Varus commanded a force of fifteen–twenty thousand men to the relief of his besieged legion. Ravaging villages en route, Varus arrived in Jerusalem with such a formidable show of force that the armed bands dispersed, leaving the citizens to their own ends. He was met outside the city walls by Joseph, cousin of Archelaus, the tribunes, senior centurions and the legion arrayed in order. Sabinus had already fled for the coast. According to Josephus:

> Varus now detached part of his army to scour the country in search of the authors of the insurrection, many of whom were brought in. Those who appeared to be the less turbulent individuals he imprisoned; the most culpable, in number about two thousand, he crucified.

By the laws of the day Varus was not acting in an unduly harsh way, nor was he overreacting to a minor local disturbance. A basic fact of political life in the Western world at the beginning of the first century A.D. dictated that the newly-proclaimed Roman Empire would not (and could not) condone revolts in its provinces or client-states. Any such attempts had to be dealt with swiftly and forcibly. Such was the case in Judaea. Israel's relationship with Rome brought an imperial power together with a regional one, a polytheistic religion with a monotheistic. Their history covered several hundred years and led to the end of the Jewish state.

Entering into history first as part of the Biblical Israel, Judaea in 167 B.C., led by the brothers Maccabeus (for "hammer"), had revolted against the Hellenistic kingdom of Syria which itself had been formed under the Seleucid successors of Alexander the Great. Under Maccabean leadership an independent Judaea was secured which would last almost a century under the rule of the Hasmonaeans.

In 64 B.C., Judaea first seriously received the attentions of the empire-builders of Rome. Pompey the Great had been "settling the affairs" of the East in Rome's interest for several years. At first delegated supreme commander for the East by the Senate in order to clear the eastern waters of pirates, a great hazard to commerce and the food supply of Rome, he had also been given authority to operate inland to a certain extent. This Pompey did to such effect that when he dedicated the spoils of his victories at the shrine of Minerva in Rome it was in these words, recorded by Pliny:

> Gnaeus Pompeius Magnus, commander-in-chief, having completed a thirty years' war, routed, scattered, slain, or received the surrender of 12,183,000 people, sunk or taken 846 ships, received the capitulation of 1,538 towns and forts, subdued the lands from the Maeotians [on the Sea of Azov] to the Red Sea, duly dedicates his offering vowed to Minerva.

Among these many countries and peoples along the seacoast of Asia (and well inland) which Pompey had conquered was Syria, formally annexing it as a province of the Republic of Rome in 64 B.C. The annexation included not only Syria but the client kingdoms of Commagene and Arabia, the ethnarchy (or people/state) of the Jews, the tetrarchy (petty state) of the Ituraeans and other minor tetrarchies in the north of Palestine. Following the Roman conquest as habitually would occur in Judaea and the surrounding territories during the last century B.C., and the first century A.D., rival claimants to the throne now presented their cases to Pompey who had not yet militarily secured the ancestral capital and religious center of Jerusalem.

The antagonists now in the year 63 B.C. were the brothers Hyrcanus and Aristobolus. Pompey sided with the senior, Hyrcanus, and invested Aristobolus in his mountaintop fortress of Alexandreion northeast of Jerusalem. Pompey commanded Aristobolus to quit the fortress and ordered all other governors to evacuate their fortresses. Aristobolus acceded, withdrew from Alexandreion, and went to Jerusalem to prepare for war.

Determined to allow no time for such preparations, Pompey force-marched on the capital. Aristobulus thereupon went to him as a supplicant promising himself, money and the city. Pompey agreed, and took him prisoner. Aristobolus's followers did not agree with the surrender, however, and barred the gates of Jerusalem. Pompey considered the strength of the walls of the city and that within them the citadel of the Temple rock was equally formidable. While planning his strategy, supporters of Hyrcanus gained the upper hand among the populace through the fear which the Roman legions inspired; the gates of Jerusalem were opened.

"The party of Aristobolus, finding themselves beaten, retired into the temple, cut the bridge which connected it to the city, and prepared to hold out to the last." Pompey resorted to practical Roman siegework, filling in the great ravine on the north side of the mount. Once this had been accomplished the general had siege towers erected on top of the earthworks.

Battering engines were brought up from the port of Tyre to attempt to breach the wall. Covering fire for this siege activity was provided by ballistae, a type of catapult in the form of a large standing, spring-operated crossbow, capable of hurling sixty-pound stones. Nevertheless, the walls held for three months.

The Temple mount fell when one tower was finally overthrown. While the legionaries fought their way in, the priests continued their libations and sacrifices, only to be killed during their ministrations. Many within died at the hands of Hyrcanus' followers, settling scores. The worst occurrence for all Jews at the time was the desecration of the Holy of Holies by the entry of the Romans. "Pompey indeed, along with his staff, penetrated to the sanctuary, entry to which was permitted to none but the high priest, and beheld what it contained: the candelabrum and lamps, the table, the vessels for libation and censers, all of solid gold, an accumulation of spices and the store of sacred money amounting to two thousand talents." (A talent in Judaea at the time was equivalent to over 1,500 ounces of gold or three thousand gold shekels.) Pompey touched none of it, however, and later ordered the custodians to cleanse the Temple and resume the customary sacrifices. So ended the first major Roman siege of Jerusalem.

Pompey next reinstated Hyrcanus as high priest for his supportive actions during the siege. The general made Judaea a tributary state of Rome while stripping it of all its non-Jewish possessions, i.e., its Greek cities on the coastal plain, and Samaria and Transjordan. Judaea became once again a purely Jewish state.

Pompey appointed his legate, or lieutenant-general, Marcus Aemilius Scaurus, as governor-general of the newly-created province of Syria which included Judaea. Scaurus was given two legions to garrison his province and its territories which stretched from Syria in the north to the borders of the kingdom of Egypt in the south. Pompey, having settled the affairs of Syria and Judaea, set out overland for Rome. With him was the former king Aristobolus, who would later be paraded through the streets of Rome as part of Pompey's triumph in 61 B.C. Many of the Jews who were brought to Rome as slaves at this time were later freed and formed a major part of the Jewish colony of Rome.

Scaurus attempted to secure the borders of his province with a campaign against the neighboring Nabataeans, an Arabic people. Faced with a severe lack of provisions the legate allowed himself to be bought off by the sum of three hundred talents paid by the Nabataean ruler, Aretas. Aulus Gabinius soon replaced Scaurus as proconsul of Syria, and in succession had to put down rebellions by Alexander, son of Aristobolus in 57 B.C., and then by Aristobolus himself, who had escaped from Rome in 56 B.C. In both of these actions Gabinius's very able lieutenant-general was Marc Antony, who commanded one legion. Gabinius also restructured the territory into five regions, each centered upon an important city.

After yet another revolt by Alexander in 55 B.C., which Gabinius crushed—killing ten thousand at the battle of Mount Tabor—the proconsul was replaced by Marcus Licinius Crassus as governor-general of Syria. In his quest for martial fame to match Pompey and Caesar, Crassus had already conceived his Parthian war. To supply his ill-fated legions for the expedition in 53 B.C., Crassus plundered the Temple at Jerusalem of all its gold including the two thousand talents which Pompey had left untouched. Soon thereafter the general and twenty thousand of his men died in the desert under the relentless attacks of Parthian horsemen.

With the death of Crassus and the annihilation of his army Syria seemed to lay open for conquest. The legate Gaius Cassius had escaped the debacle with several thousand men, however, and he succeeded in repulsing the Parthians after they had crossed the Euphrates. Cassius would later be a major conspirator against Julius Caesar on the Ides of March.

At this time the ruler of Idumaea, the region south of Judaea proper, was Antipater, another man of great ambition. Having first attached himself to Pompey's cause, Antipater courted Caesar after Pompey's murder in Egypt. When Caesar was trapped and under siege in Alexandria, Antipater led troops to aid in his relief. Caesar began his return from Egypt overland through Judaea and the provinces of Syria and Asia. He designated Antipater procurator of Judaea, the first non-Roman to hold the office since Pompey's conquest. Hyrcanus was again reconfirmed as high priest and Antipater was granted permission to rebuild the walls of Jerusalem which had been dismantled by Pompey.

As part of his reorganization of the government of Judaea in 47 B.C., Antipater appointed his eldest son, Phasael, military prefect for Jerusalem and its environs, and his second son, Herod, to the same office in Galilee. He would later be known as the Herod the Great of the Scriptures.

The assassination of Julius Caesar in 44 B.C. caused repercussions in every province and subject or allied state of the Republic. Parties coalesced among the Roman military and civil administrators, and the garrisons, as well as within the ruling cliques of the client-states. Syria, and so Judaea, had its own unique situation in that Cassius, who had helped kill Caesar, had already been appointed proconsul of Syria by Caesar before his murder. The man who had saved Syria from the Parthians was now governor-general commanding its garrison legions.

The death of Caesar was a great loss to the Jews for he had given them greater autonomy within their realm. Cassius turned to extortion to raise the wealth needed to fight Caesar's avengers, Antony and Octavian. The governor ordered seven hundred talents to be raised; Herod and Antipater produced one hundred talents each. To raise the balance, the inhabitants of four towns that did not meet their quota were sold into slavery. Having raised levies in addition to the legions of Syria, Cassius appointed young Herod procurator and marched north. Cassius died a suicide, as did Brutus, at the battle of Philippi in 42 B.C. Antony took control of the East and in 41 B.C. appointed Herod and Phasael as tetrarchs, or regional rulers in Judaea. The following year the Parthians seized an opportunity to invade again; Herod was forced to retire upon the citadel of Masada on the west bank of the Dead Sea. The Parthians then pillaged Jerusalem.

Herod found no aid forthcoming from the Nabataeans nor any other neighbors. Reaching Egypt, he received an elaborate reception from Cleopatra who was at that time seeking allies herself. Nevertheless Herod set sail for Rome. Antony presented Herod to the Senate and both Octavian and he agreed that in view of Herod's and his father Antipater's services to Rome, Herod should be king. It was thus decreed and Herod supplanted the century-old line of the Maccabees.

Of course, to be king requires a kingdom and the occupier of the throne at that time was Antigonus, a Hellenistic claimant backed by the Parthians. With the aid of Roman forces under Ventidius Bassus the Parthians were driven from Judaea in 39 B.C. and in an incursion the succeeding year the Parthian crown prince Pacorus was killed. With the reconquest of Jerusalem Herod became king in 37 B.C. Though Herod was in theory an independent king allied to Rome, in fact he had to coexist with the dominant power of the age. This he did adroitly through his political agility and astuteness. Cleopatra had long coveted Judaea and its adjacent lands as a means of restoring a semblance of the ancient Egyptian Empire. She therefore entreated Antony for them and hoped to have Herod eliminated. Though he gave her some of the southernmost tracts, Antony would not remove Herod. Herod mollified Cleopatra by leasing his own lands back, which had been detached, for an annual sum of one hundred talents.

When Octavian defeated Antony and Cleopatra at Actium in 31 B.C., Herod did not suffer. The future Augustus Caesar recognized his value as a strong client-king on the southeast fringe of the Empire and did not replace or demote him. Herod, for his part, realized that whoever represented the Roman Republic's (and later Empire's) power in Judaea at a given time was the official with whom to cooperate, and he did so. His kingdom now secure, Herod turned to his great passion—building. The palaces and citadels he had erected served three purposes: as monuments to his own glory, as places of habitation, and, most importantly, secure fortifications. In Jerusalem itself was built the Fortress Antonia (named for Antony), contiguous with and dominating the northern wall of the Temple precincts. Though it served the dual purpose of a palace, the Antonia became the base for later Roman garrisons and the symbol of Rome itself—now overlooking the Temple, the heart of Judaea.

The Temple had never been properly restored after its destruction by the Babylonians in 587 B.C. Herod spent great sums renewing its glories in the decade 20–10 B.C., utilizing the measurements and descriptions of the Bible. A thousand Levite priests were trained for the work, and services and sacrifices were never interrupted. The final details were finished in 64 A.D., six years before it would be utterly destroyed.

In time mistrusting nearly everyone (including his family), Herod built two fortresses known as Herodium on two great circular mounds southeast of Jerusalem. His major refuge, however, which he hoped to make impregnable, was Masada on a bleak mountainous plateau overlooking the Dead Sea. To enhance commerce and ensure the sea-link to Rome, Herod had an entire port city, Caesarea, constructed complete with an artificial harbor. The city was situated on the site of a Hellenistic town called Strato's Tower, south of Tyre and north of Joppa. The harbor was larger than Athens' port, the Piraeus. Caesarea was later to serve as the capital for the Roman governor-generals.

Though Herod the Great proved a solid ally of Rome and steward of Rome's interests in the region, he was not beloved by his subjects or family. The people disliked Herod because he had extinguished the Hasmonaean, or Maccabeean, line of kings which had freed Judaea from the Hellenistic monarchs of the north. In his paranoia, Herod had his first wife Mariamme I, executed in 29 B.C., two sons banished, several brothers-in-law killed, and finally, in 7 B.C., two sons executed. A few days before his own death in 4 B.C., Herod had his son Alexander executed. If the Gospel of St. Matthew is correct, Herod also had all the male infants of Bethlehem killed that same year in the hope of eliminating the Messiah (with the year 4 B.C., as currently accepted for Christ's birth).

In keeping with his character Herod had made three surviving sons heirs to the single throne. As was usual in such cases the matter went to the Emperor Augustus in Rome. The Emperor decided to divide the power, making Archelaus ethnarch (leader of the people) of Judaea. The brothers Antipas and Philip each became tetrarchs, or rulers of one-quarter of the country. Augustus himself was a beneficiary of Herod, receiving one thousand talents in gratitude for his support over the years.

After the rebellion of 4 B.C. following Herod's death had been put down by Varus, Archelaus continued to have troubles governing Judaea. Finally, in 6 A.D., Augustus deposed him and appointed a Roman procurator for Judaea. Procurators were governors drawn from the equestrian, or knightly, class of Rome. They were next in rank to legates who were usually of the noble senatorial class and had most often previously served as consuls at Rome, second to the Emperor himself as generals/administrators.

The Roman procurators established themselves in Herod's palace at Caesarea, residing in Jerusalem only during the great pilgrimage-festivals of the Jewish year such as Passover, when disturbances would most likely occur.

Also in 6 A.D., a census for tax purposes was announced, and an uprising accordingly occurred under two popular leaders, Judas and Sadduq. Sulpicius Quirinus, legate of Syria, put down the rebellion but its ideas survived to wreak much greater havoc later in the party of the Zealots. Augustus appointed three procurators from 6–14 A.D.; his successor Tiberius only two in twenty-three years.

The Emperor Tiberius first designated Valerius Gratus procurator of Judaea; he served from A.D. 15–26 A.D. His successor in 27 A.D. was Pontius Pilate who immediately caused a major controversy by introducing into Jerusalem images of Caesar in the form of medallions attached to the standards of legions. Since images were prohibited, the people and the priests protested vigorously. After six days Pilate gave in to the religious zeal and removed them.

The Roman governors of Judaea—as did Herod and his successors—accumulated much of their wealth by selling off the high-priesthood to the top bidder, then deposed that person in a year or two. This, of course, limited the position to a very few wealthy families and it became one of the major causes of the great revolt in 66 A.D. The high priest during Pilate's reign was Caiaphas, the last of four appointed by Gratus, and the same Caiaphas of the Gospel who condemned Jesus Christ to death under Jewish law. Pilate did so under Roman law.

Tiberius was succeeded by Caligula whose impiety toward any and all gods began in Rome and extended to all provinces. He ordered his statue, as a deity, erected in the Temple of Jerusalem. To effect this Publius Petronius, then governor of Syria, was dispatched with two legions and auxiliaries. Petronius was met by a large delegation of Jews offering themselves and their families for sacrifice to avoid transgressing the law of their god. Moved by this, Petronius procrastinated and sent Caligula a dispatch explaining that fulfillment of the order could result in destruction of Judaea. By the fortunes of weather at sea, Petronius's death-warrant reached him only after the news of Caligula's own assassination.

Claudius now became emperor through the power of the Praetorian Guard. The Emperor's first important appointment to procurator of Judaea was Tiberius Julius Alexander, by birth a Jew but by upbringing a Hellenized cosmopolitan from Alexandria in Egypt. He held the status of a Roman equite, or knight, and was both a capable administrator and general. A revolt led by two sons of Judas of Galilee, the rebel leader of 6 A.D., was crushed by Alexander; both sons were crucified. T. Julius Alexander served only three years in this period, from 46–48 A.D., but would return later in much more important roles. The next procurator was Ventidius Cumanus, who served from 48–52 A.D. Cumanus proved himself at least pragmatically sensitive to Jewish religious practices and laws. When a Roman soldier of the ranks, in a gesture of contempt, tore up a copy of the Scriptures and threw it into a fire, a massive uprising seemed imminent. Cumanus had the soldier arrested and executed. Cumanus was soon replaced by Antoninus Felix.

At about the same time gangs of Jewish assassins began to strike at those whose political views differed from their own. Extremists murdered moderates openly and dramatically; personal scores were avenged in public. The killers were known as *Sicarii* from the Latin *sica* for the curved dagger the murderers employed. According to Josephus "The festivals were their special seasons, when they would mingle with the crowd, carrying short daggers concealed under their clothing, with which they stabbed their enemies." The first victim was Jonathan, the high priest, after which came numerous daily murders. Along with the chaos in the streets and markets of Jerusalem caused by the sicarii, messianic impostors began to appear. False prophets claimed that through divine intervention revolutionary changes were soon to come.

In Rome in 54 A.D., Claudius died, succeeded as Emperor by his stepson Nero. The same year the procurator of Judaea, Felix, was still in office when an Egyptian appeared who gathered a following of four thousand with the promise of delivering Jerusalem from the Romans. Instead of the walls collapsing for them (as Jericho's did for Joshua), Felix led out the Tenth Fretensis Legion which proceeded to kill four hundred and capture two hundred of the believers. The Egyptian escaped. The incident was typical of the civil disorder caused by the emergence of religious fanatics attempting to revive the ancient days of the first nation of Israel.

Josephus wrote, "No sooner were these disorders reduced than the inflammation, as in a sick man's body, broke out again in another quarter. The impostors and brigands, banding together, incited numbers to revolt, exhorting them to assert their independence, and threatening to kill any who submitted to Roman domination and forcibly to suppress those who voluntarily accepted servitude." Forming into companies throughout the countryside, the brigands began a campaign of raiding wealthy country estates, murdering their owners, and burning neighboring villages.

Disorders were rampant not only in the country villages and Jerusalem but in other major cities. Caesarea was split between the Syrian residents of Greek descent and the Jewish inhabitants. Daily rioting led finally to intervention by Felix and then supreme adjudication of the issues before the Emperor Nero himself in Rome.

Felix was succeeded in 59 A.D. by Porcius Festus. Not long after his arrival, the Caesaraean dispute was resolved in favor of the gentile Syrians. In effect, Jews became second-class citizens in the Roman capital of Judaea. This produced another major cause of the Revolt of 66 A.D. Festus died suddenly and unexpectedly in 62 A.D.

During the three month interregnum preceding a new appointment, the high priest Annas II seized the opportunity to settle his political and religious scores. Annas had James the Just, leader of the Nazarene Christians of Jerusalem, executed. Many of the more pious Jews believed that such an act would incur the wrath of God on the city. The ethnarch of the Jews at this point was Agrippa II, a pragmatic supporter of Rome and great-grandson of Herod. Agrippa deposed Annas upon learning of the killing of James.

The procurator Albinus succeeded Festus; his major action in a tenure of two years was to wipe out many of the Sicarii. The many self-proclaimed messiahs, the brigands and their gangs, the political revolutionaries and religious visionaries had all been building toward a major, and possibly final, confrontation with the Roman Empire.

As ill-advised and planned as it was, the extremists were ready and organized enough to initiate a major strike against the Roman occupation. What had not been thought through, however, was that Rome could not, and would not, allow attempts at even limited autonomy by a subject kingdom which had not been approved by the Emperor and the Senate beforehand. Judaea had been treated well according to the standards of the time—the Jewish religion was intact and accepted, taxes were paid. But taxes were always being paid to some authority, if only the Temple priests, and men were not conscripted into the Roman army.

The breaking point came with the accession to office of Gessius Florus in 64 A.D., replacing Albinus. His greed was famous throughout Judaea and brigands felt they could operate freely if they split the take with the governor.

Cestius Gallus governed Syria at the same time, though unaware of happenings in Judaea. When Gallus became cognizant of the rampant corruption he took it under advisement yet made no decisive changes.

Florus, meanwhile, hoped that a rebellion would in fact occur for it would help cover his own misdeeds. In May of 66 A.D., Caesarea reached its explosive point. Because gentiles had sacrificed birds at the doors of a synagogue—the normal sacrifice to cure leprosy—the law had been violated. The Jews, insulted, sent a delegation to Florus for redress. The procurator had them arrested for removing a copy of the "Law" from Caesarea.

Ignoring the numerous signs of coming troubles, Florus ordered the Temple to deliver seventeen talents to him for "imperial service." Invoking the name of Caesar, the ordinary people demanded that Florus be removed. Malcontents mocked the procurator in the streets, begging coppers for Florus, since he seemed to need money so badly. In May Florus marched on Jerusalem, lodging in Herod's palace. Moderates begged his clemency declaring a few hotheads had instigated the incidents. But Florus no longer cared as to cause nor ultimate effect. He ordered the Xth Fretensis to attack the agora, or upper marketplace, pillage at will and kill anyone in the way.

Josephus wrote, "The troops, whose lust for booty was thus backed by their general's order, not only plundered the quarter which they were sent to attack, but plunged into every house and slaughtered the inmates." Florus had many of even the most notable citizens brought before him, scourged, then crucified at random. He carried through these punishments even though some of the victims were of equestrian rank.

With the arrival of several cohorts of reinforcements Florus attempted to force his way through the narrow streets of Jerusalem and gain the security of the Fortress Antonia, overlooking and dominating the Temple and its treasures. The crowds led by the rebels had the same objective: using their numbers and the capability of fighting from the roofs above the lanes the legion was repulsed.

Florus now decided to withdraw. After consulting the moderate elders a cohort was chosen as a garrison (*not* the one involved in the earlier massacre) and the procurator retired to Caesarea. Gallus, governor of Syria, sent his staff-officer Neapolitanus to investigate the city's situation. Joining up with King Agrippa II, the two secular administrative authorities toured Jerusalem.

Moderate Jews of the upper classes wished to stop the corruption and attendant reactive violence through the proper channels: by sending an embassy to the Emperor Nero in Rome. Agrippa saw the difficulties inherent in getting a Roman official removed from office yet he wanted to dissuade the Jews from the alternative of open rebellion. He therefore spoke to a huge crowd assembled before the palace of the Hasmonaeans. Agrippa stressed first that one bad governor from Rome did not justify war against the Emperor and the Roman people. "Look at the Athenians, the men who, to maintain the liberty of Greece, once consigned their city to the flames; . . . Those men today are the servants of the Romans and the city that was queen of Greece is governed by orders from Italy. Look at the Lacedaemonians: after Thermopylae and Plataea, after Agesilaus the explorer of Asia, they are content to serve the same masters."

Agrippa continued to recount that Philip and Alexander's Macedonians "submit to endure such a reversal of fate and bow before those to whom Fortune has transferred her favors. Myriads of other nations, swelling with greater pride in the assertion of their liberty, have yielded. And will you alone disdain to serve those to whom the universe is subject? . . . Do you really suppose that you are going to war with Egyptians or Arabs?

"I ask you, then, are you wealthier than the Gauls, stronger than the Germans, more intelligent than the Greeks, more numerous than all the peoples of the world? What is it which inspires you with confidence to defy the Romans?"

After delineating all of the provinces and client-kingdoms of the Empire and the absurdly small numbers with which they were garrisoned, from the Danube and the Rhine to the wastes of sub-Saharan Africa, from Britain and the Pillars of Hercules to the Euphrates River in the east, Agrippa asked the Jews whence help would come for the revolt. The reply was that there would be no aid from any neighboring states or former allies. "The only refuge, then, left to you is divine assistance. But even this is ranged on the side of the Romans, for, without God's aid, so vast an empire could never have been built up. . . . All who embark on war do so in reliance on the support either of God or man; but when, in all probability, no assistance from either quarter is forthcoming, then the aggressor goes with his eyes open to certain ruin."

Agrippa then issued his final warning for he believed that the Romans would not hold back in the event of a full-scale revolt, and the Roman "forbearance in the past met only with ingratitude," would lead Rome "to make you an example to the rest of the nations, they will burn the holy city to the ground and exterminate your race." This pragmatic speech made no impression on the bent-on-war extremists.

Agrippa therefore left Jerusalem to its fate. With reinforcements sent by Agrippa, the leading men of the Jews, the moderates and the chief priests, and all those in favor of peace occupied the upper city. The insurgents held the lower city and the Temple.

The principal leader of the rebels at this time was Eleazar, captain of the Temple and son of the high priest Ananias. Eleazar now ordered cessation of the daily sacrifice offered at the Temple for the welfare of the Emperor. Ending the practice was tantamount to declaring war on Rome. Joined by the Sicarii, some of the rebels overran the upper city, and notwithstanding Eleazar's connection, burned the high-priest Ananias's house and also Agrippa's palace. The public archives were also burned, destroying all debtors' records. The Fortress Antonia with its small garrison fell next; all Romans were killed. Any remaining royalists and Romans now fortified Herod's palace. While Jerusalem was in this stasis the last surviving son of the revolutionary Judas of Galilee, Menahem, raided Herod's fortress of Masada (6 A.D.). Stocked a century before, the armories there provided enough weaponry for ten thousand men, or the equivalent of two full Roman legions.

Menahem sought to make himself the leader of Judaea against Rome. Eliminating rivals, Menahem had Ananias and his brother Ezechias killed; the son of the high-priest, Eleazar, planned revenge. Ambushed unawares in the Temple itself, Menahem and his chief lieutenants were massacred. This first incident among the leaders of the revolt was a portent of the rabid internecine warfare which would cripple the ill-fated rebellion from the start.

Besides killing their own, the Jewish extremists sealed their fate by treacherous dealings with the remnants of the Roman garrison. Having made an agreement, the legionaries abandoned their fortifications. Marching out and surrendering their weapons—all under guarantee of free passage sworn by oath in a covenant—Eleazar's men proceeded to slaughter the unarmed soldiers. It was a serious mistake.

Florus realized he could not deal with the situation alone; Gallus marched from Syria with the XIIth Legion and auxiliaries. Realizing he lacked sufficient numbers to take the city he retreated. Caught in a pass in the highlands west of Jerusalem, on November 25, 66 A.D., the legion suffered heavy losses in an ambush at Beth-horon.

It was to be a hollow victory, however, for though the moderates were discredited and the extremists reinforced in their aims they had not yet faced the might of Rome when it was fully aroused. The defense of Jerusalem was placed under Joseph Ben Gorion and Annas II, a former high-priest. Eleazar and Jesus, son of Sapphias, commanded Idumaea, a region southwest of Jerusalem. Another Eleazar, son of a Zealot named Simon, held great power through possession of the booty taken from the Romans and a major part of the public treasury of Jerusalem. The general Josephus (later chief historian of the Jewish wars) shared the command of Galilee with John of Gischala.

While the unrest in Jerusalem built to a conflagration, the Jews of Alexandria in Egypt were also rising. After three Jews were burned by a mob a large number of the Jewish community attacked the amphitheater full of gentiles, attempting to burn it. Tiberius Julius Alexander now intervened. He ordered both of his legions, with two thousand auxiliaries, to attack. The dissidents were crushed.

In Palestine, meanwhile, Gallus attempted to keep the rebellion under control without aid from the extremely thin reserves available to the Emperor.

Pacifying Galilee for the moment, Gallus approached the capital. The insurgents had gathered such numbers that the Roman army lost over five hundred men—or nearly a cohort—and a tactical retreat was necessary. Agrippa tried to negotiate but to no avail.

The Emperor Nero now decided that a supreme commander was the only answer to the Jerusalem revolt. He therefore appointed a general of the guard, Vespasian, to the supreme command in Syria and Judaea. According to Josephus:

> Vespasian was one who had been a soldier from his youth and grown gray in the service; he had already restored to Roman rule the West when convulsed by the Germans; he had by his military genius added to the Empire Britain, till then almost unknown, and thus afforded Claudius, Nero's father, the honours of a triumph which cost him no personal exertion.

Vespasian wasted no time in organizing and coordinating his campaign against Judaea. Gathering his legions and auxiliaries as he advanced south from Greece (where he had been attending Nero at the Olympic games), Vespasian had his son Titus mobilize the XV Apollinaris Legion in Alexandria to join the Judaean campaign. The Jews, meanwhile, were celebrating their defeat of Gallus at Ben-horon and did not take steps to organize and unite (which would have given them their only chance for a possible—if temporary—victory over the Romans).

Vespasian now commanded the V Macedonica and the X Fretensis; his son Titus had brought up the XV Apollinaris. The auxiliary cohorts numbered twenty-three, or approximately two legions or ten thousand men. Other auxiliaries provided by client-kings raised the number by another fifteen–twenty thousand men. The cavalry amounted, at the outset, to two thousand. Judaea was not prepared for such a concerted response. Aside from several of Herod's strongholds, Jerusalem's walls were its only real defense. Given the Roman experience in—and knowledge of—siege warfare, the fall of Jerusalem became a matter of time; vicious, savage time. Fanaticism, in the end, could not stand up to disciplined Roman legions and the veteran engineers directing the siege.

The Roman order of march began with light-armed auxiliaries and archers. A heavy-armed legion, with its cavalry accompaniment, followed. The first legion had the sappers behind them clearing the way as necessary. The best of the legionary infantry with supporting cavalry escorted Vespasian. After the general came the legions of the line, eagles foremost and the ranks formed in six files.

Before attacking Jerusalem Vespasian had to attack and pacify the towns of the countryside, and the first tactical objective was the region of Galilee. The principal stronghold of the region was the city of Jotapata commanded by Josephus, Ben-Mattathias and Joseph of Gischala.

A preliminary attack by the Romans made no progress though there were many wounded on both sides. Jotapata was surrounded on three sides by precipitous cliffs; the fourth had a twisted approach track which Josephus had fortified. To take the approachable section of the wall Vespasian ordered all of his foot-soldiers to gather wood and earth to use in matching the level of the wall. While some worked on mounting the earthwork, others built protection overhead to ward off the rocks and missiles that continually rained on the engineers and their legionaries. Vespasian next brought up his catapults and ballistae, firing stones, lances and fire-brands at those manning the walls. Josephus replied by ordering his masons to raise the level of the walls.

Upon hearing of the general's intent to leave the city all of the citizens begged him to remain. Josephus, for his own reasons, hesitated. By necessity, however, he had to remain and direct the defense. Vespasian now brought up the "Ram." Iron-headed and one hundred feet long, it would take down even the strongest gate. To support the men wielding the Ram Vespasian had all of his catapult and ballistae men operating, along with all of his Arabian archers and Syrian slingers.

After fifty days the wall had not yet been breached and Vespasian himself had been wounded in the foot. Of the Roman general's men, "Each wished to be the first to brave danger in avenging his general, and with shouts of mutual encouragement, they rushed the ramparts." Finally information came that at the last watch of the night the guards were lax; a concerted effort at the gates might carry it. It did. The Romans with the losses they had suffered in the fifty-day siege showed no mercy; boiling oil had been poured on their fellow-soldiers and they replied in kind.

Josephus found himself taking refuge with forty other leaders of the city. Planning on surrendering, Josephus was stopped by those with him. Though they threatened to kill him, preferring death to slavery, Josephus decided not to die there. Instead he suggested a lottery in which the first killed the second, and so on until the last was dead. Josephus, however, fortuitously persuaded the last man not to die; the two survived.

Brought before Vespasian, it was the general's son Titus whose compassion kept Josephus from execution. Titus was twenty-seven in 67 A.D.; Josephus only thirty. The commander of Jotapata asked for an interview with Vespasian. The Roman general kept Titus and two aides with him. Vespasian had said that he would send Josephus to Nero, and that meant an unpleasant death.

Josephus, perhaps gifted with prophecy, talked his way back to life:

I come to you as a messenger of great destinies . . . To Nero do you send me? Why then? Think you that [Nero and] those who before your accession succeed him will continue? You will be Caesar, Vespasian, you will be emperor, you and your son here. Bind me then yet more securely in chains and keep me for yourself; for you, Caesar, are master not of me only, but of land and sea and the whole human race. For myself, I ask to be punished by stricter custody, if I have dared to trifle with the words of God.

Vespasian had already experienced numerous portents of an imperial future and Josephus's words reinforced the belief. His life was spared, and he became the historian of the Jewish War. John of Gischala escaped to Jerusalem.

Vespasian retired to winter quarters in Caesarea. In the spring of 68 A.D., Vespasian began the new campaigning season by reducing the cities of the seacoast and then proceeding inland. A large number of the revolutionaries had gathered at Tarichaeae on the shores of Lake Germesar in Galilee. Titus was given operational command and attacked the Jewish army on the plain outside of the city. Holding for a while against the Roman charges the rebel lines finally broke under the attack of the Roman cavalry; they fled to the city. Titus attempted to cut off the retreat but superior numbers got the rebels into the city.

The inhabitants of the city, however, had not wanted the war. Hearing the commotion inside, Titus addressed his troops. "Now is the time," he cried, "why tarry, comrades, when God himself delivers the Jews into your hands?" Titus himself was first into the breach on the unwalled side facing the lake.

Having taken Tarichaeae, Vespasian had to decide what to do with the prisoners. Liberating them would leave an army at his back; death or servitude were the choices. He offered the captives the option of a journey to the city of Tiberias. Legionaries lined the route. Upon arrival all were herded into a stadium. Twelve hundred of those old and unfit for service were killed. Six thousand of the ablest were sent to Nero in Greece for work on the canal planned for the Isthmus of Corinth. The rest, totalling thirty thousand, were sold into slavery.

John of Gischala maintained his role as one of the leaders of the rebellion. Escaping to Jerusalem, he became the virtual master of the city by playing off the priestly class, the moderates, against the Zealots led by Eleazar, son of Simon (not the captain of the Temple). While John was consolidating his position in Jerusalem the city of Gamala near the Syrian border put up a fierce defense.

As Gamala was built onto a hillside, the numbers of the attacking legionaries and the weight of their siege-engines caused landslides to occur killing many Romans and Jews. Vespasian, now sixty, led his men as only forty years in the service of Rome could have prepared him. He formed a shield-wall, linking man-to-man, shield overlapping shield and thus repulsed the enemy.

Within a few days the people of the city lost their heart for the fight. While the siege of Gamala continued Vespasian reduced the fortifications on Mount Tabor, built by Josephus. Following a bloody siege, fought partly in a thunderstorm, Mount Tabor was taken. The Romans accounted for four thousand dead; five thousand Jews killed themselves off the cliffs.

Jerusalem now became the key to subjugating the rebellion in Judaea. It was, in one place, the heart, soul and the best-fortified position available for the Jewish rebels. If it could be held, some sort of negotiated peace was conceivable (however unlikely).

The capital was now the haven for all who bore a grievance with Rome: both the legitimate ones, who strove to free Judaea, and the criminal bands who had preyed on their own people and now feared Rome's wrath. As Josephus says the brigands operated in a manner such that, "The various cliques began by pillaging their neighbours, then banding together in companies they carried their depredations throughout the country; insomuch that in cruelty and lawlessness the sufferers found no difference between compatriots and Romans, indeed to be captured by the latter seemed to the unfortunate victims the lighter fate."

Since Jerusalem lacked a single commander, and all who claimed Jewish origin were admitted entry, "it (Josephus, Book IV, 134) was just this circumstance which, notwithstanding the sedition, eventually wrecked the city; for supplies which might have sufficed for the combatants were squandered upon a useless and idle mob. . . ."

Upon mastering the city the gangs imprisoned the most noble and upstanding citizens. Knowing they could not hold them and remain safe from their kin and the Romans, they massacred them, having falsely accused them of collusion with Rome.

In order to secure the best position in the city, the gangs took the Temple mount to protect themselves from both the common people and the Romans. Mocking one of the holiest traditions of the Jewish religion, the brigands then selected high-priests by lot from any layer of society, not from the traditional priestly families. The high-priest at the time, Ananus, offered his life to them saying, "If it must be then, alone will I go and, as in utter desolation, devote this single life of mine in the cause of God."

John continued to hold sway, attempting to rouse the Zealots whom he had previously turned against, to form an alliance against Rome. To gather more allies John persuaded the leaders of the people to call up the ancient alliance with the Idumaeans, whence Herod the Great had come. They sent twenty thousand men to Jerusalem. Scorning the high priest, the Idumaeans killed Ananus and his chief aide, Jesus. Not content with their deaths the Zealots and the Idumaeans now began torturing and killing others in the upper classes.

Vespasian, having reduced Galilee and the surrounding regions, held a council of war: the subject was Jerusalem. His generals urged an immediate attack on the city. Vespasian urged caution, waiting upon the Jews to eliminate more of each other's parties, leaving the city in a weaker state for a Roman siege. The Zealots continued to take out their rage on their fellow-citizens. The wealthy, having paid a large sum, were allowed to leave; the poor were slaughtered. Since the relatives who sought to retrieve the dead faced the same fate the bodies bloated in the sun, sacrilegiously unburned.

Events in Rome now made those in Judaea of minor account to Vespasian and his top men. The first occurrence was the revolt of the Gauls under the leader Vindex. Knowing that Nero's military acumen was not to be trusted Vespasian feared for Rome itself. Accordingly, he secured and garrisoned as much of the Palestinian countryside as possible. He turned next to the citadel of Jericho.

Knowing in advance that Vespasian was on the march, the citizens of Jericho abandoned it. Those who tried to reach Jerusalem were caught and killed. The Jewish capital was now isolated. Those wishing to leave the city were stopped and either killed or detained by the Zealots.

Vespasian's timetable for the capture of Jerusalem was thrown off by events in Rome. Vindex of the Gauls had been eliminated and with him the Gallic threat to Rome. It was the imperial succession which now was the major political imperative in Rome.

The "Long Year" of 69 A.D. actually began with the death of Nero in 68 A.D. Faced by a Senate and people disgusted by his excesses and possible insanity, he was forced to suicide at the hands of a slave who drove a sword through his heart.

Within the following year (69 A.D.) four generals proclaimed themselves Caesar, the first three killed in turn until Vespasian triumphed with the support of Eastern and Danubian legions. Galba first attempted the throne followed by Otho and then Vitellius. Vespasian was a loyal Roman, and when Galba became Caesar, Vespasian recognized the accession when the news arrived in Judaea in late June of 68 A.D. Waiting upon events in Rome, Vespasian suspended most military action from the death of Nero in June, 68 A.D., until the following summer.

Titus was sent by his father in December of the same year to pay his respects to the new emperor. Agrippa, as a client-king, accompanied Titus. While enroute, the two learned of the assassination of Galba and the elevation of the general Otho who was raised up by the Praetorian Guard. Even as Otho attempted to consolidate his power the general Vitellius was gathering his army in Germany, mustering the elements of ten legions (including those in Britain).

Vitellius was acclaimed Emperor in the summer of 69 A.D., and Vespasian and Titus held back, awaiting events. Even though Jerusalem had not yet fallen Vespasian had reduced the countryside and had only four fortresses to contend with. The Roman Senate and people had been impressed by his overall strategic campaign against the Jews.

Galba's men in Spain had pushed him forth as Emperor; the Praetorian Guard had nominated Otho; the legions of Germany backed Vitellius. It was now the legions of the East and Danube who produced an emperor.

Tiberius Julius Alexander, prefect of Egypt and governor in the name of the Emperor in Egypt which was an imperial province, and thus not subject to the Senate, backed his old friend Vespasian. On July 1, 69 A.D., Tiberius Alexander administered the oath of allegiance to the two legions under his command, the III Cyrenaica and the XXII Deiotoriana. With Egypt having taken the lead the legionaries of Judaea and Syria followed suit within the next ten days. Vespasian now commanded the loyalty of eight full legions (with their attendant auxiliaries) and the troops of the client-kingdoms of the region, for a total of approximately eighty-five thousand men. Since the total legions defending the entire Empire numbered thirty, or approximately 300,000 men, Vespasian held a strong hand. Before his onset on Rome, Vespasian made one more incursion into the Palestinian countryside quelling local bands and reinforcing garrisons. Simon ben Giora, an ally of the Zealots at Masada, was driven from there to the capital.

Jerusalem now had three dissident leaders: Simon ben Giora held the city itself and its suburbs; John of Gischala controlled the outer court of the Temple and its precincts, while Eleazar held the inner court and the treasury. With Jerusalem divided and Rome in its own state of turmoil, Vespasian set out for Italy. The Emperor-designate Vespasian named his son Titus to assume command of the Jewish campaign.

In April, 70 A.D., Titus laid siege to Jerusalem. The great feast of the Passover was coming but no warnings sufficed to hold off the expected numbers of pilgrims. Every additional person meant less food for the fighters. Since Eleazar had had John's father killed, John successfully avenged the crime and Eleazar was murdered. The defense of Jerusalem now fell to John and Simon. Soon after the Zealots set fire to the granaries of the city hoping thereby to instill a desperate willingness among the population to meet the Roman army in pitched battle. There were no takers.

The result was starvation and death in the streets; rumors of cannibalism were rampant. On July 24, the Romans recaptured Fortress Antonia. Twelve days later the daily sacrifice in the Temple ended. On August 27, 70 A.D., Titus forebore from any aesthetic or religious distinctions concerning the Temple.

"Titus, now that he saw that his endeavour to spare a foreign temple led only to the injury and slaughter of his troops, issued orders to set the gates on fire." Though Titus only wished to gain entry and end the siege by August 29, the fire had gotten out of control and the Temple could not be saved. Before the Temple's end, however:

> The Romans (Josephus, Book VI, 230), now that the rebels had fled to the city, and the sanctuary itself and all around it were in flames, carried their standards into the temple court and, setting them up opposite the eastern gate, there sacrificed to them, and with rousing acclamations hailed Titus as imperator.

Though Titus might well have wanted to preserve the Temple, it burned on the anniversary of its burning in 587 B.C., at the hands of the Babylonians. The legions had lost too many men—many in an ugly manner—and were in no mood for mercy. With the Temple ablaze and now near total destruction, the soldiers burned the city. Whether Titus himself sanctioned the conflagration is not known but there was little that could be done about it once it had begun.

By September 26 the Roman army controlled Jerusalem; whatever had survived the fire was now razed to the ground. Herod's towers on the western wall of the mount alone remained. The legionaries acquired so much plunder from the Temple and the citizenry that throughout the province of Syria the glut of gold forced its value down by half.

Among the prisoners were both John of Gischala and Simon son of Giora. Both were sent to Rome for the Triumph of Vespasian and Titus. Though three fortresses—Herodion, Machaerum and Masada—still held out, the fall and utter destruction of Jerusalem meant in essence that the war had ended.

Titus sold thirty thousand prisoners at auction and held a victory review at Agrippa II's capital of Caesarea Philippi. Gladiatorial games were presented at which 2,500 Jews died in the arena. The games were in honor of the birthday of Titus's younger brother, Domitian. For Vespasian's birthday, on November 17, 70 A.D., an even greater number died in games at Beirut (Berytus).

At Rome in June 71 A.D., the Triumph over the Jews took place. Tapestries interwoven with gold and set in frameworks of gold and ivory depicted scenes of the siege and capture of the city. Each scene was in effect a moving stage upon which not only the capture of Jerusalem but of other cities and battle scenes were depicted. For each such image a general captured in the action accompanied the scene of his defeat. Even the common prisoners, seven hundred in all, had been chosen for their stature and appearance to play their part in the procession. Lastly, with the greatest acclamation, before the Emperor and his sons appeared the sacred treasures of the Temple: the golden table for shew-bread, the great seven-branched candelabrum, the Menorah, the censers and other items for sacrificial rites. Finally came a copy of the Jewish Law.

"Then followed a large party carrying images of Victory, all made of ivory and gold. Behind them drove Vespasian, followed by Titus; while Domitian rode beside them, in magnificent apparel and mounted on a steed that was itself a sight." The triumphal ended at the Temple of Jupiter Capitolinus. Here the Memertine prisoner Simon, being the chief enemy general, was executed as customary.

There remained the three fortresses in Judaea. The lieutenant-general Lucilius Bassus was therefore dispatched to Judaea to put an end to all vestiges of resistance. With the X Fretensis garrison legion and elements of others, Bassus quickly captured Herodion. Concentrating his forces, the legate now marched on Machaerus, another of Herod's constructions. This fortress had been built on a massive precipice to the east of the Dead Sea guarding Herod's eastern possessions from possible Arab incursions. Being the furthest citadel from the coast and the concentration of Roman legionary power, it had to be taken to prevent its use as a focus for another revolt.

Surrounded on all sides by exceptionally deep ravines, Herod had a city built on the first level of the mountain. A steep ascent was then dug into the slope leading to the topmost ridge. A citadel with towers each ninety feet high was constructed there with a spacious palace within. Cisterns for water and weapons for fending off a siege were also stocked.

The extremists among the Jews took possession of the upper fortress believing that the rest of the populace should bear the first shock, and also that, in the worst case, by surrendering the fortress they would save themselves. That essentially occurred: 1,700 in the town died; the rest were enslaved. Those in the citadel surrendered and departed.

Only Masada remained. Bassus had died after pacifying the rest of the countryside. General Lucius Flavius Silva was appointed governor and his major task was to crush Masada, the strongest, best-situated and armed of Herod's palatial citadels.

Though the first to fortify Masada was said to be the Maccabee, Jonathan, it was Herod who strengthened it enormously. He had the summit encircled with a wall of dressed stone nearly a mile long, eighteen-feet high and twelve-feet broad, with thirty-seven towers each seventy-five feet in height. Within were barracks, armories and an elaborate palace with four corner towers each ninety feet high. Two narrow and precipitous paths reached the summit. The first track, called "the Snake" for its twistings, led from the Dead Sea on the east of the rock in a tortuous route, turning upon itself again and again for four miles to the plateau and fortress.

The second route followed a gradually ascending foothill named the "White Spur"; its mass, however, ended well below the level of the summit and would not support an attacking army in the state it was before General Flavius Silva's arrival.

Masada was garrisoned by a large band of Sicarii (assassins who had escaped from Jerusalem). Their commander was Eleazar ben Yair, son of Jarius, a relative of the Menahem who had taken Masada back in 66 A.D., and who afterwards had been killed in the Temple for his murder of the high-priest Ananias. Eleazar, his men and their families found enormous stores of corn, wine, oil and dates, all stocked by Herod a century before and preserved by the climate. Armaments were many for Herod had feared attack by either Cleopatra backed by Antony, or his own people.

The Roman commander first ringed the entire mountain with three camps, five forts and numerous watch towers. Flavius Silva then decided that only the White Spur would support earthworks and siege towers. Since the Spur ended 450 feet short of the fort, he set his legions and Jewish prisoners to raising the bank another three hundred feet. Not considered stable enough to hold heavy siege engines, Silva directed his engineers to construct a platform of large closely-fitted stones. The result was a solid fighting base seventy-five feet high and broad.

Upon this platform the Romans built a siege tower ninety feet high and entirely encased in iron. It was armed with ballistae and other missile-launchers which kept the defenders from the walls. To breach the wall Silva brought up this tower equipped with a great battering-ram and hammered continuously until the wall was breached.

The Sicarii, however, had built an interior wall upon which the ram would have much less effect. A double wall of large beams was laid with approximately twelve feet of earth between them. The repeated pounding of the ram compressed the walls even more upon the earth within, actually strengthening it with each shock.

The Roman commander therefore decided that fire was the tactical alternative. A shower of torches rained on the wall, igniting the first and crossing the gap to the second wall. The whole began to blaze. A north wind sprang up which blew the smoke and flames toward the Romans. Just as suddenly, however, the winds reversed and the entire wall ignited. The Romans then began preparations for an attack in force on the following day.

Eleazar saw that the wall was a ruin and knew well that his four hundred men would not last long against two Roman legions. He gathered his most devoted men and began his attempt to convince them of what he thought to be the best and noblest option, suicide for all (Josephus, quoting the elderly woman survivor):

> Long since, my brave men, we determined neither to serve the Romans nor any other save God, for he alone is man's true and righteous Lord; and now the time is come which bids us verify that resolution by our actions. At this crisis let us not disgrace ourselves; we who in the past refused to submit even to a slavery involving no peril, let us not now, along with slavery, deliberately accept the irreparable penalties awaiting us if we are to fall alive into Roman hands. For as we

were the first of all to revolt, so are we the last in arms against them. Moreover, I believe that it is God who has granted us this favor, that we have it in our power to die nobly and in freedom—a privilege denied to others who have met with unexpected defeat.

This first appeal did not convince everyone, as would be expected. Eleazar renewed his impassioned plea saying, "it is by God's will and of necessity that we are to die." After speaking at great length and using every conceivable reasoning his followers were won over in a fanatic torrent.

"Like men possessed they went their way, each eager to outstrip his neighbour and deeming it a signal proof of courage and sound judgment not to be seen among the last: so ardent the passion that had seized them to slaughter their wives, their little ones and themselves." Each man proceeded to kill his family; then to make a final end, all the stores were gathered and fired.

Ten men were chosen by lot to dispatch the rest, who had lain down with their families. Of the ten one was chosen to finish the other nine. All accomplished their bloody work: 960 men, women and children were killed.

At daybreak the Legions were under arms and advancing up the causeway. "Seeing none of the enemy but on all sides an awful solitude, and flames within and silence, they were at a loss to conjecture what had happened." Two women and five children who had chosen not to die were found coming from a cistern where they had hidden.

The legionaries now found "the mass of the slain, instead of exalting as over enemies, they admired the nobility of their resolve and the contempt of death displayed by so many in carrying it, unwavering, into execution."

Some historians have suggested that Josephus fabricated, in part, the account of the mass suicide, as recounted by the old woman and the children—the only survivors. However, Josephus himself had been commander at a similar mass suicide; he decided not to end it all in that way. He admitted it for history. Nevertheless, Masada is the place where new Israeli recruits go to take an oath of fidelity, 1900 years after that end.

-------

The battles in the north of the Roman Empire, most significantly that in the Teutoberger Wald, had halted the spread of the imperial power into Germany, leaving another border that would have to be defended against hostile incursions.

In the vast lands which Rome already held, however, legionary garrisons had to keep order and see that the proper taxation went to Rome to ensure its continued supreme position in the Western world. A successful revolt in one province could easily spread to others.

When Judaea rebelled in 66 A.D., it occurred at a time of political turmoil in

Rome. In 68 A.D., the maniacal Nero was compelled to commit suicide. The following year four generals vied for the throne—Galba, Otho, Vitellius and the ultimate victor, Vespasian.

The new emperor realized full well that rebellion had to be suppressed wherever and whenever it sprang up. A successful one anywhere could be disastrous. Even an unsuccessful one could have widespread repercussions if it were of sufficient magnitude to draw legions away from (already) thinly-held frontiers. Since Judaea was the land-link between the commerce-rich province of Syria to its north and grain-rich Egypt, which fed the city of Rome, rebellion there had to be quickly and ruthlessly crushed.

The revolt of Judaea, therefore, compelled Rome to respond rapidly with full force under the command of Vespasian. The fanatic resistance of the Zealots and the Sicarii, with their excesses even against their own people, heightened the intensity of the fighting.

The prolonged siege of Jerusalem, lasting over four months, reinforced Rome's will to crush Judaea so completely that no other province would soon consider seriously rejecting Rome's will by force. With the fall and destruction of Jerusalem the "diaspora" (or dispersion) of the Jewish people began, lasting nearly two thousand years until the establishment of the modern state of Israel in 1948.

After the last stand at the Temple in Jerusalem, Vespasian's son Titus, having taken command upon his father's accession to the throne, ordered two legions (of twenty-five available) to invest a desert plateau held by less than five hundred fighters. The legions spent two years on the siege of a nearly impregnable fortress. Such was the implacable will of Rome.

Though revolts would continue sporadically throughout the Empire, the following century would see Rome reach the zenith of its peace and power.

To this day recruits and conscripts to the Defense Force of the modern nation of Israel journey to the bleak mountaintop of Masada as part of their initiation into the service. There they remember the nationalist and religious spirit of the Zealots; how they died with their families for the land, Judaism, and a distant future for their people. The oath of the new soldiers taken there reflects that heritage.

# 6

## STAMFORD BRIDGE AND HASTINGS, 1066 A.D.

THEN HAROLD OUR KING came upon the Norwegians by surprise and met them beyond York at Stamford Bridge with a large force of the English people; and that day there was a very fierce fight on both sides. There was killed Harold Fairhair and Earl Tosti, and the Norwegians who survived took to flight; . . . Some were drowned, and some burned, and some destroyed in various ways so that few survived and the English remained in command of the field. (The primary source is the "Anglo-Saxon Chronicle," Editor, Whitelock, 1961.)

Harold Godwinson, King of the English, had defeated the last true Viking invasion of England. Within three weeks, however, Harold would face perhaps the most formidable descendant of the Vikings: William of Normandy.

The Duchy of Normandy began as a Viking realm in the tenth century A.D., under the wandering warrior, Hrolf, who according to the sagas was 'a great Viking,' so large that no horse could bear his weight. He went everywhere on foot and thus became known as Hrolf the Ganger.

Hrolf is better known to history as Rollo, son of Earl Rognvald of More in Iceland and brother of Earl Turf-Einar, an early Norse earl of Orkney. Starting his raiding career in the Baltic, he went on to the Oslo Fjord in Norway. For that raid he was exiled by the Norwegian King Harald Fine-Hair. Rollo proceeded to the Hebrides, then to the Viking bands which were harrying both coasts of the English Channel in the late ninth century A.D.

Some of these bands went up the Seine River in France, seizing Rouen and several other towns. After a reverse at Chartres in 911, they withdrew. The

French king, Charles III, took this opportunity to secure his western, coastal flank against more Viking raids; he held a parley with Rollo. Charles ceded the lands already held by them to the Norsemen and they in turn swore oaths of allegiance to the king. Northmandy-Normandy had been founded. By the Pact of St. Clair it was ensured that Viking garrisons would hold Rouen, Lisieux, Evereux, and all lands between the Bresle and Epte Rivers. Also, the Vikings would become converts to Christianity.

Both a superior fighter and ruler, William held good claim to the English throne. He was born in September, 1027, the bastard son of Duke Robert I of Normandy and Arlette, a tanner's daughter. Orphaned in 1035 at the age of eight when his father died while on pilgrimage, he managed to remain alive until he was old enough to defend his lands under arms. At the age of twenty, with the aid of the King of France, Henry I, William defeated his rebellious barons at the battle of Val-es-Dunes, near Caen.

Following up on that victory he destroyed the castles of the rebels, eliminating their power centers. This would be William's pattern for the rest of his life: win in battle, but if possible destroy in peace, conquering by default. Laying waste to the area around which the local lord or baron was connected removed the base of operations from which the knight fought. William borrowed his military-political policy from the Romans, who would attack and devastate (if necessary) the towns and strongholds of the objective territory or tribe in order to subjugate. Without those bases all was lost to the enemy. William capitalized on this to the extent that lords would not stand up to him in open battle. Until 1064, William waged constant war against either the neighboring counties of Brittany or Anjou, his own vassals in Normandy, or the King of France.

Duke William of Normandy, ever since he had won his first decisive battle over his rebel barons at Val-es-Dunes at age twenty, was a man of singularly fixed purpose: firm consolidation and extreme extension of his personal power. Though he gave due thought to, he did not care about the opinions of his vassals, the Church, or his people—save only as to how it effected the furtherance of his aims. This ruthlessness first occurred on a large scale following the victory at Val-es-Dunes after which he destroyed the castles and laid waste his own countryside to permanently ensure his hegemony in Normandy. In 1048, the year after Val-es-Dunes, William proposed marriage to Mathilda, daughter of Baldwin V, Count of Flanders. This alliance would secure his northeastern frontier. Pope Leo IX objected on the enigmatic grounds of "affinity."

Five years later William married Mathilda anyway. Recognition, however, was granted by then Pope Nicholas II in 1059 with the condition that William build two monasteries at Caen, near the coast. The Duke agreed and earned the Papacy as an ally. The following year, 1060, a great stroke of luck came to the Duke with the death of King Henry I of France, leaving his infant son Philip I as King. This resulted in Baldwin V, William's father-in-law's elevation to Regent. Thus France became, if not an ally, at least a non-active enemy of Normandy. This development also created the possibility, albeit limited, that William could somehow become King of France.

By 1064 William had subjugated the counties of Maine, to the direct south, and Brittany, to the southwest. The Duke had now secured all his flanks and he considered one great land ripe for expansion: England. Just twenty miles distant over water, it had been sovereign in itself, for the most part, for over five hundred years. Since the first invasion by Julius Caesar in 55 B.C., until the last Roman legion left the island in 410 A.D. to defend Rome itself from the barbarian tribes of the north, England had lived divided by a variety of kingdoms and local rulers.

The Danes had invaded and held a large part of the island for several lengthy periods, once during the ninth century until driven out by Alfred the Great, and the second commencing in 991 with a victory at the battle of Maldon. The native line of Anglo-Saxon kings returned in 1042 with the accession of King Edward the Confessor.

The English and Danes had been exchanging control over the throne of England through dynastic rivalries and inter-marriage for nearly two centuries. Edward was English-born but French-bred for he was the son of Emma, daughter of Duke Richard I of Normandy, and Ethelred, King of England. Edward was in exile when Harathcnut, the last Danish king of England, ruled. Upon Harathcnut's death in 1042, Edward was summoned back from exile by a people happy to have an English king again. Following a long delay caused by a remnant of Danes protesting the succession, Edward was crowned King on April 3, 1043.

Edward came to be called "Saint" because of his pious, devout and monk-like character. Simple and well-meaning, he was loved by the people and imparted a certain spiritual, central order to the land after centuries of disorder and foreign invasion. His basically Norman upbringing meant that he brought with him a French entourage to London. All of this would set the stage for William.

As his chief adviser and principal commander of his armies, Edward chose, or had chosen for him, Harold Godwinson, Earl of Wessex, whose House including his brothers Gyrth and Leofwine controlled a great region encompassing Middlesex and Essex, Norfolk, Suffolk, Cambridge and Sussex. Harold's father, Godwin, was a low-born man of ferocious and aggressive ambition.

Godwin, along with two other great earls, Leofric in the northern midlands and Siward in Northumbria, controlled much of the revenue-gathering of the land and in turn this controlled the army. Godwin had such power that in

1044 he contracted the marriage of his daughter Edith to the King. Thus, by Godwin's death in 1053, his son Harold was Edward's brother-in-law. Through a succession of bouts among the major earls, Harold emerged as the pre-eminent military leader, and so commander of the armies. In the summer of 1065 Harold, in this capacity of most important earl and commander-in-chief, sailed for Normandy. What exactly his mission was has never been agreed upon. There are two major possibilities.

The first and most important is that Harold was to convey to Duke William, the King's cousin, that Edward had chosen the Duke to be his successor as King of England. The second possibility is that his mission concerned the release of his brother Wulnoth and his nephew Haco, both of whom had been hostages to King Edward and were being guarded by a cousin in Normandy.

Two Norman chroniclers support the first theory in slightly different versions. Both William of Poitiers and William of Malmesbury agree basically that Edward, realizing death was near, wished to confirm an earlier promise, perhaps made in 1051, concerning his successor. Harold was shipwrecked on the voyage and captured by Count Guy of Ponthieu. William ordered Harold set free and brought to him by Guy.

"There, Harold, well proved both in ability and courage, won the heart of the Norman; and still more to ingratiate himself, he of his own accord, confirmed to him by oath the castle of Dover, which was under his jurisdiction, and the kingdom of England, after the death of Edward."

The swearing of fealty to William is recorded in the Bayeux Tapestry, the great work which reproduces the epic story of William, Harold and the battle of Hastings. The tapestry itself is twenty-three feet long and twenty inches wide and was commissioned by Odo, Bishop of Bayeux, within twenty years of the Conquest. Though the actual nature of Harold's mission is obscure, the fact is that Harold came into William's hands somehow and did swear an oath of fealty, whether under duress, free will, or as he had been directed to by Edward.

The validity of the oath-taking is affirmed by the fact that William, after Harold returned to England, informed the Pope, the Emperor of Germany, and Western Europe at large that it had occurred. Harold did not refute it.

Soon thereafter, in October 1065, a major political crisis developed in England. Harold's brother Tostig was Earl of Northumbria, near the Scottish border. Unpopular with the thegns, or land-holders of his earldom, Tostig was deposed by them while he was away from his lands with Edward at Brentford. The thegns next offered the earldom to Morcar, brother of Edwin, Earl of Mercia. Morcar accepted and joined forces with Edwin at Northampton. Harold attempted to reconcile the parties in a council at Oxford, but failed.

Edward saw no recourse but to exile Tostig. The Earl thereupon took his wife and sailed across the Channel to his brother-in-law, Baldwin of Flanders. Another piece of luck had befallen William. The House of Godwin now split, with Harold positioning himself for the throne of England and his brother now living with the father-in-law of the main contender for the throne.

Edward, though in his forties, was sickly and worn out. He held his usual Christmas court at London, but the tide was ebbing. "And King Edward came to Westminster at Christmas and had the minster consecrated which he had himself built to the glory of God and of St. Peter and of all God's saints. The consecration of the Church was on Holy Innocent's Day (December 28). And he died on the eve of the Epiphany (January 5, 1066), and was buried on the Feast of the Epiphany, in the same minster . . ."

Just before his death, King Edward the Confessor,

> *the wise ruler entrusted the realm*
> *To a man of high rank, to Harold himself,*
> *A noble earl who all the time*
> *Had loyally followed his lord's commands*
> *With words and deeds, and neglected nothing*
> *That met the need of the people's king.*

Whether Edward had in fact named two successors, Harold and William, or a successor who already owed allegiance to the other, is unclear. The most important fact is that both Harold and William felt legally entitled to the throne.

Nonetheless, England needed a strong king immediately. The kingdom's enemies were building on four fronts: William in Normandy, King Harald Hardraada in Norway, the embattled Tostig with Baldwin of Flanders, and Malcolm Canmore, a Scottish chieftain.

The Witan, or royal council, assembled to choose the new king. Comprised of bishops, earls, abbots and the more important thegns, the Witan consulted on matters of national importance. Without hesitation the Anglo-Saxon Harold was elected king over the foreigner William. Though not of royal blood, Harold had proven himself an able general in the border wars against the Welsh; added to this, most importantly, were Edward's words on his deathbed.

On January 6, 1066, the day Edward was buried in his new church at Westminster, Ealdred, Archbishop of York, crowned Harold King of England. Upon hearing of Edward's death and Harold's succession, William sent an envoy to remind the new sovereign of his oath. Harold, in turn, was engaged in consolidating his newly-won power. To engage the north as an ally which had lately thrown over his brother Tostig, Harold married the Earl of Morcar's sister, Ealdgyth, and so bolstered his stature there.

William, at this point, had no such internal nor external difficulties. The victory at Val-es-Dunes fifteen years earlier had served to solidify his base of power in Normandy. From the mouth of the river Scheldt in the north to the Loire in the south, all ports were his or an ally's. His eastern flank was secured by his father-in-law, Baldwin, who held Flanders and the Regency of France.

William had conquered Brittany in the west, and Maine in the south. In 1060, the year in which King Henry I of France died, fate had intervened again as Geoffrey Martel of Anjou also died. He was a powerful and long-time enemy of William, but after his death civil war broke out over the succession. The last threat on the continent had been eliminated. Harold and the Channel became the main enemies.

King Harold's forces consisted of two major divisions. The first, and by far the more formidable, was the "housecarles." Basically a Norse institution, dating back to at least the early ninth century, this type of fighting man could be found throughout history in many tribes and states. Essentially the housecarles were the retainers of either the royal or a noble (land-holding at least) household. The warriors received food, lodging and some pay, and in return were always available for duty (as opposed to those warriors in a strictly feudal organization who were called up at need for the campaigning season).

The second major division was the "fyrd." Raised in times that threatened war, the fyrd constituted the national militia and 1066 took the threat to that extreme on several occasions. The fyrd was raised on the basis of the amount of land either the earl, bishop, abbot, thegn or a town controlled. The standard levy was one fighting man per "five hides," a hide being, for the most part, a plot of land of 120 acres. For each man so levied, two shillings had to be provided for each of the months he served, along with food and sundries. At the end of sixty days the fyrd disbanded, the vital flaw in its concept, and particularly so for Harold.

Though the housecarles rode to battle as did some of the fyrd, the English fought on foot. The one recorded instance, in 1055, in which they tried to mount a charge all went awry:

And then they gathered a large force with the Irishmen and the Welsh, and Earl Ralph (a Norman in England) gathered a large force against them at Hereford town, and there battle was joined. But before any spear was thrown the English army fled because they were on horseback, and many were killed there . . .

Though inept with the horse, the English were fierce fighters on foot. The standard weapons were three. The spear was used for both hurling and thrusting. The two-edged sword, a precursor of the broadsword, could be utilized both to hack and to thrust. And the long-handled "Danish" axe—first developed as a weapon for boarding enemy ships—was extended over the shields of the English line and out against the oncoming foe.

The housecarles, being of a higher status, wore coats of forged link-mail and ironbound helmets. Any of the fyrd who could afford it wore the same. The shields they all carried were of major importance for the essence of the English defense was the great shieldwall. Just as in Greek warfare the shields were interlocked—the English shields were so linked that any thought of individual or small unit mobility defeated the unitary mass and singular purpose of the wall. The shieldwall was intended to be a great rock upon which the waves of the enemy would break again and again until the point where a general advance by the defenders would finally crush the exhausted attackers. It was defensive in deployment but with an ultimately offensive purpose.

The English had no archers at that time, though they would later have the best in Europe. William, however, believed in the mixed-arms concept of warfare and utilized numbers of bowmen in his army who employed both crossbows and the short Norman straight-bow. The main Norman strength lay in the mounted knight. All wore chain-link armor, full helmets, and wielded a lance. When the lances had either found their mark or shivered, the knights drew sword or mace. Protected by kite-shaped shields down to the lower leg on their non-sword side, the Norman knight could wreak much havoc but only if he could get at his foe. While the shield-wall held this was nearly impossible.

Since the cavalry were the mobile strike unit, the archers needed a stable support that would also constitute an actual battle line. The Norman and other French men-at-arms provided this line, armed in basically the same fashion as the men of the English fyrd.

Under the Norman feudal system, each baron, bishop or eminent knight held his lands under obligation to the Duke. In time of war each of these land-holders was responsible for supplying a certain allotment of fighting men, both knights and foot, to the Duke. When called up for duty the term of service was forty days, less than that of the English. In addition, William could not compel any of his vassal lords outside of the duchy of Normandy to fight overseas; they would have to volunteer.

In order to make the invasion an "international crusade" then, William dispatched envoys to the Pope, the Emperor, and the major courts of Europe. Through several high-ranking churchmen, especially Lanfranc, the Prior of Bec, the Duke gained the blessing of Pope Alexander II for his cause. He also received a consecrated Papal banner to use as a standard in battle. The case of legitimacy had already gone by default in the papal court; Harold had not contested. The German Emperor, Henry IV, promised aid if needed. The King of the Danes did likewise, but sent no help. Now that he had Papal consent, William began active preparations for the invasion.

A war council of the barons of Normandy was summoned in the spring of 1066 in the town of Lillebonne, west of Rouen. By now the ambassadors had returned with favorable tidings. Tostig had also come with support from Baldwin. The assembly, however, was not united for such a daring enterprise: England was a large and rich country, capable of fielding a much larger army than that which the Duke could raise and transport across the Channel. But the Duke's eloquence and promises of land and wealth for the victors prevailed, and preparations began for a fleet to be constructed, particularly horse-transports.

Once the Norman chivalry had assented to the plan, mercenary volunteers soon arrived. Given the Papal blessing, land-hungry knights seeking estates in England arrived by the hundreds. Knights came from the counties of Brittany and Maine, from Flanders, Anjou and Poitou, from Burgundy, the Aquitaine, central France and southern Italy.

Such a gathering of knights and lords, in a cause blessed by the Pope, directly presaged the First Crusade which would begin nearly thirty years later, in 1095. Though William had succeeded in assembling a large army for those times, perhaps ten thousand fighting men in all, Harold could more than double that number if he were able to bring to bear all his forces against a single enemy. Here again, fate intervened on William's behalf.

Tostig, Harold's brother and the ousted Earl of Northumbria, remained deeply embittered by his brother's refusal to restore his domains. He therefore approached William and asked permission to raid the eastern coasts of England. Since this would serve to harry Harold, and even possibly provoke the summoning of the fyrd prematurely, the Duke agreed. Tostig sailed first to the Isle of Wight where he still held estates, and then continued on at the head of sixty ships to raid Sussex and Kent. The northern fyrd was raised by Earl Edwin, and in May he defeated Tostig and drove him off with only twelve of his ships remaining. Tostig then sailed for Scotland and his blood-ally, Malcolm Canmore, King of the Scots.

King Harold, however, felt that Tostig's raid might well be the advance guard for William's invasion force and so he ordered a general mobilization of the national fyrd. That step proved premature with disastrous consequences to follow. Arriving with his housecarles, Harold ordered coastal defenses rebuilt and the fyrd to stand ready. A small fleet of perhaps one hundred ships were ordered to station off the Isle of Wight.

On the continent mercenary knights were swelling William's embarkation camps at the town of Dives, northeast of Caen. The fleet which had been constructed under the Duke's orders numbered somewhat over five hundred ships, many of which were horse transports, essential to his tactical strength in the mounted knight.

Earl Tostig continued to seek a strong ally to press his claims to both the

North, and possibly even the crown itself, of England. Coolly received in Scotland, he tried King Svein of Denmark and was rebuffed there also. The Earl next tried Norway, the kingdom of Harald Sigurdson, known as Hard-raada, "the greatest warrior of his age in the North." Harald had served in the Varangian (Viking) Guard of the Byzantine Emperors in Constantinople, and had visited the Holy Land.

Harald Hardraada (for hard-counsel) did not rule with even the limited consent of his lords and warriors. His decision to make war was final. Hard-raada was the successor to Magnus of Norway, who by treaty also had a claim to the throne of England through the last Danish king, Harthacnut. Tostig played upon this claim, and finally convinced this Norse king to make the last great Viking raid in history. "Then ("Anglo-Saxon Chronicle") King Harald and the earl talked long and frequently together; and at last he took the resolution to proceed in summer to England, and conquer the country. King Harald sent a message-token through all Norway, and ordered out a levy of one-half of all the men in Norway able to carry arms." Harold of England now was faced by two great expeditions being marshaled against him: in the far north, and the near south.

The northern struck first. Tostig again led an advance party, gathering the remnants of his own supporters among the Channel and northern islands. Knowing through Tostig that Duke William might beat him to the great prize of England, King Harald Hardraada sailed from Bergen in late July 1066. With a fleet of three hundred ships, each manned by forty warrior-sailors, Harald commanded well over ten thousand men in his assault on England. The fleet sailed first to the Shetlands and Orkneys, then south to link up with Tostig near the mouth of the river Tyne. After plundering and burning the seacoast town of Scarborough, the Vikings proceeded up the river Humber to York. There the brother earls Edwin and Morcar had gathered the northern fyrd against another onslaught, much greater in number than Tostig's earlier attempt.

On September 20, the English fyrd was arrayed outside of York at a place called Gate Fulford, flanked by the river and a ditch.

> When King Harald saw that the English array had come to the ditch against him, he ordered the charge to be sounded, and urged on his men. He ordered the banner which was called the Land-ravager, to be carried before him, and made so severe an assault that all had to give way before it; and there was a great loss among the men of the earls, and they soon broke into flight, some running up the river, some down, and the most leaping into the ditch, which was so filled with dead that the Norsemen could go dry-foot over the fen.

Harold Godwinson had not been lax, however. Massing all available house-carles, mounted, and members of the fyrd which he could now newly raise (as their earlier term of service had ended several weeks before) the King force-marched north, day and night, to York. The English army had covered nearly two hundred miles in less than a week and arrived only four days after the victory of Harald Hardraada at Gate Fulford.

On September 25, Harald, Tostig and most of the Vikings marched to Stamford Bridge, northeast of York, planning to reconfirm their conquest of Northumbria. King Harold's approach and his security measures had been so thorough that the overconfident Norse did not realize they were now to face the King of England with a large part of his national forces.

Tostig counseled a return to the ships to bring up the rest of the army and rearm with the mail shirts which had been left behind because of the late summer day heat. King Harald refused and planted the banner "Land-ravager" where he would make his stand. Tactically, Hardraada arrayed his warriors in a large circle with shields facing in all directions.

Harold of England now sent a deputation to the Norse. Tostig was invited back to rejoin Harold, being offered Northumbria and one-third of England overall to rule with his brother. Tostig then asked, "But if I accept of this offer, what will he give King Harald Sigurdson for his trouble?" The horseman replied, "He has also spoken of this and will give him seven feet of English ground, or as much more as he may be taller than other men." Tostig's final word was, "We shall rather all take the resolution to die with honor, or to gain England by a victory."

The Norse armed circle withstood attack after attack, by both housecarls on horse and afoot, and fyrd-men. They had a shieldwall themselves, and while it held intact the English lost many in frustrated attacks against it. When the Norse thought that the English were weakening the wall disintegrated at certain points through the eagerness of Viking warriors for individual combat, thereby giving the English an opportunity to counterattack.

Harald Hardraada stepped into the thickest part of the battle, swinging his great-sword with both hands. All gave way before him, until an arrow cut his windpipe.

> *Unhelmed, unpanzered, without shield*
> *He fell among us in the field,*
> *The gallant men who saw him fall*
> *Would take no quarter; one and all*
> *Resolved to die with their loved king,*
> *Around his corpse in a corpse-ring.*

Those who had advanced died with him. The banner "Land-ravager" still stood, and Tostig took over the command. Harold again offered peace, but the Northmen rejected it.

Near sunset the men who had been left at the ships came up at the run; under the command of Eystein Orre the charge became known as "Orre's Storm." Exhausted, they removed their armor and threw themselves into the battle. Most died; ". . . darkness fell before the slaughter was altogether ended." King Harold Godwinson had defeated the last great Viking invasion of England: Hardraada had died, as had Tostig, Harold's brother, and thousands of their warriors. But Harold had also lost many of his best men of the housecarls and they were irreplaceable when the time came—within three weeks—to face William and his knights from Normandy.

Harold, in a chivalrous gesture, gave quarter to all of the surviving northmen, including Hardraada's young son Olaf, on the condition that all swore oaths "to always keep peace and friendship with the country." The Vikings who returned to the north filled twenty-four ships out of the original three hundred, a loss of well over five thousand men.

While Harold and the English forces were dispensing with the threat in the north, William continued his preparations for his assault on southern England. By mid-August 1066, William had amassed a fleet and army ready to land in England. The backbone of his army—his mounted knights—numbered approximately three thousand men, the bulk being Norman. Men-at-arms constituted the heavy infantry and numbered from two–four thousand. The archers counted perhaps two thousand. William's army of conquest therefore numbered from seven–nine thousand men, a formidable force in any battle of the period: given the extensive English losses at Stamford Bridge, a masterful host for Harold to challenge.

William's first major task after the gathering and organization of his armies was to cross the Channel with minimal loss of craft, men and horses. The Duke hoped to avoid interference from the English fleet, which though small due to cutbacks by Edward the Confessor, remained a skilled and experienced foe. He therefore decided upon a nighttime crossing. The Duke knew that because of Tostig's first raid the fyrd had been called up by July 8, and its term would end on September 8. His own soldiers could also disband by then if they had not already crossed the Channel. William's gravest concern lay in getting three thousand warhorses—massive steeds trained for battle—into transports, across twenty-five miles of open water, and on to shore again. His learned monks could tell him that the Romans had done it first under Julius Caesar in 52 B.C.

Norman knights from Sicily had arrived, and they brought with them invaluable knowledge of their own amphibious operations against the Saracens in southern Italy and Sicily. The exact design of the horse transports is not known but the numbers of the fleet, including supply ships, approached seven hundred vessels.

By late August the fleet was assembled and ready for embarkation at Dives, a town approximately halfway between present-day Cherbourg and Le Havre. The Channel winds blew contrarily every day and William's army grew restive. Gaming, drinking and reworking weapons, gear and harness grew increasingly more tedious. Finally on September 12, a westerly wind sprang up. Seizing the opportunity to shorten the final crossing by a number of miles, the Duke embarked the fleet and sailed northeast to St. Valery, a town at the mouth of the river Somme, almost directly across from Hastings.

A favorable cross-Channel wind came from the south on September 27. The day was spent in a feverish haste to load the transports and sail that evening. Just as Harald Hardraada had feared to find England already conquered by William, so also did the Duke fear a victory by Harald. He did not yet know of Stamford Bridge. Within twelve hours the most important cargo—the warhorses—had been loaded. At 9 P.M., William signaled that lanterns be lit on all vessels. His flagship, the "Mora" (fate in Greek), had been given him by his wife, Mathilda. It mounted the largest torch and all captains were ordered to take their courses from it. Only two ships were lost in the unopposed crossing. The English fleet was on the Thames near London, disbanding as the fyrd had done.

At 9 A.M., Thursday, September 28, 1066, William of Normandy set foot on English soil near the town of Pevensey, west of Hastings. On his first step down he slipped and fell with both hands on the ground. Many feared the ill-omen but William rose and said, "By the Splendor of God, I have taken possession of my kingdom; the earth of England is in my hands." Scouts were dispatched immediately while the knights armed themselves in full array, ready for battle should the English be nearby to contest the landing. Engineers and carpenters immediately set to work constructing a stockaded camp to provide a base of operations. The ships, taking advantage of high tide, were beached by noon.

A Saxon thegn from Sussex witnessed the landing from some low foothills north of Pevensey. After gleaning what knowledge he could from what he recognized as the long-awaited Norman invasion, he set out north to warn the King. Resting little, the thegn rode night and day to York where Harold was resting his men, celebrating his great victory, and settling the affairs of the northern earldoms.

By the first days of October William would have learned of Harold's victory at Stamford Bridge, and also would have surmised that the victory would have been a dear one against Hardraada and his Vikings. York was 190 miles from London, Hastings just seventy. Though some of the Duke's counselors advised him to take London, William held to his original plan: secure a position on the English coast, provide a safe haven for his fleet if matters were to go awry, and wait for Harold to come to him.

Harold was impetuous and aggressive in war, and his victory at Stamford

Bridge happened due in large part to those qualities. William knew he faced a staunch opponent who had just defeated one of the greatest warriors of the age, and he wanted to do battle with the King near the coast and not well inland away from the fleet. The Duke obviously held the English forces in great esteem.

William deliberately sent out raiding parties to ravage the Sussex countryside—Harold's own earldom—to further goad him to attack. Harold needed no further persuasion than his own character dictated. Flushed with the crushing of the Vikings, Harold felt that fate would grant him a second major victory to save England. On October 2, riding at the head of his elite housecarls who had survived Stamford, Harold sent out the call for the fyrd to be raised again. He knew full well that the only fyrd-men he could gather on the route to Hastings would be those whom he could call up in the shires through which he passed on the march south. London was nearly two hundred miles to the south. Only with his mounted troops, the housecarles, could Harold arrive by the night of October 5–6. The King remained there until October 11, allowing the footmen of the fyrd and those from surrounding shires to join him. Councils were undoubtedly held and the wisest course seemed to have been to remain in London and fortify it further, gather all of the national fyrd, and organize for battle when fully prepared.

At the same time, though, Sussex and the lands south of London would have to be sacrificed—either allowing the Norman invader to pillage and forage at will or necessitating complete destruction of the land by the English themselves, leaving the Normans without supplies.

Harold's impulsive character accepted neither of these options. Whereas William was cautious in order to achieve his ultimate goals and would probably have stayed in London, Harold chose battle as soon as feasible.

Perhaps the only man who could have changed Harold's mind was his brother Gyrth. Earl of East Anglia, Gyrth had fought at his brother's side and commanded his own housecarls and fyrd-men. Gyrth advised Harold to stay in London and gather all of the nation's forces. Gyrth meanwhile would lead the housecarls and the fyrd available against William. Sussex would have to be stripped of its produce and animals, and William would be forced to battle Gyrth. If Gyrth should win it would be the same as if Harold had won; if Gyrth should lose, at least the King would not be in danger and he would be in London preparing an even greater army to push the invader into the sea.

In a lay of the period, Gyrth spoke:

> *Fair brother, if Thou wilt give me the command,*
> *Whilst thou here in London dost take up thy stand,*
> *The Fortune of War with the Duke I will try. . . .*
> *Now if I in the combat am vanquished and taken,*

*Whilst thou, (if God wills it), in Life dost remain,*
*Reassembling thy forces from near and from far,*
*And attacking, again try the fortune of War;*

"But Harold rejected Gyrth's counsel; and said, that by none but Himself, should his forces be led."

*How could We, said He, o'er this Land sorrow bring?*
*Or ruin a People who own Us a King?*
*We will never harry or injure a Land,*
*Which trusts both for Rule, and for Weal, to Our hand.*

Challenges had been forwarded by both sides. William reminded Harold of his oath and the King denied it, stating it was taken under duress and that Edward's deathbed designation of him as king superseded all oaths or promises. Harold offered battle one week hence—Saturday, October 14, 1066.

Both contenders for the throne of England proceeded on that timetable. William believed that Harold would fulfill his promise to meet in battle and not encastellate himself behind the fortifications of London. He was correct. Harold remained in London for six days organizing his housecarls and gathering members of the fyrd from over ten shires. He did not, however, have the men of the north. The earls Edwin and Morcar had decided their men had suffered and died enough against Hardraada at Gate Fulford. They would not be able to provide a viable fighting force again for at least several months.

On either October 11 or early the next day, Harold left London for the last time with his vanguard of housecarls. He had already appointed a rallying-point for the fyrd and any volunteers: a spur of the Downs seven miles north of Hastings known familiarly as "The Place of the Hoar Apple Tree." The Hoar Apple Tree had been the assigned spot for the mobilization of the southern fyrd in June when Tostig was undertaking his first raid.

Leading his housecarls, Harold arrived at the assembly point late on October 13. Mounted members of the fyrd accompanied him and foot-soldiers of the fyrd would continue to arrive all night, exhausted from their forced-march from London sixty miles to the north.

Certain Norman chroniclers, no doubt somewhat prejudiced, claimed that the English spent the battle's eve drinking, singing and gambling, while the Normans were devout and prayed. It seems highly doubtful that men exhausted from a great battle against the Vikings in the north, who then took part in two forced-marches with a few days rest between, would stay awake carousing. In any case, they slept deeply.

So heavy was their sleep, in fact, that Harold did not have all the time he needed to properly array his men in battle ranks. "And William came against him by surprise before his army was drawn up in battle array."

King Harold's venue to give battle was a good one. Having opted to oppose William near the coast the King chose a fine defensive position at which infantry would hold their own against mounted knights. The site was a ridge called Senlac, and later by the Normans "Battle," seven miles north of Hastings.

Senlac is a ridge which stands at the head of a spur jutting out from the Wealden Hills. The spur is approximately 250 feet high, and the ridge itself, at its highest, 275 feet. The actual frontage for the English army to form on was about six to seven hundred yards. The slope in front of the line dropped one hundred feet over a distance of four hundred yards, forcing cavalry to labor more in the ascent. The flanks of Senlac fell off precipitously, entirely unsuited to a cavalry charge. The western edge had a ravine with a stream and brushwood choking it, and on the east the steep slope dropped off to a local road. The entire position commanded the High Road to London from the south of England, and it is this fact which must have been central in Harold's tactical planning.

If Harold merely intended to fight a delaying action protecting London he could have done so further north with the far greater forces he could have raised in the meantime. The other alternative is that—flushed with his sudden surprise victory at Stamford Bridge—he hoped to do the same to William, who might well not expect a weary and not fully-manned army to come against him. A combination of the two seems likely: if victory could be gained with a sudden onslaught, good; if forced to hold the London road, reinforcements would be coming, and Sussex would know the King had not deserted it.

To man the ridge the English set out sometime after dawn on Saturday, October 14, from the "Hoary Tree," about a mile distant. The Normans had more ground to cover, six miles from their camp to Telham Hill which stood across a small boggy valley from Senlac Ridge. Therefore, they must have arisen, eaten and armed before dawn, around 5 A.M. The English upon reaching Senlac deployed the shieldwall at the crest of the ridge. The front to be held by this solid mass was some six to seven hundred yards long. The front rank had to stand "shield-to-shield, shoulder-to-shoulder," just as in the classical Greek phalanx.

The shields overlapped and each man would need only enough space to wield his great axe, or spear, over the shields. Allowing two feet per man, then, the first rank numbered about one thousand men. Half of these at least would be housecarls, located at the center where the Norman cavalry assault would be the worst. Harold had placed his standards at the highest point, in the left of the English center. The King stood under his banners, the "Dragon of Wessex" and his own personal banner, the "Fighting Man."

Behind the first rank of the shieldwall the English spread their ranks slightly, to perhaps three feet of front per man, so that each succeeding rank contained seven–eight hundred men. If the total phalanx including the shieldwall numbered ten ranks in depth, then Harold commanded 7,500 men at Hastings, perhaps 2,500 of which were housecarls, equal in battle to the Norman knights.

William, seizing the initiative, marshaled his army in three divisions. The center was composed of Normans, perhaps four thousand total, half of which were knights. The Duke commanded them personally. The knights were the third echelon; preceding them were the men-at-arms, and before them came the archers. The wings were organized in the same pattern. A battalion of archers first, followed by one of heavy infantry, and finally the cavalry. The left flank consisted in the main of Bretons, commanded by Alan, Count of Brittany, and it numbered approximately 2,500 men. The right wing had French mercenaries and volunteers from all over Western Europe; Count Eustace of Boulogne commanded perhaps 1,700 troops.

At 9 A.M., with the sound of Norman trumpets echoing, William ordered a general advance. The archers and crossbowmen went first, and "in such wise the Norman foot drawing nearer provoked the English by raining death and wounds upon them with their missiles. But the English resisted valiantly, each man according to his strength, and they hurled back spears and javelins and weapons of all kinds together with axes and stones fastened to pieces of wood."

Under the fury of the English reply the Bretons on the Duke's left flank broke. With archers and infantry fleeing downhill the battalion of knights riding in support were likewise thrown into disarray. This opened the flank of William's center to attack. The roots of Harold's ultimate undoing, much later in the day, first manifested themselves here. Under strict orders not to break the shieldwall, men of the fyrd on the English right flank pursued the Bretons downhill. William ordered a counterattack from his central reserve of Norman knights and several hundred of the fyrd died.

Given the temporary collapse of the Norman left, this might have been Harold's one chance to achieve a decisive victory that day—but only if he had employed his elite housecarls as shock troops and attacked the Norman center at the same time. It would have thrust back their infantry on the cavalry just as the English right had done. Instead, unsupported, the right sustained heavy losses. With full support the Normans might have been routed, losing foot-soldiers and retreating with only their knights to the base and a fleet which faced the newly-called up English navy in the Channel.

At almost this same juncture—very early in the battle—William was unhorsed and lost to the view of his men. Though Hardraada had Tostig to replace him, the Normans were in a precarious position, as the battle-leader was all-important in early medieval warfare. If he fell, his army quite often went down with him; the individual and regional battalions were left without a center.

With the English charging downhill in large numbers (though not in a general advance), William rose over his dying steed and "Staying their retreat, he took off his helmet, and standing before them bareheaded he cried: 'Look at me well, I am still alive and by the grace of God I shall yet prove victor. What is this madness which makes you fly, and what way is open for your retreat. . . . You are throwing away victory and lasting glory, rushing into ruin and incurring abiding disgrace.' "

Remounted, the Duke solidified his center and shored up his left flank, all in preparation for making an irreparable break in the English shieldwall. But the wall would not yield. To avoid the confusion and carnage caused by Norman bowmen and infantry thrown down headlong by the tough English infantry, William decided to lead the battle himself with his knights as the main strike force. The first phase of the battle, until an equilibrium had been restored, lasted to nearly noon. At that point, the Duke began his cavalry attacks. Since the most favorable slope for a charge was fixed on the English center, it also would close on King Harold, his standards and housecarls—the best of the English army.

Throughout a long hot afternoon Norman knights on their destriers, or warhorses, charged in company-sized groups, attempting to cleave a hole in the shieldwall that would shatter the whole and destroy the defense. Harold's order-of-the-day still stood: Do not break the shieldwall.

When the English foot-soldiers first swept down on the Normans at 10 or 11 A.M., it seemed an excellent tactic as it almost served to unravel the whole of the Norman line. Yet William, a great tactician, decided that having the English, at least the fyrd-men, break their own line themselves was the way to Norman victory.

Accordingly, late in the afternoon, the Duke ordered small company as-saults to end: the time had come for a master stroke meaning either victory or death. William ordered his archers to the fore with instructions to provide high-angle fire. This fire was intended to pass over the ranks of the charging Norman knights, over the shields of the front line of the shieldwall, and into the ranks of the men beyond, who had stood for eight hours under continuous attack. William then chose to use a *ruse de guerre*, a feigned flight by his knights after an advance. Using this advance-retreat ploy he drew hundreds of the fyrd to their deaths. Though Harold tried to control the fyrd, the line was too long and confusion reigned.

King Harold's housecarls remained true to their orders and held their position around the standards, protecting the King and his brothers. As dusk began to descend William tried yet another feigned retreat; even more of the fyrd died. At the same time Count Eustace of Boulogne advanced on the Norman right, driving the English left back onto the center or into a full retreat.

Harold's housecarls held steadfast to their positions. Sworn to guard the king, they held their places at sundown. King Harold might have been struck in the eye by an arrow, as shown in the Bayeux Tapestry, or hilted by a squad of Norman knights who charged at the standard with the intent of killing Harold; both seem possible. Wounded by an arrow, a Norman sword ended the life of a king who ruled nine months and nine days.

Harold's brothers, the earls Gyrth and Leofwine, died defending him and the standards. The housecarls did not surrender. Leaderless, knowing their king was dead, they fought on taking as many Normans as they could. The housecarls fought so savagely and well that Count Eustace, commander of the Norman right flank, ordered a halt.

Duke William came upon this and immediately countermanded, ordering a full charge. The housecarls subsequently died around the last Anglo-Saxon King. The Norman knights did such a job of hacking at the King's body that only with difficulty was it identified later. Duke William, soon to be king, ordered the body to be buried on the seashore. England was now joined to the continent through blood and history. Slightly less than one year after Harold was crowned king, William, Duke of Normandy, a descendant of the Vikings, became King of England on Christmas Day, 1066.

————

The battle of Hastings, perhaps more than any other conflict since the defeat of the Moslems at Tours in 776 A.D., marked a watershed for Western civilization. At Hastings tribal and provincial England died and the beginnings of the modern state were born.

Ironically, the battle of Stamford Bridge three weeks earlier had seen the country show a united front to the invaders from Scandinavia, the last of the great Viking hosts to assault the British Isles. In that battle the age of Viking conquest of territory—not mere plundering—ended. When Harald Hardraada got his six feet of English earth, and more, the age was over.

The Viking "Ragnarok" at Stamford, however unintentioned, led to King Harold Godwinson's final defeat at Hastings. The members of the English fyrd, called up to meet one threat to the land, were up to the challenge. But in less than three weeks they had to face another, more fearsome foe, Duke William of Normandy. Exhausted by their forced march from the north to the Channel near Hastings, the housecarls of Harold and the English fyrd had to fight a pitched battle against a fresh force whose major strike unit was the mounted, armored knight, a force not yet a true fighting arm of the English army.

While defeating Harald and the Viking invasion, King Harold laid himself open to the greater threat. Both had to be dealt with, but the Norman incursion proved to be fatal to English independence. King Harold, his brothers and his housecarls, knew that day what import the battle had: at sunset their land would be free or conquered territory.

Duke William's victory united England to the continent of Europe as it had once been as a province of Rome. Six centuries had passed since then. The last stand of Harold Godwinson and his housecarls and fyrd led to the beginnings of the modern English state, all initiated by the descendant of an early Viking conqueror of western France.

William spent the next six years after Hastings conquering various holdouts in England, Wales and Scotland. He did this ruthlessly, and to great effect, and thereby formed the country now known as Great Britain.

# 7

## WATERLOO

### PRELUDE

IN OCTOBER 1795, in the sixth year of the French Revolution, the Paris mobs rose again. The aim of the rabble this time was to overthrow "The Directory," the ruling junta of five created by the French Constitution written earlier that same year. The Directory had replaced the Jacobin Party under Robespierre, last and perhaps most brutal of the major revolutionaries.

A young officer of the French Artillery had worked in the planning office of the War Ministry in Paris for less than a year. Though he had proved his worth in battle several times since his graduation from military school, the shifting tides of French politics had kept him from advancing up the ranks. When word reached the Directory that the mob had risen it sent for the officer, Napoleon Bonaparte. Realizing the target of attack would be the Palace of the Tuileries, Napoleon ordered a cavalry officer who had served with him in Italy to bring artillery to the Palace. Arrayed in formation covering the approaches to the Tuileries, Bonaparte ordered the cannon to be loaded with grapeshot, ammunition which consisted of about fifty pellets—each larger than a musket ball—wired together. When the crowd charged Napoleon fired a "whiff of grapeshot" and two hundred died instantly. The mob dispersed. Soon after, Napoleon was appointed "General de Division"; ten days later he became Commander of the Army of the Interior. The career of the first, and perhaps greatest, general of the modern era of warfare had begun.

Napoleon Bonaparte was born into a large family of lower-class nobility on August 15, 1769, on the island of Corsica, a recent addition to the kingdom of France. Through connections with a French baron a place was secured for the nine-year-old Napoleon at the French military academy at Brienne. An exceptional student, particularly in history, geography and mathematics, at the age of fifteen he entered L'Ecole Militaire in Paris, the training-ground for future French officers. Within a year, in November 1785, Napoleon became a probationary lieutenant with La Fére Artillery Regiment in Valence. At Valence the young officer learned the basics of handling, loading and targeting artillery; most importantly, he began to learn how to command men.

The period of burgeoning revolutionary sentiment held both great danger and almost unlimited promise for a young officer. Coming from an outlying province and having (at best) only a tenuous connection to the *ancien régime,* the real nobility of France, Napoleon weathered the political storms fairly well. In fact, the neophyte commander used his furloughs to travel to Corsica hoping to help foment a revolt there which would liberate the island from France, whether it was ruled by the Revolution or the feudal nobility.

The authoritarian side of Napoleon's character came to the fore in 1792, however, upon his return to Paris from a furlough in Corsica. The French government had just declared war on Austria. Looking forward to action in the field, Napoleon was in Paris on June 20 when the mobs began to form. Bonaparte and two friends decided to follow them to the Tuileries: there they saw King Louis XVI accepting the tricolor of the Revolution. Napoleon now wrote to his brother Joseph that "the Jacobins are madmen," and that he would have ordered the troops to fire on the "canaille"—the rabble. And when Napoleon witnessed the slaughter on August 10 of Louis's Swiss Guards, who had been ordered not to fire on the rabid mob, he became firmly convinced that strong central rule by one man was necessary to maintain order. To Joseph Napoleon he again wrote, "If Louis XVI had shown himself on horseback, he would have won the day."

The overthrow of the King and the seeming success of the Revolution led the other dynastic powers of continental Europe—Prussia, Austria and Holland—into what became known as the "War of the First Coalition," aimed at crushing revolutionary France and halting the spread of its ideas. Monarchical England, commanding the seas, joined in.

This war for France's survival became a people's war. More than half of the officer cadre were nobles who had by now fled or were dead. The National Convention turned to universal conscription to fill the ranks—75,000 men were drafted. Young officers like Napoleon had their chance at this moment for rapid advancement.

Bonaparte himself was a supremely ambitious opportunist. As a Lieutenant-Colonel assigned to the army of Italy to fight the Austrians there, Napoleon passed through Toulon in September 1793. The city was besieged by a French force seeking to oust the Royalists and drive off a supporting British fleet.

Quickly sizing up the strategic situation with due and deliberate preparation, Napoleon helped the commanding general direct an assault on the key defensive points. The city was taken, and Bonaparte was wounded for the first time. But within three days Napoleon, twenty-four years old, was a General of Brigade.

In March 1794 Napoleon was appointed Artillery Commander for the army of Italy, and shortly thereafter led a successful offensive on the Mediterranean coast. He began at this point to plan on a larger scale, a skill at which he would become the master of the age. Italy, with its various states and kingdoms, belonged for the most part to the Austrian Empire. Napoleon therefore started to plan a grand strategy to drive Austria from northern Italy.

His planning talent, however, brought him back to Paris and the War Ministry. The "whiff of grapeshot" brought him to "General of Division," and soon after, in March 1796, command of the army of Italy. Upon arrival in the Maritime Alps the new commander found the army unpaid and lacking in food, clothing, and even muskets. Napoleon immediately enspirited his divisional commanders—Berthier, his chief-of-staff, Massena, Augereau and Serurier, all of whom would become Marshals of France through merit, not privilege as in the past. With alacrity the men were reprovisioned and rearmed where necessary, and the campaign began.

The strategic plan was to split the Austrian army from its ally, the King of Sardinia, defeating one and then the other. Napoleon would use this grand concept often, lastly at Waterloo. The Austrians were driven off; a decisive charge later by Colonel Murat (who would also be a Marshal) against the Sardinians brought an armistice.

By May 10 the Austrians had been brought to bay on the banks of the Adda River at Lodi. With enemy fire a scant two hundred yards distant, Napoleon personally placed his artillery: his grenadiers and his cavalry won the day. Years afterward, Bonaparte wrote, "It was only on the evening of Lodi that I believed myself a superior man, and that the ambition came to me of executing the great things which so far had been occupying my thoughts only as a fantastic dream."

The end of June 1796 saw Napoleon in possession by conquest of Milan and Lombardy, the Piedmont, the Republic of Genoa, part of the Duchy of Parma, part of the Republic of Venice, and the Duchy of Mantua. His men were paid in silver not the worthless paper "assignats" of the Revolution, and this gained for him their supreme loyalty.

Austria struck back on July 28 with a new army of fifty thousand men under a veteran cavalry general, Count Würmser. Though Napoleon also had fifty thousand, he could spare only thirty thousand men to guard the northern passes through the Alps. Both armies split their forces but Bonaparte's decisiveness and quick maneuvering kept the Austrians from registering significant tactical gains.

Finally, "in a fight to the death" at Arcola on November 17, the French (though losing twice as many men) scored their first thorough victory over the Austrians by forcing their retreat. The date January 14, 1797 brought the conquest of Italy for the French Republic. With a mixture of bold leadership, a willingness to delegate authority for troop movements to individual commanders under an overall plan, and the ability to inspire an army outnumbered two to one, Napoleon crushed the army of the Hapsburgs at Rivoli.

Bonaparte pushed his army of Italy to within one hundred miles of Vienna the following month. With full diplomatic powers from the Directory, he dictated terms in the Treaty of Campo Formio (October 17, 1797) which guaranteed the natural frontiers of France, adding Belgium and lands along the Rhine to the Republic. In addition, Lombardy and two new Republics—Cisalpine and Ligurian—were formed as dependencies.

With the Austrian Empire at bay for the time being and Prussia and Holland inactive, Napoleon turned his sights on Great Britain. "Let us concert all our activity on the navy and destroy England. That done, Europe is at our feet." Realizing England possessed nearly absolute command of the seas at this time, the General decided to strike at British power in an unexpected place, the East. Egypt became the target.

Possession of Egypt would interfere with English trade in the eastern Mediterranean, and ultimately with India, a relatively new possession of England. On July 1, 1798, a French army of thirty-two thousand men disembarked near Alexandria (founded by Alexander the Great, one of Napoleon's heroes and models). Alexander had taken Egypt bloodlessly; Napoleon would fight for it. Admiral Horatio Nelson had nearly intercepted the French fleet on its voyage: on August 2, 1798, Nelson destroyed that fleet at the "Battle of the Nile." Napoleon and his army were cut off from France.

Undaunted, Bonaparte met and defeated the Mameluke Turkish forces of Egypt at the "Battle of the Pyramids" on July 21. The victory could not be decisive, however, with his army severed from France and he wrote to Joseph, "glory is stale when one is twenty-nine; I have exhausted everything; there is nothing left for me but to become really and completely selfish." Which he proceeded to do when, after fruitlessly invading Syria, he made secret plans to return to France with the few remaining frigates of the fleet.

Napoleon had received news that a Second Coalition had formed against France. Fighting had been renewed in Italy, on the Rhine, and in Holland. England was blockading France's Atlantic coast. All these events were enough to end the Egyptian adventure after a year and a half of effort. The General left behind an army of nearly thirty thousand men in the valley of the Nile under General Kléber; they had been virtually abandoned for want of a fleet.

After returning to Paris Napoleon put a good face on the events in the East. On November 10, 1799, he led a coup to replace the ineffectual Directory. He emerged from the "L'Orangerie" as the preeminent Consul with broad powers from this "coup de Brumaire." Bonaparte prepared to fight the Second Coalition against France. His first military action after the coup occurred in the courtyard of the Palace Orangerie. A thousand soldiers had been gathered there, the "Grenadiers of the Legislature and Directory." In 1795 while military commander of Paris, Napoleon had ordered them to restore order in the city. Now he was greeted with cries of "Vive le général Bonaparte!" The General rechristened the unit as the "Guard of the Consuls." This was the birth of the Guard which would remain with Napoleon to the end at Waterloo.

General Murat became Commander-in-Chief of the Guard. On December 24, 1799, Napoleon elevated himself to "First Consul." His first decree as First Consul on January 3, 1800, established a total complement of two thousand men for the Guard, infantry, cavalry and artillery. Their ranks would swell dramatically, for at Waterloo the Guard numbered ten times as many.

The Austrian Empire's army threatened to drive the French out of the lands won by Napoleon in Italy. Dividing his army into five columns, Bonaparte advanced through the Alps. The main French force under Napoleon traversed the Great St. Bernard Pass with cavalry and artillery during a spring of melting snow and avalanches. Confronting a larger Austrian force at Marengo, Napoleon was repulsed even after committing his reserves. A column under General Desaix marched to his relief. Upon arrival Desaix said, "This battle is completely lost, but there is time to win another." He did, and died saving the day. Napoleon claimed credit for this victory at Marengo.

Napoleon had demonstrated the Revolutionary army's power based on a national citizen-army rather than a professional-mercenary one. He next turned to securing peace with the monarchies to free his hand domestically. Through the Treaty of Luneville with Austria in 1801, the Peace of Amiens with England and the Concordat with the Papacy in 1802, Napoleon gained needed time for internal consolidation. The following year he reorganized the many semi-feudal states of Germany into a French-dominated entity. The borders were secure.

With that security and his seemingly unstoppable military and political successes, Napoleon's drive for supreme power reached its apex. On December 2, 1804, with Pope Pius VII watching, Napoleon crowned himself Emperor. The Guard had become the "Imperial Guard." The new Emperor had only one active enemy at this time—England. Abrogating the Peace of Amiens in 1803 over the possession of Malta, England faced Napoleon alone.

Though he lacked a viable navy, Napoleon still assembled an army of nearly 200,000 men at the Channel port of Boulogne. Despite vigorous efforts at shipbuilding all plans for invasion ended with English Admiral Horatio Nelson's tremendous victory at Trafalgar on October 21, 1805. Though Nelson died, ships of the French fleet were either captured or destroyed.

The Emperor turned to his alternative target, the German states. Austria, Sweden and Russia had now joined England in a Third Coalition against France. With 200,000 men Napoleon force-marched from the English Channel to the Rhine. In less than a month the Emperor had fifty infantry regiments and 180 squadrons of cavalry ready to invade Germany. At about the same time that Nelson destroyed the French fleet (and along with it any possible threat to English soil), Napoleon and his Marshals, particularly Michel Ney, had decisively defeated the Austrians at Ulm, northwest of Munich.

Ney was only one of an extraordinary group of men whom Napoleon raised to the highest military rank possible, Marshal of France.

Ney and the other Marshals rose through the ranks by merit. Social status no longer mattered, but rather courage and initiative in battle, loyalty in adversity, and the special ability to utilize delegated authority to their chief's best advantage became the criterion for advancement.

Ney had been a sergeant major in 1792 and a colonel in 1794. By 1796, he had become a general of brigade; in 1799 he became a general of division. In 1804, Ney received his sword as a Marshal of France.

The senior marshals each commanded a corps in the French army. A corps was unlike any unit seen up to that time in Europe. The corps had a major component of infantry, approximately fifteen–twenty thousand men, and artillery of forty guns (eight- or twelve-pounders). With this force Napoleon expected a Marshal to hold an enemy army—whatever its size—in place or at least contain it until the "masse de décision" could be brought to bear on the battlefield.

The "masse" would be comprised of several corps in most cases and would equalize a battle begun by a single, much outnumbered corps. Napoleon began his brilliant career with this strategic innovation and used it at Waterloo. Overall army strategy centered, of course, on Napoleon, assisted by his immediate staff, the "Maison." Composed of experienced and vigorous aides-de-camp, they delivered the Emperor's orders night and day. Close coordination in action of the semi-independent corps would have been impossible without these aides.

On the first anniversary of his coronation as Emperor, Napoleon won his greatest victory at the Battle of Austerlitz. With seventy-three thousand men and 139 guns, the Emperor faced eighty-five thousand men and twice as much artillery. The emperors of Russia and Austria both took the field in person, and thus Austerlitz became a battle of three emperors. Russia provided the majority of the allied troops.

Tsar Alexander took command himself. Though not yet thirty, Alexander overruled his Field Marshal Mikhail Kutusov, the commander of the allied forces, and decided to offer battle to Napoleon. It was precisely what the Emperor wished. Eleven days before the battle Napoleon chose a plateau northeast of Vienna for a showdown. He had selected an elevated plain in a triangular shape. His strategy formed from his first reconnaissance of the heights of Pratzen was to draw the Russo-Austrian armies into a sack from which they could not free themselves. And everything occurred precisely as Napoleon had planned. Austerlitz was to be his most perfectly scripted and carried out battle.

With roughly half of the members of the allied armies available, Napoleon ordered Marshal Davout, commanding twenty-seven thousand men, to force-march from nearly eighty miles away. The Emperor had selected Pratzen to draw the allies in to an attack from which they could not withdraw. Marshal Davout had received his orders on November 29. On December 1, Davout arrived with his Corps having covered nearly eighty miles in forty-six hours. By the next morning the Emperor was ready.

To draw the Russians in, Napoleon retreated from the heights and had a small screen of cavalry under Marshal Murat retreat as though stunned by the enemy's numbers. The ploy was accepted and the allies occupied the plateau. On the night of December 1 Napoleon, as was his habit, rode to survey the battlefield's terrain and his probable dispositions. At 3 A.M., he slept.

The Russians attacked at 6:30 A.M. Napoleon had always performed on two- or three-hour naps, and he was prepared for the attack. With Davout's Corps the French still fell short of the allies' numbers by nearly fifteen thousand men. Utilizing the preferred bait of the plateau position, Napoleon waited for allied descent from there that would lead to an opportunity for a French victory.

The Russians took the offering and attempted to overwhelm the French on the low ground. Napoleon's massed guns and a charge by one thousand of his heavy cavalry—the cuirassiers—helped to carry the battle. The victory enabled Napoleon to curtail the Tsar's efforts at military action in the West while also blunting Austria and Prussia's efforts in the East.

Austerlitz gave the Imperial Guard its first chance as a division-sized fighting unit. In October 1805, the Guard numbered 4,500 infantry, 1,600 horse and 770 artillery, marines and gendarmes. On the march the Guard was led by the chasseurs de cheval, its light-armed cavalry. Horse-artillery followed with the rest of the chasseurs. Supplies for the artillery, administrative and corps wagons were followed by the Emperor's personal wagons. Horse grenadiers and artillery completed the Guard's retinue in the rear.

Napoleon apparently always intended the Imperial Guard as his absolute strategic reserve; they would be committed to battle only in the most desperate circumstances. The Guard would deliver the decisive winning-blow in an engagement or hold a lost field as necessary. It would do both during the three days of Waterloo.

Following the debacle at Austerlitz, the Austrian Empire dropped out of the

Third Coalition against France. Napoleon advanced on Vienna. Prussia ill-advisedly decided to fight and at Jena on October 14, 1806, the Prussian army was crushed. The first Prussian units to engage the French column under Davout consisted of cavalry led by the sixty-six-year-old Blücher. He failed to halt the French advance; at Waterloo he would help turn the tide at the crisis of the battle.

Napoleon's sights turned further east, intent on creating an independent Poland under his suzerainty. Securing Warsaw, the French crossed the Vistula River north into East Prussia and moved forward against the Russian forces in early 1807. A vicious battle at Eylau was fought in a blinding snowstorm; the standoff produced twenty-five thousand casualties on both sides.

On June 14, Napoleon trapped a Russian army of sixty thousand with its backs against the town of Friedland with a river beyond. More than twenty thousand Russians died in the fighting itself or drowned. Within a month Emperor Alexander of Russia had signed the Treaty of Tilsit with Napoleon, recognizing the French Emperor as virtual ruler of all of Europe west of Russia.

Only the Iberian Peninsula had not yet been considered for conquest; in late 1807 its turn came. Five years of warfare there against Spanish guerillas and a British expeditionary force yielded nothing but costly losses in men, money and time for the Emperor, who led his forces personally for only one short campaign (November 1808–January 1809). Sir Arthur Wellesley, later to be the Duke of Wellington, had arrived in Spain in August 1808. The two generals did not cross swords then; it would happen seven years later at Waterloo.

A Fifth Coalition formed in 1809 consisting of Austria, England, Spain and Portugal. The latter three countries fought Napoleon's Marshals in Iberia; Austria fought on the Danube. In the two-day battle of Wagram on July 5–6 1809, armies of approximately 150,000 men each fought until the Austrians had lost forty thousand, the French thirty-two thousand. The French won a major victory.

Napoleon now had only one continental enemy to concentrate on, the Russian Empire. To Caulaincourt, his ambassador to Russia, Napoleon said, "Admit frankly that it is Alexander who wants to make war on me." Caulaincourt demurred. The Tsar had told the ambassador, "If the Emperor makes war on me it is possible, even probable, that we shall be defeated, assuming that we fight. But that will not mean that he can dictate a peace."

"Your Frenchman is brave; but long privations and a bad climate, our winter, will fight on our side. With you, marvels only take place where the Emperor is in personal attendance; and he cannot be everywhere, he cannot be absent from Paris year after year," the Tsar said.

Napoleon gathered together the Grand Armée of over 600,000 men, perhaps the single largest army to take the field on a campaign in history since Xerxes and the Persian Empire invaded Greece and the West. Having garrisoned his supply depots in Poland, Napoleon invaded Russia with 550,000 men—440,000 from France and the remainder from twenty other states. The Imperial Guard numbered forty-one thousand infantry of the Old and New Guards and 6,200 Guard Cavalry. The Cavalry Reserve consisted of forty thousand men—cuirassiers, chasseurs, hussars, dragoons and lancers.

The Russian armies could bring together a quarter of a million men because it had the vast European regions of the motherland itself with which to work. Napoleon's main line of advance had 300,000 troops to the Russian General Peter Bagration's 127,000. Divided by command rivalries, the Russian army finally decided to face Napoleon near the town of Borodino, southwest of Moscow.

On September 6, 1812, with roughly comparable numbers of 125,000 men and six hundred guns on each side, the battle deteriorated into an artillery duel killing men by the hundreds. The French then launched direct infantry assaults. Ney and his men stormed the outworks of the line. An all-out attack by the Old Guard might well have crushed the Russian army; Napoleon hesitated. Marshal Bessières, commander of the Guard Cavalry in the campaign, reminded his commander that "Sire, you are eight hundred leagues from Paris." The loss of the Guard could mean the downfall of the army and the Empire. The Russian general Kutusov was relieved to be able to retire after sundown. His army had lost forty-four thousand men in fourteen hours, the French thirty-two thousand. Napoleon, over two thousand miles from his capital, stated simply, "I dared not to risk my last reserve." For the first time the Emperor's will had failed. He wanted to force a peace on Alexander, but he could not bring himself to take the risk involved in eliminating the Russian military or its later capacities.

Nevertheless, on September 14, Napoleon entered Moscow. Expecting to be met by the city elders the Emperor instead was confronted by some elderly citizens, mental patients and criminals who had not left. Tsar Alexander had abandoned Holy Moscow to the invader. He would not surrender.

Napoleon took over the apartments of the Tsar while the Guard quartered in Kremlin Square. On the evening of September 15, flames broke out in the poorer wooden quarters of the city. Looters, and not the Tsar's orders, had caused it, but it served Russia just the same. The massive destruction of Moscow produced a vast ruin of a city incapable of supporting the French army for the winter. Napoleon's choices devolved on retiring to a much smaller city, such as Smolensk, or a full retreat to Poland and French sovereignty. He delayed a month before accepting the inevitable. On October 19, 1812, four months after crossing onto Russian soil, Napoleon ordered a full withdrawal. The Russian winter set in early and the Cossacks arrived soon after to harrass the flanks and rearguard.

The morning of October 25, Napoleon called Caulaincourt to him: "This is a bad business . . . I beat the Russians every time, but that doesn't get me anywhere." Calling for his horse, Napoleon set out to reconnoitter the enemy positions. With eight generals and only a dozen cavalrymen the group rode smack into a Cossack encampment. Outnumbered four to one, the French chasseurs protected the Emperor until four squadrons of the chasseurs came up and drove off the Cossacks.

The Emperor was safe but as the days of the retreat went by he began to fear more and more for his political authority in Paris. Ney commanded the rearguard, holding off the Cossacks and Russian regulars as they advanced. Confronted by eighty thousand Russians on the road from Smolensk to the west, Ney attacked at a numerical disadvantage and was repulsed. The Russians asked him to surrender. Ney replied, "A Marshal of France never surrenders." As Marshal Caulaincourt says, "The efforts of all the Don Cossacks were vain." They couldn't kill off Ney and the rearguard.

On December 5, 1812, Napoleon left the remnants of the Grand Armée behind and headed for Paris. His marshals and chief generals concurred in the move. Within a week the Emperor had reached Warsaw escorted by Caulaincourt in a covered sledge. On December 18, the Emperor was in Paris preparing a new army to defend France from the inevitable attack which would follow news of the debacle in Russia. Over fifty thousand of 550,000 Frenchmen came out capable of fighting. Winter and the great distances of the Russia heartland had won.

Napoleon, meanwhile, gathered new levies to fill his ranks. Between January and March 1813, the Emperor conscripted 530,000 new troops. He needed them to confront the Sixth Coalition against him: Russia, Prussia, Sweden, Austria and England. In August Napoleon met the allied army near Dresden. Over two days of rain-soaked fighting the French inflicted thirty-eight thousand casualties on the enemy versus losses of ten thousand men. Ney attempted to capture Berlin but was repulsed.

In October, Napoleon met the allies at Leipzig. He had concentrated 185,000 troops; the Allies had gathered 260,000 men for the first day of the battle on October 16. By October 19, they would have 370,000 men. The French would finally field a thousand guns, the allies 1,500. The "Battle of the Nations" cost the French seventy-three thousand casualties, the Allies fifty-four thousand. Added onto the Russian campaign's losses, Napoleon had lost more men than he could afford.

Napoleon now fell back on France to restore his position. In a series of brilliant holding actions, he held off three allied armies, his Marshals dealing with each in turn. France, however, had been drained to its limit by Napoleon. On April 6, 1814, the Emperor sarcastically announced to his generals, "Neither you nor the army need shed any more blood. Resign yourselves to living under the Bourbons and to serving them faithfully. You wanted peace, now you can have it. But the peace that you long for will destroy more of you as you lie in your feather-beds than war would have done in your bivouacs."

Upon his abdication Napoleon was given the island of Elba off France's southern coast as his domain. He retained the title of Emperor and had one thousand of his Old Guard to defend him. Napoleon bided his time until Paris was ready for his return. On February 26, 1815, the Emperor returned from exile. The European powers of Great Britain, Austria, Prussia and Russia had been meeting at the Congress of Vienna planning to remake the face of the continent with Napoleon gone. His return now threw them into turmoil.

Landing near Marseilles, Napoleon advanced north toward Paris. Ney, serving the restored Bourbon King Louis XVIII, promised to bring Napoleon back "in a cage." Near Grenoble the Emperor first met troops of the line sent to stop him. Approaching their formation, the Emperor Napoleon opened his greatcoat and said, "Here is your Emperor. Shoot him if you wish." The soldiers cheered and ran to him.

Back in Paris Napoleon organized an army once again, the Armée du Nord. By the beginning of June 1815, he had gathered 120,000 men. Four corps of the line were formed and the reserve had an additional corps along with the Imperial Guard. The Guard numbered twenty thousand men; the cavalry thirteen thousand. Napoleon had his Armée concentrated near the border of Belgium.

The allies reacted rapidly. The British organized a composite army of 105,000 men. Of these approximately thirty-five thousand were British; the rest were German and Belgian troops under the command of the Field Marshal, the Duke of Wellington. The Prussians provided an army under the command of Field Marshal Prince Blücher, who had fought Napoleon at Jena. Under himself and his Chief of Staff Gneisenau, Blücher had 120,000 men. Thus Napoleon faced double his numbers.

Consequently, he employed his standard tactic, the "masse de décision." This grand maneuver entailed splitting the enemy force, attacking that formation which provided the best target first, then proceeding to the second. At 3 A.M., on June 15, 1815, Napoleon's last army crossed the border into Belgium. The first target was the town of Charleroi. It was taken by 3 P.M. Napoleon intended to concentrate his attack on the British and Prussian forces. Ney was given command of the left flank with forty thousand men. He advanced on June 16 to Quatre Bras, a crossroads town south of Brussels. Wellington was in the capital and received notice of the incursion at a dress ball given by the Duchess of Richmond. He dispatched available units forward immediately.

While Ney closed on Quatre Bras, Napoleon concentrated on the Prussians at the town of Ligny, east of the crossroads. Napoleon anticipated that the Prussians under Blücher would be much more willing to come to the aid of Wellington than vice-versa. The Emperor was correct and proceeded to direct his main effort against the Prussians.

Ney had his written orders from Napoleon by 11 A.M. He was to contain the Anglo-allied forces at Quatre Bras, defeat them and be prepared to shift his avenue of attack to support the Emperor against the Prussians at Ligny. Ney ordered Marshal Reille to follow him to Quatre Bras, executing any other orders the Emperor might issue. Ney then proceeded with the corps under Reille to the crossroads accompanied by one thousand cuirassiers under General Kellermann, and a further 2,500 light cavalry. Ney had a total of nineteen thousand infantry and 3,500 cavalry in hand. With them he would take on Wellington, commanding ever-increasing numbers.

Ney waited on further orders from Napoleon; the Emperor realized that he had the whole of the Prussian army awaiting him. General Blücher had at least eighty-three thousand men while Napoleon faced him, on the attack, with sixty-five thousand.

On June 16, Ney waited until 1:30 P.M. to attack the allies. He had expected the crossroads to be winnable at any time and waited on orders. When he finally unleashed his attack the British had gathered ten thousand men under the Dutch Prince of Orange. Reinforcements continued to arrive all day. Ney had but one corps with which to break Wellington; he used it and his cavalry to the utmost.

At 2 P.M., Ney attacked with every man available. The French did not break the allies but took half their cannon. Wellington arrived with reinforcements and took charge. By this time Ney had received his second order from the Emperor: defeat the allies in front of him and bring his men to bear on the Prussian right flank at Ligny. Napoleon was outnumbered by almost twenty thousand men and the arrival of the impetuous Ney could stave off what would be a decisive defeat.

Ney would not come, however; Wellington had arrived with thousands of reinforcements. At 4 P.M., the Prince of Brunswick's corps arrived on the field for the allies. The Prince was shot and died that night. Ney now sought to use his infantry reserve, Count d'Erlon's corps. But due to heavy fighting at Ligny, Napoleon had already ordered d'Erlon to march his troops there and decide the battle. As it turned out, d'Erlon arrived at neither battle; he was Ney's reserve, but the Emperor's order took precedence.

Ney was not one to admit a drawn battle was unwinnable. At 5 P.M., Ney was maddened by the loss of d'Erlon's corps to Napoleon's battle at Ligny. Faced by such a loss—with the order to defeat Wellington still standing—Ney summoned his cuirassiers. Each cavalryman bore plate armor on the chest and back; they all carried a straight long-sword and two pistols. They were the most feared of the French cavalry. Charging on heavy Norman and Flemish horses the cuirassiers could demolish an infantry formation not prepared for them (in square).

Ney ordered his cuirassiers to charge the crossroads, Quatre Bras. There were one thousand of the heavy cavalry charging into the center of twenty thousand men, with more allied soldiers arriving all the time. General Count Kellermann took command of the attack. The Emperor had ordered Ney again to break the allies. Napoleon wrote, "The fate of France is in your hands." The cuirassiers were sent ahead without proper preparation.

At this point Ney was wild: the Emperor had ordered him to eliminate Wellington and march to Napoleon's aid. Everything was now on the board; there was nothing available in reserve. Kellermann had only one thousand men with three thousand waiting behind the lines, having not been brought up. Ney reiterated that "The fate of France is in your hands."

General Kellermann would not argue the point. To keep his cuirassiers from questioning what might happen, he mounted his horse and gathered his men behind him. To keep them from knowing what awaited, Kellermann attacked at top speed on the crest of the hill. Kellermann's heavy cavalry approached the ridge with an increasingly thunderous noise. Reaching the British Sixty-Ninth Regiment's Square, they crushed it, and then eliminated two squares of recently arrived Brunswick infantry. Crashing through the center of the allied line, Kellermann and his cuirassiers reached the crossroads at Quatre Bras. There they found artillery of the Dutch, English and Brunswick, along with infantry fire. Kellermann's horse was shot out from under him; his cuirassiers remounted him and retired to the French lines after sustaining heavy losses. Total French losses at Quatre Bras were four thousand; the allies lost 4,700. Ney, though he failed to take the crossroads, had contained Wellington and prevented him from aiding Prince Blücher at Ligny. Blücher was left to fight Napoleon and the Guard.

With eighty-three thousand men the Prussians had a solid numerical advantage on ground they had chosen. Taking advantage of local villages and chateaux, Blücher formed his line on these strongpoints. Napoleon's objective was to defeat the Prussians and drive them as far east as possible from the British and other allies. The Emperor arrived a little after 10 A.M., to reconnoiter the Prussian positions. He realized there were at least two corps awaiting him with more on the way. Napoleon had not expected to face over eighty thousand Prussians at Ligny, but he quickly adjusted to the new tactical situation.

Finally at 3 P.M., Napoleon signaled to attack. A gun of the Guard fired three times, and the first French line advanced. The line was composed of tirailleurs or skirmishers whose mission was to soften up the enemy line by sniping/fighting in a loose formation. Ney had again been issued an order to attack the Prussians' right flank. By now he could not. Napoleon decided to crush the Prussians unilaterally; if necessary he would use the Imperial Guard to ensure the victory. As Napoleon's attack developed, Blücher fed in reinforcements massed against the center, and thus depleted his reserves. Though Napoleon always wanted to reserve the Old Guard for the absolute last stroke, he knew that this battle called for an early commitment of his ultimate fighting force, the Guard.

Attacking with infantry of the line, the French pressed the Prussians back on the right and in the center. Finally, Napoleon decided to attack with the Guard. While deploying them, his aides saw a column coming from the west. The Emperor hesitated, not knowing whether the column was d'Erlon's or the British. After sending out riders it was determined that it was indeed d'Erlon.

Ney had continued his attempts to take Quatre Bras. Contravening Napoleon's orders, Ney commanded d'Erlon to rejoin him and participate in taking the crossroads. D'Erlon marched back and forth on June 16, uncertain where he should be. By nightfall he had not decided where his forces belonged and his corps of twenty-one thousand men went unused.

Napoleon deduced that the only victory available to the French was at Ligny. He sent one final order to Ney at 4:30 P.M. "The salvation of France and the fate of the Army depend on your execution of the Emperor's orders."

After the confusion caused by d'Erlon's approach, Napoleon had the Guard prepare to attack. Blücher positioned his troops on the forward slopes of the hills he was holding. Wellington, through his experience in Spain, had always kept his troops on the reverse flank of a hill to deflect the impact of artillery. Although the Duke had met with Blücher early on June 16, the Prussians remained in their forward positions. Napoleon directed his artillery against the center of the Prussian line. Though outnumbered by over twenty thousand men, Napoleon decided he could crush the Prussians using his strategic reserve, the Guard. At 6:30 P.M., the Emperor ordered the Guard forward. Ten thousand men, each with twenty years experience, attacked in a tremendous onset just as a thunderstorm broke. The Prussian center crumbled; after heavy fighting three corps were sent into headlong retreat.

Prince Blücher ordered his infantry, "Stand fast, brave lads." He then summoned all his remaining cavalry squadrons. Leading his hussars of the Seventh Uhlans personally, Field-Marshal Blücher, at the age of seventy, charged the French line. As darkness fell Blücher's horse was shot from under him. In its death throes it rolled over, severely bruising him. His aide-de-camp stood over him while the French cuirassiers charged by, not knowing that they had the enemy commander under their hooves.

For several hours the fate of the Field-Marshal was unknown. His chief of staff, General Gniesenau, retreated toward the town of Wavre from which he could regroup the Prussian army and be able to aid Wellington's army when Napoleon assaulted them. This seemed inevitable for the French had lost (at most) ten thousand men to almost twenty-five thousand Prussians. The Emperor and his Guard had secured a great victory; the English and the Dutch and German allies were next.

Though Napoleon had lessened the total odds against him from over two to one to slightly less, he still could not face the entire enemy with an army which could not afford to take many casualties. Also, an immediate full-scale attack after Ligny would be contrary to his overall strategic concept of throwing his main force at one enemy formation while holding the other at bay with one of his self-contained army corps.

The Duke of Wellington decided to retire north from Quatre Bras on a line which would enable him to defend the road to Brussels. The Duke chose a ridge called Mont St. Jean for his infantry and artillery and with several farmhouses in front of it as his position. It was several miles south of the village of Waterloo.

After the costly battles of Quatre Bras and Ligny, both the French and allied armies rested. Of the allies only the Prussians were on the march, retreating. Early on the morning of June 17, Wellington inspected the situation at Quatre Bras. The Duke allowed the men to have a cooked breakfast before marching to their new positions near Waterloo. At this time (9 A.M.) Wellington informed a Prussian liaison officer that he intended to offer battle to Napoleon at Mont St. Jean, provided he would have the support of at least one of the Prussian army's four corps. The Duke now issued his orders for the retreat.

Meanwhile, the Emperor was visiting the wounded at Ligny. He had already decided that the final clash would not occur that day. Ney was ordered to seize control of the crossroads when possible; the rest of the day would be spent regrouping and coordinating all forces for the supreme effort the following day.

Marshal Grouchy had been in command of the reserve cavalry. Napoleon now gave him the equivalent of two corps, approximately thirty-five thousand men, and orders to pursue Blücher and prevent the Prussians from aiding Wellington at Waterloo. The Emperor and the Imperial Guard would destroy the allied army and reestablish France's preeminent political position on the European continent. Victory would ensure that the French people would support Napoleon in raising another Grand Armée capable of opposing successfully the other allies when they attacked, including the Russians and Austrians. Given time those empires could raise an additional 400,000 men to destroy Napoleon; their preparations were already underway, albeit slowly. Russia and Austria were not in a great hurry to face the Emperor again.

The Duke of Wellington arrayed his forces on the ridge of Mont St. Jean late on June 17. The position was two miles south of Waterloo, anchored by the large chateau-farmhouse of Hougoumont directly in front of his right flank, and La Haye Sainte, much smaller but commanding the Brussels road and the center of his line.

The Duke's line occupied roughly three-and-one-half miles of frontage, of which two miles were held in depth. His crack troops—those which he depended on most—were, of course, British. He deployed them along the line concentrating on his center-right wing, at the end of the avenue which presented itself to Napoleon between the farmhouses of Hougoumont and La Haye Sainte. If broken there the entire line would fall to pieces. Wellington ordered Hougoumont garrisoned by one thousand men, composed of companies from the Guards' brigades whose sappers set to work reinforcing the walls. La Haye Sainte had a posted garrison of under four hundred, too few for the task later.

In all Wellington had twenty-four thousand British, twenty-three thousand German and twenty thousand Dutch and Belgian troops, for a total of slightly over sixty-seven thousand. He had 156 cannon on the field. The infantry of the line carried, for the most part, a "Brown Bess" musket; it could be fired three times a minute and was accurate to seventy-five yards. The Anglo-Dutch army had somewhat over ten thousand cavalry available, roughly comparable in numbers but not in overall quality to the French.

The best British cavalry regiments were the Horse Guards, the Union Brigade and the Scots Greys. The King's German Legion also provided an effective strike force. The Scots Greys, though lacking the body armor which the French cuirassiers wore, carried the same type of heavy straight sword used to thrust and kill. The lighter cavalry used curved swords for hacking and cutting, or lances for thrusting.

Formed up in a front line two men deep, Wellington had a Dutch-Belgian division on his far right; the forward right wing had two English brigades, a Hanoverian brigade and a joint Anglo-German brigade. Napoleon's main target for attack was defended, on the center-right, by two Guards brigades and a Hanoverian and Anglo-German brigade.

The chateau of Hougoumont had elements of the Coldstream Guards and companies of Hanoverians and Nassauers as the outpost's garrison. The man who would lead the first attack on the British line at Hougoumont was Prince Jerome Bonaparte, Napoleon's younger brother. The attack was intended as a diversion in order to draw troops away from Wellington's center, where the main thrust would occur.

On the morning of June 18, 1815, the Emperor rose with the expectation of attacking at 9 A.M. Assembly was slow but it was the state of the ground which caused the main delay. The soil was soaked from the heavy rains of the previous two days. Artillery could not be maneuvered and sighted properly on marshy ground. The average piece weighed nearly two tons and could not be positioned effectively in a mire.

The French attack began with an artillery bombardment at approximately 11:30 A.M., at least two hours later than Napoleon had planned. Always superbly able to adapt to the exigencies of time and weather, the Emperor gave Prince Jerome the go-ahead to take Hougoumont. After the initial artillery assault Jerome launched a brigade of the Second Corps against the walls of the farm. The advance had to proceed first through the orchard outside. The French were caught in a murderous crossfire and repelled with heavy casualties. Jerome now ordered a second brigade to the walls. Lieutenant Legros [nicknamed L'Enfonceur the Smasher], a huge officer wielding a sapper's axe, assaulted the main gate. Legros forced his way into the courtyard with a half-dozen men; all died under heavy fire. The attacks on Hougoumont were continued, for the Prince refused to back off, regroup and rethink the attack.

The problem of overly independent actions by individual commanders affected Napoleon's overall plans to a great and perhaps fatal degree at Waterloo. All Marshals were expected to operate at their own discretion within the bounds of the major plan which had been developed by Napoleon. The Emperor undoubtedly wanted possession of Hougoumont but not at the expense of men thrown away for no gain. The loss of men did not bother Napoleon but failure to accomplish the goal he wanted did. Prince Jerome, against the sensible advice of his staff, continued to throw men at the walls with considerable losses. Jerome did not accept his orders as a simple diversionary maneuver (though capturing the chateau would certainly help the overall tactical situation) and thus wasted men.

The British, meanwhile, poured reinforcements of Coldstream and Scots Greys into the chateau and orchard of Hougoumont, respectively. By 1 P.M., the situation had stabilized for the allies, and the French were at a distinct disadvantage in attempts to dislodge the new troops. At 1:30 P.M., the pressure of that initial fight had all but ended, for Ney had completed his preparations for the second phase of Waterloo, the assault on the center of the allied line. Somewhat over two thousand Guardsmen and allies had held off ten thousand French for two hours. At the end of the day Wellington remarked, "You may depend upon it, that no troops but the British could have held Hougoumont, and only the best of them at that!"

Napoleon had planned the major attack on the center and left-center of the British line, but Ney would have operational control at the front. The main battle lines of the armies were separated by undulating ground and distances of 1,000–1,500 yards. About halfway between the armies the ground rose slightly before dropping off again. Napoleon ordered most of the eighty artillery pieces he would use to support Ney's attack to be positioned there, giving his gunners a major advantage.

Just after 1 P.M., a devastating barrage broke onto the British line. Many of the French guns, with effective ranges of over one thousand yards, were mauling British formations from half that distance. The French twelve-pounder cannon fired a ball of 121 M.M. caliber. At that short range the shot ripped its way through rank upon rank, crushing all men in its path. Many British survivors could not remember ever having experienced such a firestorm.

The drums began to beat the "pas de charge" for the French advance at 1:45 P.M. Eighteen thousand men of the First Corps under d'Erlon proceeded across the fields in four divisional columns. The cry of "Vive l'Empereur" went up throughout the ranks. The four infantry columns were covered on the left and right flanks by cavalry units, and field artillery came along in support. At the same time Prince Jerome renewed his pressure on the English right at Hougoumont.

Napoleon had initiated this massive attempt to rupture the allied line using one-quarter of his entire strength even though he had just obtained intelligence that a strong force was advancing from the east toward his right flank. At first the troops were hoped to be Grouchy's, to whom the Emperor had dispatched orders earlier in the day to retire toward Napoleon's position, keeping his forces between the Prussians and the French right.

Instead, a Prussian courier captured by the Seventh Hussars revealed that thirty thousand men of the Prussian IV Corps under General Bülow were approaching the weak French right. Napoleon retained his unshakeable composure. He could have easily cancelled the attack and ordered a withdrawal south to Charleroi to await Grouchy and his thirty-four thousand men in order to reform with fifty percent more strength. Rejecting that option, he turned to his chief of staff, Marshal Soult, and exclaimed, "This morning we had ninety chances in our favor. Even now we have sixty chances, and only forty against us." So saying, he ordered two cavalry regiments to the right flank, followed thereafter by ten thousand infantry of General Lobau's VI Corps. They were to hold off the Prussians until the issue was forced at Mont St. Jean.

Count d'Erlon then received his order to advance. Two serious mistakes were made, however. Three of the four divisions marched in column, that is, with fronts only two companies in width, yet with great depth. This tended to reduce the amount of fire-power at a given moment while at the same time presenting a very compact formation for artillery to plow through. Also, if fanning out motions into line were not performed speedily and efficiently, the battalions would bunch up, disordering the attack. One division did advance in a line three deep, thereby giving more men the opportunity to fire.

The second error was in the lack of cavalry support for the infantry. Most French attacks under Napoleon began with an artillery barrage followed by cavalry charges, with infantry coming up last. The optimal results would be threefold. First, artillery fire would force the enemy to fan out into line to reduce its casualties, for many could die from one canister shot, or even a ball, in a dense formation. Second, the cavalry would try to catch the enemy reforming into the tight-knit squares which formed the four-sided wall of bayonets intended to repulse horsemen, but which would again provide compact targets for the approaching infantry. If all was synchronized closely, the enemy would suffer severely, and, most likely, crack.

The first brigades of the allies to receive the attack were the King's German Legion garrisoning La Haye Sainte, athwart the road to Brussels at the center of the line, and the English Ninety-Fifth, which were entrenched in a sandpit slightly to the east of the farmhouse. Advancing through heavy fire, d'Erlon's men burst on La Haye Sainte which had not been properly fortified; one of its main gates had even been broken up the night before for firewood. The King's German Legion did not retreat, however. Having lost the adjacent orchard, it fell back on the buildings. A battalion of Hanoverians sent up as support was crushed by a regiment of cuirassiers who came up suddenly from the edge of the sandpit.

The companies of the Ninety-Fifth, though they had delivered a murderous enfilade on the French columns, fell back on the rest of their brigade at the main line. The French swept on, utterly routing Bijlandt's Dutch-Belgian brigade which had already received a severe mauling from the artillery. That brigade went to the rear and was not seen again that day. Sensing victory the columns began to deploy into line to increase their firepower.

At this movement General Picton ordered his brigades to advance on the ridge and fire; arrayed in line two deep, three thousand men fired in volley at a range of fifty yards, a distance at which it was almost impossible to miss. The French still came on. Picton, already wounded, cried out, "Charge, charge, hurrah," and turned to Kempt, one of his commanders, and ordered, "Rally the Highlanders." The next moment the general fell dead with a bullet through the temple. Infantrymen on both sides were now using bayonets.

Further east, German brigades were forming squares to receive the charge of the cuirassiers. The allied infantry was exceedingly hard-pressed, and in increased danger from French cavalry. At this point either Wellington himself, or the Earl of Uxbridge, commander of the allied cavalry, ordered a counter-attack by the British heavy cavalry.

Sir William Ponsonby's Union Brigade of nine hundred men—the Royals, Scots Greys and Inniskillings—along with over 1,200 horse of the Household Brigade, made up of squadrons from the First and Second Life Guards, the

Royal House Guards and the King's Dragoon Guards, were directed to repel the French.

The Household Brigade had the immediate advantage over the cuirassiers who were coming upslope, and with British mounts being heavier the French were scattered. Their dispersal threw their own infantry into confusion with ranks being broken by the retreating horsemen. The Union Brigade charged into the French ranks and wreaked havoc. Unprotected infantry were again helpless against heavy cavalry: two thousand prisoners were taken, and two Eagles captured.

D'Erlon's attack was in full retreat; the British, with relatively few casualties, should have stopped there. The Scots Greys, however, were enflamed. With cries of "Scotland forever!" they charged across the valley and were immediately followed by the rest of the heavy brigades. Napoleon greeted this exuberant charge with fresh cavalry reserves. The Greys, Royals and Inniskillings were met by two regiments of lancers who dispatched many, including the commander, Ponsonby. A French lancer named Urban was prepared to capture Ponsonby when several Scots Greys rode up to his rescue. Rather than lose his captive, the lancer killed him with one thrust and turned on the would-be rescuers. He killed three. The Second Life Guards and the King's Dragoon Guards had two regiments of cuirassiers receive them. The British lost over one thousand cavalry in that magnificent, ill-advised charge.

At Hougoumont the fight continued. Napoleon ordered his howitzers to fire "carcass projectiles" intended to set the barn and other outbuildings ablaze. By 2:45 P.M., the barn was on fire. Wellington ordered the chateau to be held with an injunction that the commander "should keep your men in those areas which the fire does not reach." This order left many wounded to burn as the able manned the wall.

It was now 3:30 P.M. Wellington, with d'Erlon's corps in retreat, had ordered his infantry to fall back on the reverse slope of Mont St. Jean to blunt the effect of the French artillery. More guns had been brought up to concentrate on the British right center. The cannonade was unprecedented in its intensity. Captain Mercer of the English artillery, who remained at his battery—disregarding Wellington's orders to retire into the square upon the approach of the cavalry—said that the French fire was so heavy that, "so thick was the hail of balls and bullets that it seemed dangerous to extend the arm lest it should be torn off."

Marshal Ney now arrayed what would be the greatest charge at Waterloo. Hoping the withdrawal of large numbers of the English redcoats and allies signaled the beginning of an allout retreat, Ney and several of his commanders believed a massive cavalry charge would break the line. In committing his forces this way he risked a great loss in men and horse for the chance to achieve total victory.

Ney marshalled over five thousand cavalrymen aligned in three divisions; the cuirassiers would lead the attack. Glistening in their steel breastplates and horse-hair plumed helmets, the heavy cavalry followed the artillery barrage of the massed battery. The attack was sent through the gap between Hougoumont and La Haye Sainte. The distance between the farmhouses was only one thousand yards, and given the range of British muskets, Ney and his cavalry commanders had to collapse the front to only seven hundred–eight hundred yards. Each line would deploy perhaps 250 mounts. Though three horses had already been shot from under him in leading d'Erlon's attacks, on his fourth mount he led the French cavalry against the allied line.

The array was brilliant: General Milhaud's cuirassiers led the onset, followed by the light cavalry of the Guard, the Grenadiers à cheval. A British officer related the spectacle:

> . . . [they] shone in burnished steel, relieved by black-horse-hair crested helmets; next came the red lancers of the Guard, in their gaudy uniforms, and mounted on richly caparisoned steeds, their fluttering lance-flags heightening the brilliance of their display; while the third line, comprising the chasseurs of the Guard, in their rich costume of green and gold, with fur-trimmed pelisses 'à la hussard,' and black bearskin shakos, completed the gorgeous, yet harmonious, coloring of the military spectacle.

After the Guard cavalry came squadrons of multi-colored hussars, dragoons with tiger-skin headdresses and carabiniers in white.

Wellington ordered his infantry to prepare to receive cavalry: "Form square." Normally a battalion of five hundred would deploy into a square sixty feet on a side, with 125 men per side. At Waterloo, however, given the uneven checkerboard formations the squares became rectangles. Three companies comprised of 150 men each would be in front and rear, and two of one hundred men apiece on the sides.

The British square had four ranks. With bayonets fixed the first rank knelt, their muskets set on the ground. The second rank stood low behind, their bayonets backing the first. The third and fourth ranks actually did the firing over the wall of steel in front of them. The bayonets were intended for the horses, the musket fire for the riders. In between and in front of the squares stood the artillery positions. The Duke had ordered the gun crews not to fire until the last possible moment before the French sabers reached them and then run for the nearest square.

The leading cuirassiers began to ascend the ridge, abandoning the unhurried, calm trot they had used in crossing the valley. As they gained speed and neared the top, the French guns fell silent. Only the steady drumming of thousands of hooves could be heard. At less than a hundred yards the British opened fire. Though cannister and round shot tore through man and horse, leaving bloody heaps on the ground, the French came on.

At the last moment the gunners ran for safety. Now the French had their turn. The cuirassiers thrust at any target available with their three-foot long swords while the horses wheeled from the bayonets. When a man fell in first rank, he was immediately replaced by one from behind. Colonel Gronow, standing in a First Guards square, said that even during the first charge, at 4 P.M., his square was, "A perfect hospital, being full of dead, dying and mutilated soldiers."

The waves of cuirassiers beat again and again trying to break the squares, until at 4:15 P.M., Wellington unleashed what was left of his heavy cavalry along with some light regiments and repelled the French. The gunners re-charged and fired while the French artillery could reply with their men out of the way, raking the squares.

Marshal Ney reformed his squadrons. Slightly after 4:30 P.M., he led the second charge. Colonel Mercer had stood with his battery in the first attack against the Duke's orders to steady an allied square near him. He later wrote,

Every man stood steadily at his post, the guns ready, loaded with a round-shot first, case over it . . . It was indeed a grand and imposing spectacle . . . I allowed them to advance unmolested until the head of the column might have been about fifty or sixty yards from us, and then gave the word, 'Fire!' . . . The effect was terrible. Nearly the whole leading rank fell at once; and the round-shot pene-trating the column, carried confusion through its extent . . . Still, however these devoted warriors struggled on, intent only on reaching us.

Ney pressed attack after attack with his forty squadrons, some severely depleted. But just as he had earlier erred in not supporting d'Erlon's infantry with cavalry, he now reversed the error and left the cavalry without infantry support, which was less than a mile away. No one was sure after the avalanche of charges how many had in fact been made, but it was at least seven and possibly ten.

Napoleon was incensed that Ney was squandering horsemen, but once committed he supported "the bravest of the brave" with even more cavalry. Perhaps fifteen thousand horsemen charged the ridge of Mont St. Jean, but the squares, severely wounded, still stood. Ney had four more horses shot from under him. At nearly 6 P.M., he at last thought to bring up six thousand of Count Reille's men and some field artillery, but it was too late.

All through the great French infantry and cavalry attacks of the afternoon, the Prussians were advancing inexorably toward the east flank of the battle. It was a two-pronged approach, as circumstances dictated. The IV Corps under General Bülow were the first Prussians to approach the battlefield at 1 P.M., when they were mistaken for Grouchy's corps. The Prussians's overall plan was to attack in force the weak and recessed right wing of the French. Fear that Wellington's center might crack before they could arrive forced Blücher to alter his plans significantly. The Fourth Corps would continue on toward Napoleon's right with the Second Corps following. He would then have First Corps proceed to Wellington's direct aid on the English left flank. The Third Corps was engaged with Grouchy at Wavre, far away to the northeast. Even disengagement by Grouchy would not get him to the field that day.

The old Prussian's moves were intended to keep the Emperor off-balance. He could be attacked in the right and rear while simultaneously the British could receive reinforcements on their line. The attack on the French rear came at the village of Plancenoit, which Lobau was holding. The village was actually behind Napoleon's command post and consequently near the Guard, none of which had entered the battle, save for the cavalry.

Plancenoit erupted into a savage street-by-street fight, often with the bayonet. By 6 P.M., Plancenoit had been captured by six Prussian battalions. Napoleon now ordered eight battalions of the Young Guard, with twenty-four guns, to retake Plancenoit. This they did, driving the Prussians back to the east of the village. Soon, however, seven more battalions of the Fourth Corps arrived. Attacking in columns from several directions, the Prussians pushed the Young Guard out.

At the same time as this action was occurring at Plancenoit, Napoleon searched for his next point of attack. Time was scarce and the British line had to be broken. The Emperor decided that La Haye Sainte must fall.

Ney was once again given the call. For the first time in a day of massive attacks, the Marshal made the coordinated assault for which the French army was famous. Utilizing two regiments of infantry and sappers, some cavalry and guns, Ney took the farmhouse near the center of the British line. A sapper, Lieutenant Vieux, broke down the wooden gate with an axe, and the infantry stormed in. Out of four hundred men of the King's German Legion who fought it out hand-to-hand, only forty-two escaped to the British line.

Napoleon occupied a fortified position only three hundred yards from the center of the allied line. From there his guns began to riddle the already disastrously-thin ranks. Remnants of the cuirassiers charged and met two battalions of the King's German Legion. One was annihilated, its colonel killed and flag captured; thirty men survived.

Ney hoped to complete the rupture of the line and sent to Napoleon for more men. The Emperor replied, "Some troops! Where do you expect me to get them from? Do you want me to make some?" Without a cavalry reserve, due to losses sustained in Ney's impetuous charges, Napoleon had only the Imperial Guard left. However, they were the most valuable troops on the battlefield; Napoleon refused to commit them yet.

If the Guard had followed the cavalry charges along with Reille's Corps, the day might have ended in a French victory at 4:30 P.M. Again, with La Haye Sainte's capture, the British center was near collapse, and the Guard could be committed. Napoleon hesitated while the Prussians drew nearer. Ney was asking for six or seven battalions of the Guard with which, he asserted, he would split the allied line. With Wellington done for, the Prussians could then be dealt with piecemeal, as their advances were spread over broad areas and at lengthy distances, brigade by brigade.

Napoleon had eight fresh battalions of the Old Guard—well-seasoned veterans all—and six battalions of the Middle Guard. Nevertheless, he could not be certain that the Duke's men would, in fact, give way to a full assault. More importantly, his own right flank and rear was threatened. In case of defeat, his line of retreat would be cut. He therefore decided to secure the flank first before a final attack. Napoleon ordered eleven battalions of the Guard to form squares in a line from La Belle Alliance to Rossommé, facing east to Plancenoit. Two battalions, one each of the Second Grenadiers and Second Chasseurs, were sent to support the Young Guard and secure the village.

Within twenty minutes the bayonet charge of two battalions of the Old Guard had routed fourteen battalions of Prussians. The Guard had retaken Plancenoit, secured Napoleon's flank, and given their Emperor one last chance to crush the British and their allies. It was 7 P.M., and there were two hours of light remaining in which to attempt a breakthrough. Napoleon envisioned a familiar battlefield scene; it had happened on many battlefields before: The Old Guard, never defeated, would be ordered at the last moment to deliver the coup de grâce. But never before had they faced such odds.

Wellington, sensing Napoleon's final surge, reinforced his center with forces from both flanks. His instinct was confirmed by a French traitor. A carabinier galloped across the valley, sword in sheath, shouting, "Long live the king! Get ready! That bastard Napoleon will be upon you with the Guard before half an hour." Thus informed, the Duke instructed his gunners not to duel with French batteries but wait for the attack and concentrate all their fire on the Guard.

Nine battalions of the Guard formed up to advance in column on a two-company front. The battalions were to deploy into line upon approaching the allied positions. While the Guard arrayed itself, it was becoming apparent to all on the French line that large numbers of troops were appearing on the northeast horizon. Napoleon had an aide-de-camp immediately gallop down the line announcing that Marshal Grouchy had finally come: "Vive l'Empereur! Soldats, voilà Grouchy!" The line took up the cheer of "Vive l'Empereur!"

The mood did not last for long, however, for cannon fire was heard from that direction. The cry now became, "Voyez! Ces sont les Prussiens!" At this point it did not matter, for those who would fight to the end for Napoleon would do so no matter what the odds.

Count Reille and d'Erlon's men, and all others able to fight, were ordered to support the Guard on its flanks and in the rear. What little remained of the cuirassiers, lancers of the Guard, dragoons and hussars accompanied the flanks. With the drums beating the "pas de charge," Napoleon placed himself at the head of the Guard at the beginning of their final advance. It is possible he intended to lead the attack, and that he was dissuaded by his staff for at La Haye Sainte he handed over command to the unkillable Ney for one last throw against the British.

Ney, riding his fifth horse of the day (and eighth over the past two days!) at first led the Guard directly up the road toward the British center. Four battalions of Grenadiers marched in column, followed by four battalions of Chasseurs. Each battalion numbered five hundred men. The column formation had two companies marching parallel, with two light field guns between each formation. The front rank of each company would present seventy-five to eighty muskets in firepower and bayonet.

One battalion of Grenadiers was detailed off to hold a secure position facing Hougoumont on the left flank of the advance. As the column moved closer to the allied line, the cool and steady professional advance of the Guard became disjointed, perhaps through having to keep formation over the thousands of dead—men and horse—or through the shroud of smoke hanging everywhere.

The result was that the Chasseurs fell back behind the Grenadiers and to their left, while two battalions of the Grenadiers themselves fell back to the left of the First Battalion, Third Grenadiers, which remained closest to the original attack route. The Guard thus began to advance in echelon; it would not be possible to deploy into one solid (though thin line) to deliver all their fire at once. Nor would it be possible for the individual columns to attack specific enemy units simultaneously, for the differences in distance and ground to be traversed had changed.

The Guard marched into a cul-de-sac. The allied line curved in front of the advancing columns, and at two hundred yards the artillery erupted with everything it had. Cannister and ball ripped the ranks, which closed up and continued on, with shouts of "Vive l'Empereur!" Ney lost his fifth horse of the day. He marched on, sword in hand, next to General Friant of the Grenadiers.

The First Battalion of the Third Grenadiers led the attack. As the right front echelon, the battalion broke and scattered the Thirtieth and Seventy-Fifth English regiments. A Brunswick corps in its path was overborne. Artillery batteries were captured. General Friant, wounded, had to leave the attack just before a counterattack by three thousand bayonets of Chasse's Dutch-Belgian division backed by artillery. The Grenadier Battalion was thrust back by the sheer weight of the six-to-one odds against it, and retreated down the slope.

The second echelon, comprised of the First and Second Battalions of the Fourth Grenadiers, cut deep into the Thirty-Third and Sixty Ninth Foot English Regiments, next to where the Third Grenadiers had struck. Though thrown into disarray the remnant of the regiments did not yield their positions.

The third echelon, with one thousand men of the Third Chasseurs, advanced almost unopposed to the ridge by infantry. The "old bearskins" found the British guns abandoned, no crews to be seen. It seemed that nothing stood in their way to collapse the allied middle.

Amidst French exultation at the coming victory, General Maitland of the First Foot Guards shouted, "Up Guards. At them!" One thousand five hundred Guardsmen, four-deep, rose from the far slope of the ridge where they had lain among the grain. Standing together as one, they delivered a volley which killed three hundred of the French Old Guard. The French were packed nine-ranks deep and therefore had much less musketry to bring to bear, but they stood and returned the fire with great loss. The Chasseurs desperately tried to deploy from column into line, but their own dead and wounded hampered their movements.

Wellington now saw that the Chasseurs were close to breaking and ordered Maitland's Foot Guards to charge. The disordered Chasseurs retreated down the slope followed by the Foot Guards. English artillery stopped firing because the fighting was at such close quarters. Near Hougoumont, however, the English held up, for the fourth Guard echelon, two battalions of the Fourth Chasseurs, was advancing to the rescue. The Foot Guards raced back up their hill, under covering artillery fire.

The Chasseurs and Grenadiers regrouped and attempted the ridge once more; they could not have numbered more than 1,500. Raked with fire from the front and both flanks, these remnants of the Guard retreated down the slope. An overwhelming cry of despair went up from the French ranks, "La Garde recule," or "The Guard retreats." Well-founded or not, it was enough to shatter the morale of men who had fought for ten hours straight on the third day of the battle which would determine the destiny of their country. Some panicked; others did not.

Napoleon, the ever-prepared commander, had kept three battalions of the Guard in reserve for just such a setback. Though most of the army and even the Emperor realized it was all over, still he formed up these final battalions to support those he had sent forward. Soon he decided that these last three battalions of the Guard would cover the retreat. The Guardsmen did not have to be ordered to do so: they knew the day was lost and that it fell to them to try to stem the oncoming tide from Mont St. Jean.

That tide was released by Wellington. When he saw that the Chasseurs had been thrown back, the Duke made a gesture that was forever etched in the memories of the combatants. Taking off his hat, he pointed to the French and waved it three times. All who saw him knew what was meant—everyone able was to charge the French.

The French ranks were in turmoil. With the retreat of the Guard, all order was lost. Some units broke and ran while others formed up around their Eagles. The only battalions that held themselves in perfect order were the Second Battalions of the First and Second Chasseurs and the Second Battalion of the Second Grenadiers of the Guard.

Under their Generals Cambronne, Roquet and Christiani, the last squares of the Guard were surrounded by the English cavalry of Generals Vivian and Vandeleur. Unable to break the squares, artillery was ordered to the point-blank range of sixty yards. Napoleon ordered them to withdraw, maintaining formation in square.

At about this time Ney tried to rally the troops once more. Standing in the road with a broken saber he shouted to d'Erlon, "D'Erlon, if we come out of this, you and I will be hanged." Finding a brigade of two battalions of the line intact, he stopped their orderly retreat with the words, "Come and see how a Marshal of France dies!" Unfortunately, he could not find a bullet or sword to kill him. The brigade was soon repulsed.

The Prussians continued to pour in from the east. In Plancenoit the Guards were outnumbered more than five to one, with little more than three battalions fighting three divisions. Upon the insistence of his chief-of-staff, Marshal Soult, Napoleon finally acquiesced and gave the order to withdraw from the shelter of the Guards square next to La Belle Alliance.

The remnants of the Chasseurs and Grenadiers continued to withdraw slowly, covering the Emperor's departure from the field, along with the rest of the army's retreat. The squares were blasted into triangles, and finally thin wounded lines. English officers asked the Guard to surrender. General Cambronne of the First Chasseurs replied with the single eloquent word, "Merde!" It has since been rendered as "The Guard dies but never surrenders." With a vicious cannonade British artillery ended the existence of the Imperial Guard at Waterloo. It was 9:00 P.M.

Strewn about over nearly three square miles were the bodies of fifty thousand men. The dead were almost evenly divided between the French and allies. Tens of thousands of horses also lay in the moonlight. Scattered among these bodies were the wounded, prey to the ravages of Belgian peasants who attacked the helpless like vultures, killing those who could not resist and robbing all, French and allied alike.

———

On the slopes of Mont St. Jean revolutionary France—embodying its people's army, and especially the Guard of the Emperor—died. It would revive three decades later, but it would be twice that long before true descendants of the Revolution would appear again, in the Commune of 1870.

When five thousand men of the Old Guard died around their Eagles with fifteen thousand other Frenchmen, twenty-five years of the revolution came to an end. Even if the embodiment of an egalitarian movement became an emperor, the common man, the soldier, still believed that Napoleon stood for him, and that the royalty of Europe was the enemy.

At Waterloo the monarchs of Western Europe and their armies felt the need to crush, once and for all, this symbol of the upstart underclasses. They would tolerate no more such disturbances to the peace of the continent.

As the final day's battle developed both sides fully realized that its outcome meant either the eclipse, or a new dawn, for the Emperor. The commanding generals spent the lives of their troops in accordance with the magnitude of the battle. But with Napoleon holding back at the end, the Imperial Guard was squandered; they fell too few, too late.

Napoleon went to Paris and abdicated in favor of his son, the Prince of Rome. Neither would survive to take power in France again. The Emperor Napoleon died in exile on St. Helena in 1821 at the age of fifty-two; his son died in Austria at age twenty-one in 1832.

The Iron Duke Wellington assessed the battle of Waterloo in his own laconic way, saying "it was a damned nice thing—the nearest run thing you ever saw in your life."

In defeat, Napoleon had much time to analyze the battle and its political and military possibilities while in his final, fatal exile on the rock of St. Helena in the south Atlantic. Speaking to his personal surgeon, the Irish doctor Barry O'Meara provided by his British captors, Napoleon declared that if the Prussians had not arrived:

> . . . the English army would have been destroyed. They were defeated at mid-day. But accident, or more likely destiny, decided the Lord Wellington should gain it. . . . . It was the greatest folly to disunite the English and Prussian armies . . . He might have lost everything. But he has been fortunate; his destiny has prevailed; and everything he did will meet with applause. My intentions were, to attack and destroy the English army. This I knew would produce an immediate change of ministry. . . . The people would have said, What is it to us who is on the throne of France, Louis or Napoleon; . . . They would have made peace. . . .
> Peace would have been permanent. . . .

Instead of a Napoleonic peace, however, the allies of the last confederation against the former Emperor of Europe from the English Channel to Moscow now were finally free to impose their collective will upon the continent.

The direct results of the allied victory at Waterloo were the breakup of the First French Empire, and ultimately, the rise of nationalism and centralization of government in Germany under Chancellor von Bismarck and Italy under Garibaldi, both nearly half a century after the battle.

The fate of Europe and most of the world has been intertwined with that of the Franco-German relationship ever since.

Victor Hugo wrote in "Les Miserables":

To this word of Cambronne, the English voice replied: 'Fire'! the batteries flamed, the hill trembled, from all those brazen throats went forth a final vomiting of grape, terrific; a vast smoke, dusky white in the light of the rising moon, rolled out, and when the smoke was dissipated, there was nothing left. That formidable remnant was annihilated; the Guard was dead. The four walls of the living redoubt had fallen, hardly could a quivering be distinguished here and there among the corpses; and thus the French legions grander than the Roman legions, expired at Mont St. Jean on ground soaked in rain and blood in the sombre wheat-fields. . . .

# 8

# THE ALAMO, 1836

THE MEN OF GONZALES answered the call. They were the only ones. In the middle of the night on February 29, 1836, thirty-two men from a town seventy miles northeast of San Antonio crept through Mexican lines besieging the former Franciscan mission of the Alamo. The men had come because they valued freedom for themselves and their families, and for Texas, above their own lives. The thirty-two men of Gonzales were joining a force of 153 men under the command of Col. James Bowie. Bowie was ill with fever, however, and active command had passed to Lt. Col. William B. Travis. Next in the chain of command of the garrison was Col. David Crockett of Tennessee.

It was during a storm on the night of February 29 that the small reinforcement sneaked into the Alamo. The reinforcements knew beforehand that their chances were minimal, but they joined the doomed garrison nevertheless. (It would be only two more days before everyone finally knew the fort was lost.) The leaders of the band from Gonzales were Capt. Albert Martin and Lt. George Kimball of the town militia, "the Gonzales Ranging Company of Mounted Volunteers," which was formed the day before. The men varied in age from fifteen to forty-eight-years-old.

The men formed up, among them Isaac Millsaps: he was forty-one and his wife was blind. He left seven children behind. The wealthiest man in town, Thomas R. Miller, joined in. He lived near Jacob Darst, a forty-eight-year-old man who would go down fighting at the Alamo. As the small group headed out of town, a boy named William King stopped Kimball and asked if he could join the party. His father was needed at home, with nine children to feed.

137

William, the oldest at fifteen, was allowed to join. None of the men and boys who left Gonzales on Saturday, February 27, ever saw the town or their families again.

The troubles that led to the Alamo and eventual independence and statehood for Texas began in 1830. By that year, over seventy-five percent of Texas's settlers were from the United States. Texas was at the time the northernmost province of a recently-independent Mexico, which had won its freedom from Spain in 1821.

Texas was huge, comprising fully one-half of the territory of Mexico, and colonists were needed in abundance to settle it. In an effort to lure them, the new constitutional government of Mexico offered large land grants and exemptions from trade duties and taxes. There were two consequent obligations: the new colonist must swear allegiance to the Mexican central government and become, at least nominally, a Catholic.

Those requirements proved no problem to the thousands holding dreams of owning their own land in a vast new region far from the already increasingly crowded cities of the East. They came by railroad, coach, and riverboat to New Orleans, the thriving commercial portal which led to Texas.

Laws passed in 1824–1825 allowed settlers to live for ten years in Texas free of taxes and trade duty. Each family could receive 4,428 acres of land for $30. This colonization program was handled by contractors called empresarios, who in turn received huge amounts of land for their services in establishing colonies. One of the most successful was Stephen A. Austin.

Austin proved a solid Mexican citizen, at first, on the strength of his oath of allegiance as did many of the other settlers during the first decade under Mexican rule. But by 1830 political, social and civic attitudes had changed. The heavy influx of colonists and traders brought with it the seeds of a crisis.

Slavery was forbidden by the Mexican constitution but many new Texans openly and flagrantly flouted the law. Smuggling became common and taxes were all but completely forgotten. The Mexican government could not fail to react to such complete rejection of its laws in a state that by now was over three-quarters non-Mexican. In April 1830, the government took steps to remedy all four major problems. It made further American immigration illegal, outlawed slavery, imposed new taxes, and established trade restrictions. The Texans next realized that Mexico actually meant to enforce the law with the establishment of a string of garrisons by Gen. Manuel y Terán across Texas.

Soon there arose increasingly vocal objections by many Texans to Mexican laws, and ultimately, Mexican rule itself. One of the key leaders in this movement, later to be known as the "war party," was Lt. Col. Travis. He arrived in Texas in May 1831, by way of North Carolina, his birthplace, and Alabama, where he had married and settled. But the marriage failed, and like so many others he had come to Texas to begin anew. He began his law practice and settled in.

By June 1832, Travis had become deeply involved in the political situation. The local commander of the Mexican garrison at Anahuac, Col. John Bradburn, had cracked down on smuggling. Travis and a friend, Patrick Jack, attempted to rile the colonel with a warning that a hundred angry colonists were planning to take the town. Bradburn awaited an attack all night; in the morning he found it was a joke. He was not amused and arrested both of them. Settlers now became truly angry and marched on Anahuac. They found the prisoners tied to stakes in the ground and were promised the pair would be killed if anyone fired. Travis, in his first show of heroics, called on them to fire at the oppressor. Instead, the colonists withdrew and laid siege to the town.

The siege lost its motive, however, with a revolutionary change in the central government of Mexico. General Antonio Lopez de Santa Anna had overthrown the seemingly anti-American government of President Anastacio Bustamente. Supposedly a liberal, Santa Anna temporarily suspended customs duties, relieved Col. Bradburn of duty, and released Travis and Jack. Austin felt vindicated that no real violence had occurred.

Austin and the members of the so-called "peace party" now began to draft resolutions that would give semi-autonomy to Texas, nominally separating it (governmentally) from the local Mexican state of Coahuila. They also sought repeal of anti-slavery laws, along with tax exempt status. These demands, of course, contradicted the 1830 Mexican laws. Nevertheless, Stephen Austin felt the liberal President Santa Anna could be reasoned with, and traveled to Mexico City convinced he could gain separate, though Mexican, statehood for Texas, along with a constitution his peace party had drafted. Austin arrived in the capital in mid-1833. After several futile months he found himself imprisoned. He remained there for a year until his release on bond in early 1835. He was still detained in Mexico City.

The Customs House at Anahuac had reopened. Its commander, Capt. Tenorio, took up the anti-smuggling campaign. While the leader of the peace party was held powerless in Mexico, Travis decided to take action. He hated the Mexicans, and Santa Anna had become, in Travis's and many other Texans's eyes, just another anti-American Mexican dictator. On June 27, 1835, Travis and twenty-five men seized the Customs House. The captain departed for the garrison town of San Felipe, while colonists throughout the area were shocked that Travis had gone that far. Too far, many thought, and Travis had to timidly withdraw. The peace party moderates still held the upper hand.

The war party seemingly lost any momentum it had, but Santa Anna restored it for them. Enraged by Travis's cavalier treatment of a garrison commander, and much worse, the seizure of the Customs House, the Mexican President sent troops north. Four hundred men under Gen. Antonio Cos, Santa Anna's brother-in-law, were ordered to enter Texas and establish martial law. Travis and other rebellious colonists were to be arrested.

Where the Texans before had wanted to be semi-autonomous with a greater voice in their own affairs, they were now threatened with a military occupation and martial law. Santa Anna had incited what Travis and the war party could not: Texas was uniting against Mexico.

In view of the impending threat, "Committees of Public Safety" began to form all over Texas; Travis had been vindicated. To a friend on August 31, Travis wrote, "principle has triumphed over prejudice, passion, cowardice and knavery. . . . And now let Tories, submission men and Spanish invaders look out." The following day came the startling news that Stephen Austin had returned from Mexico.

A crowd of a thousand Texans anxiously waited to hear what the moderate leader would say at a banquet in his honor in Brazoria. He declared that the people felt that they "would not unite with any armed force sent against this country; on the contrary, it would resist and repel it, and ought to do so . . ." On September 19 came word that Gen. Cos was preparing to occupy in force San Antonio de Bexar, the town formed around the former Franciscan mission, the Alamo. Austin issued a proclamation that "War is our only recourse."

The local garrison commander, Col. Ugartchea, was zealously searching houses, confiscating weapons, and breaking up potentially rebellious groups of colonists. Ugartchea learned that the men of Gonzales had refurbished an old six-pounder gun given them as protection against the Indians. He dispatched Lt. Casteñada with one hundred men to seize it.

Mexican forces arrived at Gonzales on September 29. They found no cannon, but eighteen armed men under Capt. Albert Martin. The men had with them an unfurled homemade banner which read, "Come and Take it." Casteñeda hesitated, and finally encamped nearby across the Guadalupe River. The Gonzales Committee of Safety sent out calls for help, and by October 1 the Texans numbered 167. That night the Texan force crossed the Guadalupe.

In a fog-shrouded dawn the men approached the Mexican camp bringing with them the six-pounder, which Martin had buried in an orchard. The Texans believed Casteñeda planned to attack that day; they wanted "first licks." A shot sounded, perhaps by accident, and then the fog lifted. The forces were three hundred yards apart. Muskets fired on both sides and the six-pounder gave out a hail of nails, horseshoes and scrap. The Mexicans broke and ran.

Texas won another victory a week later. On October 9, Capt. Collinsworth captured the fort and arsenal at Goliad. Two cannons and hundreds of muskets were captured, and volunteers now had weapons and ammunition reserves. Two days later Austin arrived in Gonzales and was elected commander of the "Volunteer Army of Texas." With four to five hundred men Austin marched against Cos at San Antonio. The banner of the small army was white with a black design: a lone star at the top with a cannon barrel below, then at the bottom, "Come and Take It."

Appeals to the states were sent out. From the town of Nacogdoches a letter was sent to Philadelphia. Printed there in the *Gazette* of October 24, 1835, the town asked, "Call on those friends of liberty who aided the Poles and the Greeks, and they will I trust hold out their help to their suffering countrymen. Furnish us with cannon and ball, rifles, muskets, powder, blankets. Lose no time . . ."

Volunteers poured into New Orleans. Companies from the South included Maj. Ward's Georgia battalion, Capt. Duval's Kentucky Mustangs, Capt. Shackleford's Red Rovers of Alabama and Capt. Burke's Mobile Greys. Dragoons under Lt. Wheelock arrived from Boston via New York. A company of Germans came from Pittsburgh by steamboat.

New Orleans would not be outdone, however. Meetings were held in taverns and on the streets planning the export of material aid and manned expeditions to Texas. At the Arcadia Coffee House a crowd pledged $10,000 in a few minutes. Adolphus Sterne, visiting from Nacogdoches, declared that the cause had to have not only money, but fighting men. He had fifty rifles with him which he had just purchased; anyone who would take one and fight for Texas could have it free. Hundreds pushed forward to the rifles. Grey uniforms came out and the "New Orleans Greys" were born. Many would die at the Alamo. For all who volunteered to help in the Texas struggle the recommendation was to bring a "good rifle and one hundred rounds of ammunition."

The first company of Greys crossing the river Sabine into Texas were met by a girl with a banner. On a field of azure blue, edged in gold, bold black letters proclaimed "First Company of Texan Volunteers! From New Orleans." In the center a flying eagle bore the legend "God & Liberty." Sterne and the local residents welcomed them at Nacogdoches. Toasts were raised, but even at this point opinions were divided as to whether the cause should seek full independence or the rights promised them under the Mexican Constitution of 1824. Subsequent events would overtake that discussion.

On October 27, a reconnaissance-in-force, some ninety men under colonels Bowie and Fannin was scouting possible campsites near San Antonio. The following day began with another fog-enshrouded battle at the end of which there were sixty Mexicans and one Texan (Capt. Richard Andrews, the first casualty of the revolution) dead.

By November 1 General Cos and his eight hundred men were entirely cut off garrisoning San Antonio and the Alamo. As the siege dragged on without an attack, morale dropped on both sides. The Texans had no concerted leadership; the Mexicans nowhere to go. On December 2, two American residents from San Antonio—Sam Maverick and John W. Smith—escaped through Mexican lines. They brought news that the Mexicans were starving and low on ammunition and morale. They also brought maps and a plan of attack.

General Burleson was in command, with Austin back to the States to seek more aid and Travis occupied with the newly-created consultative government of Texas. While the general hesitated, an old plainsman named Ben Milam rallied the men with, "Boys, who will come with old Ben Milam into San Antonio?" Two hundred and forty of the Texans attacked on December 5, fighting house by house into San Antonio. Milam died of a sniper's bullet, in Sam Maverick's arms. On December 9, Cos began surrender negotiations. Three days later he began a withdrawal from San Antonio, leading the last 1,105 Mexican troops in Texas. Over-zealous Texans seriously reduced the effect of the victory, however. Dr. James Grant, holder of lands to the south, and Col. Francis Johnson proposed taking the war into Mexico, to Matamaros. The men who enthusiastically followed them stripped San Antonio of supplies and headed south.

While his brother-in-law was in the process of losing Texas, Gen. Santa Anna had begun to organize the Mexican Army of Operations for the "Texas Campaign." There were nine instructions for Gen. Don Joaquin Ramirez y Sesma, "who has been placed in command of the First Brigade to reinforce the City of Bejar (San Antonio) or battle its besiegers." The ninth point was this:

The foreigners who wage war against the Mexican Nation have violated all laws and do not deserve any consideration, and for that reason, no quarter will be given them as the troops are to be notified at the proper time. They have audaciously declared a war of extermination to the Mexicans and should be treated in the same manner.

And finally,

Not being able to foresee all the situations which the General of the First Brigade might encounter, it is therefore left to his valor and wisdom to act to anticipate them, charging you above all not to engage in any action whatsoever in which a successful outcome is not assured. In spite of this, you should not fail to take advantage of any charge which might arise because of the enemy's negligence or cowardice.

Colonel James Neill, left in command at San Antonio, wrote on January 7, 1836, to the new Provisional Governor Henry Smith, that, "We have 104 men and two distinct fortresses to garrison, and about twenty-four pieces of artillery. You doubtless have learned that we have no provisions nor clothing in this garrison since Johnson and Grant left."

The governor ordered Travis to reinforce Neill. Travis, with thirty men under his command, was slow to follow orders to proceed to San Antonio and the Alamo. "You can plainly see that the Alamo never was built by a military people for a fortress," wrote Green B. Jameson to Sam Houston, the commander of the army of Texas appointed by the new government.

Jameson, though not an engineer, knew well enough the weak points of the Alamo. The Mission of San Antonio de Valerio was founded in 1718 by the Franciscan Order with the purpose of ministering to the local Indian tribes. The mission compound itself was completed in the 1750s. In 1801, with the abandonment of the region by the tribes which the mission served, the Spanish army secured the mission as a fort, whereupon it became known as "the Alamo," from the cottonwood trees which grew around the precincts. The Alamo consisted of a large rectangular plaza of nearly three acres, with the chapel forming a wing on one side. It was situated four hundred yards from San Antonio, with clear land all around—providing a field of fire of 360 degrees. The plaza compound had walls nine-to-twelve-feet high and about two feet thick.

The strongest point of the Alamo was its church. It would prove a great defensive position if attacked by unaccompanied infantry, but with Mexican artillery present, the church could only be used to shelter noncombatants and provide a defensive position of last resort. The walls of the church were four feet thick, and it rose some twenty-five feet high. Though roofless, the second story provided a parapet for artillery.

Between the front of the church and the plaza wall was a gap of fifty yards. Jameson and his men set to work to close the gap with a wood and earthen embrasure. The finished earthworks stood six feet high, with gun embrasures inset. The walls of the compound had no firing positions: there were no loopholes for firing muskets, nor parapets for the men to defend the tops of the walls. The Texans soon had places ready for the Kentucky long-rifles of the volunteers.

Colonel James Bowie arrived at the Alamo on January 19, 1836. He was under orders from Gen. Sam Houston to blow up the Alamo or oversee its destruction by Col. Neill. San Antonio would be abandoned and the artillery withdrawn to Gonzales and Copano. Houston had entrusted Bowie with the mission because, "There is no man on whose forecast, prudence, and valor I place a higher estimate."

Bowie was one of the best-known men in the Southwest. He had grown up in the Louisiana bayous. Bowie met up with the pirate Jean Lafitte, who had helped Andrew Jackson defend New Orleans in 1815, and struck up a trading relationship. Bowie and his brother Rezin bought slaves for $1 a pound and later resold them in New Orleans for $500–$1,000 apiece. The money went into land speculation.

With thirty men Bowie rode in to the Alamo on January 19, 1836. The men there were dispirited, low in ammunition and without medical supplies. Bowie could have carried out Houston's orders, but he hesitated. The Alamo was the only fortress that stood between the imminent invasion of Texas and all the settlers' towns to the north and east; Bowie decided to hold it, and if necessary, die there.

Bowie learned from local contacts that Santa Anna was marching on Texas with 4,600 men. The colonel knew many of the residents because San Antonio was his home town: Bowie had married into the local upper-class, the Vendremedi family; his wife and children had died of fever there. He cared only for his town and for Texas; his own life did not matter with his family gone. For the record, Bowie wrote that, "Colonel Neill and myself have come to the solemn resolution that we will rather die in these ditches than give it up to the enemy."

Bowie and the men were firmly entrenched on February 3, when Travis and thirty men rode in to the Alamo. Travis wasn't happy with his appointment and upon arrival he met Bowie, a rival for command and a personality to reckon with. Travis's arrival had increased the garrison by one-quarter.

An arrival later in the week raised the garrison's morale to its highest level. On Sunday, February 8, Davey Crockett arrived with a dozen of his "Tennessee Mounted Volunteers." Each of them was worth ten ordinary men. The garrison wanted a speech from the ex-congressman, and Crockett obliged:

I have come to your country, though not, I hope, through any selfish motive whatever. I shall identify myself with your interests, and all the honor that I desire is that of defending as a high private, in common with my fellow citizens, the liberties of our common country.

The same week that Travis and Crockett arrived, three brothers named Taylor from Liberty, Texas, came. They would die together in the Alamo. By February 10, 1836, the garrison numbered 142 men, all of whom were willing to stand the test. That night a celebration was held to welcome Crockett and his men. As the party rolled on to 1 A.M., a messenger rode in with word of the Mexican advance. Travis, Bowie and Crockett conferred and decided not to spoil the party. The Mexicans weren't close enough yet to worry about. Neill, however, not included in the discussion, had decided that his time was done. He left on the next day for "twenty days' leave."

As his last act Neill appointed Travis to succeed him. This was reasonable for Travis was the ranking regular army officer, but he was only twenty-six; Neill was forty-six. Bowie was there, too. He was forty and one of the most redoubtable fighters in the southwest. The volunteers wanted an election, and Bowie won in a landslide.

To celebrate, Bowie got roaring drunk, along with many of the men. He had an underlying illness and alcohol exacerbated it. Travis was upset with him, but had come to the conclusion that Bowie had been correct in his assessment of the Alamo's strategic importance. He wrote the governor on the thirteenth, "It is more important to occupy this post than I imagined when I last saw you. It is the key to Texas . . ."

With the new day, Bowie realized they would have to work together to hold the Alamo. They agreed to keep their separate commands but confer on major steps. They wrote a joint plea to the governor: "There is no doubt that the enemy will shortly advance upon this place, and that this will be the first point of attack. We must therefore urge the necessity of sending reinforcements as speedily as possible to our aid."

The men were well satisfied with the joint command: they were short on most things, but not fighting spirit. By the middle of February Almeron Dickinson, artillery commander, had all his guns in place save three. After several messengers arrived bringing news that Santa Anna was entering Texas, finally on February 20 credence was given to a man who said he had seen the Mexican army fording the Rio Grande. That evening at nine Travis held a war council in his quarters. The consensus was to ignore the news. Santa Anna would come, they felt, but not until spring when the weather and fodder were better.

The Mexican army crossed the Rio Grande on February 16, though, and five days later was twenty-five miles from San Antonio and the Alamo. At dawn on the twenty-third a lone courier rode into town and advised the local Mexican residents to get out—Santa Anna was coming.

Travis watched the withdrawal not knowing its cause; he finally placed a sentinel in the church steeple. Shortly after 1 P.M., the church bell pealed. "The enemy are in view!" Two men went out to check the sentinel's story; they ran into the Mexican cavalry vanguard. The alarm was rung again, and all who would fight for the Alamo ran towards it. Captain Dickinson rode in to town for his wife and child. He yelled to his wife Susannah, "Give me the baby! Jump on behind me and ask no questions." As the men and their families went through the main gate a Mexican woman spoke softly, "Poor fellows, you will all be killed."

Within the Alamo it seemed there was only one man in control: Sgt. William R. Ward, normally an inveterate drunkard, was stone cold sober as he supervised the guns which commanded the gate. The women and children were placed in the chapel, the strongest point. It also served as the gunpowder magazine. Travis sent out another message for help.

While Travis was writing his letter, Crockett walked in. He wanted a position to defend, to do something: "Colonel, here am I. Assign me to a position, and I and my twelve boys will try and defend it." Travis knew immediately where he wanted Crockett—behind the wood and earthen palisade, between the church and the south wall, the weakest part of the defense. If there was anyone who could hold that gap it was the marksmen from Tennessee. Numbers would not count at first, only a clear, steady fire.

Travis finished his letter, "The enemy in large force is in sight. We want men and provisions. Send them to us. We have 150 men and are determined to defend the Alamo to the last. Give us assistance." At least 5,500 Mexicans were now marching on the Alamo. The invading army had an advantage of forty to one. James Butler Bonham rode to Goliad to ask for aid from Col. Fannin, who had 420 men. Fannin didn't feel he could leave Goliad, a well-prepared fortress. Fannin's ultimate end might have made him wish he had gone to the relief of the Alamo.

Travis and Bowie asked again for aid from Goliad:

> We have removed all our men into the Alamo, where we will make such resistance as is due to our honour, and that of the country, until we can get assistance from you, which we expect you to forward immediately. In this extremity, we hope you will send us all the men you can spare promptly. We have 146 men who are determined never to retreat. We have but little provisions, but enough to serve us till you and your men arrive. We deem it unnecessary to repeat to a brave officer, who knows his duty, that we call on him for assistance.

Despite these impassioned pleas, Fannin would not leave his well-prepared position to aid the men of the Alamo.

Santa Anna ordered a red banner to be raised from the tower of the Mission de Concepcion. The red banner meant that blood was the order of the day: quarter would not be given. Travis had the raising of the death-banner answered with a shot from the garrison's big eighteen-pounder. The Mexican guns answered, but they were no larger than a twelve-pounder.

By 3 P.M., on February 23, the Mexican army had filled Military Plaza in San Antonio. After Travis fired the cannon shot it was learned Santa Anna wanted a parley. Bowie still wished to be conciliatory but would not sacrifice demands for independence. He sent a message to Santa Anna offering to negotiate as equals. The general was incensed. An aide to Santa Anna wrote, "The Mexican army cannot come to terms under any conditions with rebellious foreigners to whom there is no other recourse left, if they wish to save their lives, than to place themselves immediately at the disposal of the Supreme Government . . ."

Travis's messenger was told that the Texans's only hope was to surrender, laying down their arms and promising never to take them up again. The courier agreed to return with Travis if the Texans agreed to the demands; if not the garrison would resume fire.

Bowie and Travis were now locked in a debate over who would command the fort. While they discussed the command, Gregorio Esparza, a skilled artilleryman, and his family approached the Alamo. The watch opened a window in the Alamo's church to allow the Esparzas to enter.

While the two commanders bickered over responsibilities, nature intervened. Bowie had been ill for some time, possibly with some form of the fever which had killed his wife and children. On the day after the Mexican army arrived, Bowie collapsed. He handed over command to Travis on February 24.

The Mexicans began building earthworks that day about four hundred yards from the fort. Though still out of rifle range, each day they would advance their lines toward the walls. That afternoon Mexican artillery opened up with a five-inch howitzer and several nine-pounders. Until the end of the siege the garrison would sustain an intermittent barrage every day. The Texans decided to conserve their ammunition and fire only at well-selected targets.

Late on the twenty-fourth, Travis issued a general appeal to all who believed in freedom:

To the People of Texas & all Americans in the World.
Fellow citizens and compatriots—I am besieged, by a thousand or more of the Mexicans under Santa Anna—I have sustained a continual bombardment and cannonade for twenty-four hours and have not lost a man—The enemy has demanded a surrender at discretion, otherwise, the garrison are to be put to the sword, if the fort is taken—I have answered the demand with a cannon shot, and our flag still waves proudly from the walls—I shall never surrender or retreat. Then, I call on you in the name of Liberty, of patriotism and everything dear to the American character, to come to our aid, with all dispatch—The enemy is receiving reinforcements daily and will no doubt increase to three or four thousand in four or five days. If this call is neglected, I am determined to sustain myself as long as possible and die like a soldier who never forgets what is due to his honor and that of his country.
—Victory or death.

At the end of the day the garrison took count: no casualties, even though several artillery pieces had been hit. On February 25 a new breastwork was erected by the Mexicans. At 10 A.M., their bugles sounded. The first advance against the Alamo had begun. The Texans held their fire 'til point-blank range; then artillery Captains Carey and Dickinson gave the order to fire. At the same time "Crockett's boys" from Tennessee opened up with their "squirrel rifles."

The Mexicans, however, were able to take cover among a group of shacks that had sprung up around the fort. Originally used by commonlaw wives of the soldiers, the huts were excellent cover from the long rifles. The Alamo's main gate opened and a squad of Texans rushed the huts and put them to the torch. They succeeded and the Mexicans lost their cover; the Texans now had an open field of fire. Miraculously, there were still no casualties at the Alamo. More batteries were placed near the Alamo. Travis wrote an appeal to Sam Houston, commander-in-chief of the Texan Army of Volunteers. Someone had to take the message: it fell to Juan Seguin, commander of the Tejanos, the Mexican members of the garrison. "If they overpower us, we fall a sacrifice at the shrine of our country, and we hope posterity and our country will do our memory justice. Give me help, oh my Country!"

Regardless of the possible arrival of outside help the Texas marksmen kept up a steady and deadly fire when targets were available. Captain Rafael Soldana of the Tampico battalion reported that:

A tall man, with flowing hair, was seen firing from the same place on the parapet during the entire siege. He wore a buckskin suit and a cap all of a pattern entirely different from those worn by his comrades. This man would kneel or lie down behind the low parapet, rest his long gun and fire, and we all learned to keep at a good distance when he was seen to make ready to shoot. He rarely missed his mark, and when he fired he always rose to his feet and calmly reloaded his gun seemingly indifferent to the shots fired at him by our men. He had a strong resonant voice and often railed at us, but as we did not understand English we could not comprehend the import of his words further than they were defiant. This man I later learned was known as "Kwockey."

A relief campaign was in the making. Fannin had received Travis's first appeal; he prepared a column to march to the Alamo's relief. On February 26 he started out with over three hundred men and four guns. En route several of his wagons broke down and Fannin suddenly lost his nerve. He returned to the presumed security of Goliad.

The next day Travis's appeal met its only positive reply. Thirty-two men from Gonzales mounted up for the seventy-five-mile ride to the Alamo, now an entirely surrounded fortress. They left wives, children and family behind— there was no guarantee that anyone else would come to help. But they approached enemy lines anyway shortly after 2 A.M., on March 1. A horseman appeared, and offered to guide them into the Alamo. One of the guides from the fort, John W. Smith, didn't trust the fellow and suggested they shoot him. The rider galloped off. Startled guards on the Alamo's walls fired a round at the party, wounding one man in the foot. His reaction, cursing in English, convinced the guards that the men were Americans, and the company entered. The gates closed behind the only reinforcements the Alamo would receive.

The fort now had 183 men to defend it against two–three thousand Mexicans.

To keep up morale, Crockett found an old fiddle and would challenge John

McGregor, a Scotsman, to musical duels on his bagpipes. They played to keep up the Texans's spirits while blotting out the relentless serenade ordered by Santa Anna—choruses of bugles and drum rolls followed by barrages from the Mexican artillery.

Travis decided to send out his most trusted messenger, James Butler Bonham to see Fannin. Like Travis, he was a lawyer originally from South Carolina, a romantic who would die for his beliefs. Houston wrote of him, "His influence in the army is great, more so than some who would be generals." Bonham met Fannin in Goliad on February 29, who would not alter his position. He would stay at Goliad and hold the well-manned fort.

On his ride back to the Alamo, Bonham met Ben Highsmith, a messenger who had attempted to penetrate Mexican lines. Highsmith tried to warn Bonham not to attempt to get into the Alamo, but he replied, "I will report the result of my mission to Travis or die in the attempt." At 11 A.M., on March 3, Bonham charged through Mexican lines and entered the Alamo, keeping his sworn word to his commander. The somber news was that Fannin was not coming to help, and thus they could expect no further assistance.

This was the decisive day of the siege. After it was known that Fannin was not coming, Greene Jameson, directing work on the fortifications, had the men dig more trenches in the large open square and reinforce the walls with the earth. Soon after the news about Fannin, shouts and cheers rang from the village. Texans who still held hopes ran to the walls.

There they saw an end to all hope: a Mexican reinforcement column of one thousand men under Gen. Gaona had just arrived. Santa Anna now had at least 2,400 men and ten guns around the Alamo. The reinforcements were all hand-picked companies including the Zapadores, nearly two hundred fighting sappers who would help breach the walls.

That night courier John W. Smith prepared to set out once more through the Mexican lines. He would carry the last personal messages of the garrison along with yet another appeal from Travis. The commander of the Alamo asked for at least five hundred pounds of cannon powder, two hundred rounds of six, nine, twelve- and eighteen-pound cannon balls and ten kegs of rifle powder. He asked again for all the help that could be sent, and stressed that the Alamo might well be "the great and decisive ground."

To his friend Jesse Grimes, Travis wrote, "Let the Convention go on and then make a declaration of independence, and we will then understand, what we are fighting for . . . But under the flag of independence, we are ready to peril our lives a hundred time a day." Travis would die not knowing the convention had declared the independence of Texas the previous day.

Finally he wrote one last note to a friend who had been taking care of his only son:

Take care of my little boy. If the country should be saved, I may make him a splendid fortune; but if the country should be lost and I should perish, he will have nothing but the proud recollection that he is the son of a man who died for his country.

The men wrote their last letters to loved ones also. Isaac Millsaps, who had left his blind wife and seven children in Gonzales, wrote:

We are in the fortress of the Alamo a ruined church that has most fell down. The Mexicans are here in large numbers they have kept up a constant fire since we got here. All our boys [from Gonzales] are well and Capt. Martin is in good spirits . . . Col. Bowie is down sick and had to be to bed. I saw him yesterday and he is still ready to fight. . . . I have not seen Travis but two times since here. He told us all this morning that Fannin was going to be here early with many men and there would be a good fight. . . . I hope help comes soon cause we can't fight them all . . . If we fail here get to the river with the children. All Texas will fall before the enemy. . . . I don't know what else to say they is calling for all letters, kiss the dear children for me and believe as I do that we'll be well and God protects us all . . .

Travis gave his packet of letters to Smith, as did the men. The colonel added two more afterthoughts: reinforcements should bring ten days' rations, and also Travis would order the big eighteen-pounder to fire three times every day—morning, noon and night—to let anyone coming know that the Alamo still was fighting.

Around midnight the north gate opened and a party of Texans went out as skirmishers. Firing at will as a distraction the Texans attracted Mexican patrols to them while the enemy guns also opened up. Smith galloped out the main south gate and headed east.

Though Travis still held out hope that reinforcements would come (as in his request for cannon shot and powder), everyone knew the end was just a matter of time. The morning of March 4, a new Mexican battery, positioned only 250 yards from the north wall, opened up. It was near enough to the walls to be exposed to musket fire, and its dangerous proximity showed that assault was imminent.

The walls had now come under such intense firing that cannon balls were passing through them and even the earth behind. Jameson and his men worked feverishly to shore them up. Enemy batteries commanded a field of fire at all points. Travis described their sites as being "in Bexar, four hundred yards west; in La Villita, three hundred yards south; at the powder house, one thousand yards east of south; on the ditch, eight hundred yards northeast, and at the old mill, eight hundred yards north."

The feeling of entrapment grew enormously. Crockett wanted to make a sortie and take the fight to the Mexicans. "I think we had better march out and die in the open air. I don't like to be hemmed up." The main advantage of staying in the Alamo was, of course, that the Texans could kill many more Mexicans from within. Every day they held was a day gained for Sam Houston to raise more troops and gather supplies.

All through the fourth the Mexicans worked at constructing scaling ladders. Bowie had himself carried out to urge the men to stand by Travis and hold the fort to the end. Most of the local Mexicans who had remained inside the mission decided the situation had gotten serious enough to escape whereupon Travis decided he would offer that same alternative to his men.

By March 5, the Mexicans were on the north side only two hundred yards from the wall. There still had not been a Texan killed. Late in the day the Mexican cannonade slacked off. In the lull Travis ordered a general assembly in the square. Addressing the men he said that there was no realistic hope of help coming. The garrison had three choices: surrender, escape, or a last stand and fight to the death. A fight to the death with the casualties they could inflict on the Mexicans might indeed delay their advance and help Texas.

Travis declared he would remain but that every man had the right to decide for himself. Travis unsheathed his sword and drew a line in the sand. He asked all that would stand with him to cross it. Crockett crossed, Bowie had himself carried across, the entire garrison except one man crossed the line into history. That man, Louis Rose, was a veteran Napoleonic soldier, and knew that by leaving he could live to fight another day. He climbed the wall after dark and successfully penetrated Mexican lines.

Major General Santa Anna, meanwhile, had called his war conference of senior officers for consideration of the final assault on the Alamo the previous night. For an egotist such as Santa Anna the occurrence was highly unusual. He normally made all decisions unilaterally. This time he had wavered, wanting to be assured the Texans could be taken by storm.

Two of his leading battle commanders wanted to attack. His brother-in-law, Cos, wanted to wait for more heavy artillery, as did the senior Gen. Castrillón. An officer pointed out that there were no doctors or medical supplies for their wounded. Santa Anna answered that was fine, for the men would know, going into battle, that it "was not as bad to die as to come out wounded."

With such clashing opinions Santa Anna dismissed the council and reverted to form; he would decide alone. Enough time had been wasted and the Alamo was, after all, only his first target. The attack would take place on Sunday, March 6.

Santa Anna's battle plan called for four columns of infantry to attack simultaneously. Cos would strike at the northwest corner and Col. Duque at the northeast. Colonel Romero's column would attack from the east with Col. Morales attacking the south wall. The cavalry under Gen. Sesma would be deployed on the eastern side of the Alamo to saber the Texans who were expected to try to escape.

The best troops were to be kept in reserve under Santa Anna's command with the batteries facing the north wall. For the reserve he had chosen the grenadier companies from his five battalions, and the crack Zapadores. In total, four hundred men.

The first-line attacking force numbered 1,100 men. Cos and Duque each had about 350 men to hit the northern corners. Romero had three hundred, while Morales had only one hundred men. However, Morales's target was the shoulder-high palisade of logs defended by Crockett and his "twelve boys" from Tennessee.

The battle orders for the Mexican force were detailed. Overcoats and anything that might slow them down were forbidden. Chin straps were to be down, shoes and sandals on, and all weapons, particularly bayonets, in perfect condition. The grenadiers were issued six packages of cartridges each, the others two packages. Every man had two spare flints. Ladder carriers would sling rifles in the assault.

At 5 P.M., on March 5, the grenadiers joined the Zapadores at the north end of the Alamo. The other attacking battalions found their assembly areas. By 10 P.M., all firing had stopped. At 1 A.M., on March 6, the four columns moved forward to their attack positions.

Travis had decided to try one last plea. A sixteen-year-old, Jim Allen, was known to be a great rider with a very good mare. He left, riding bareback slumped around his horse's neck, and raced through enemy lines toward Goliad and Fannin.

With the Mexican bombardment ended, Travis sought to use the time to repair the walls as much as possible. The closeness of the Mexican guns had threaded them in many places. The men were ordered to rest after doing as much as they could at night. Travis went into the church where the women and children were. There he gave fifteen-month-old Angelina Dickinson a heavy gold ring with a black cat's-eye stone he had been wearing. Putting it on a string, he placed it around her neck as a memento. Finally he went to bed.

At 5 A.M., only one man was making the rounds of the walls, Adjutant John Baugh, officer of the day. Nearly two thousand Mexican troops were formed and ready for a signal. All crouched to hide the white in many of their uniforms. The tension, fear and expectation of battle built until one soldier finally shouted "Viva Santa Anna!" Others took up the cry.

At this point Santa Anna had to unleash the attack or abort it entirely. He therefore ordered his bugler to sound the attack. The call passed down the lines from company to company. Captain Baugh was not the only man on duty—pickets were outside the walls but nothing was heard from them. He concluded they had been overrun already.

Baugh ran for the barracks shouting, "Colonel Travis! The Mexicans are coming." Travis jumped from his bed, grabbed his sword and double-barreled shotgun, and headed for the walls. Though they could not yet be seen, there was no doubt the Mexicans were coming. Bugles and cries split the night. Travis shouted to his men, "Come on, boys. The Mexicans are upon us and we'll give them Hell!" On the north wall Travis turned and saw some of Juan Seguin's loyal Mexican men. He said to them, "No rendirse, muchachos!" By now, leading Mexican attackers had reached the fort's defensive ditch—cannon could not sight on to them. Ladders began to go up. Travis leaned over the wall and fired his shotgun point-blank down a ladder. At the same time a musket ball caught him in the forehead. He fell back within the walls, dying.

The attacking columns were receiving heavy fire from the walls. The guns firing from the church held down the columns attacking from the east and the south. The Adama Battalion, attacking from the northwest, was hit by grapeshot. Just two salvos killed forty men. To the northeast, grapeshot raked the Tolucas Battalion, and half a company died. That battalion's commander, Duque, was badly injured by the fire and fell. His infantry continued their headlong onslaught and crushed their commander to death. The columns hesitated at the fire and casualties and retired to reform. They advanced a second time, were ripped, and fell back.

In the third attack a chance movement by the troops of two columns helped decide the day. Romero's column on the east side headed north toward the Toluca (Duque's) column, while at the same time Cos's column from the northwest also joined the Tolucas. Both could have done so because they knew Santa Anna held his reserves in back of that area, and therefore it would be the safest from which to attack.

The Texans did not care for the situation's fine points. Many of the men, especially the sharpshooters, had four or five guns lined up next to them. Each man could account for five Mexicans, but the pre-dawn light might hamper their shooting. The Texan guns continued to wreak havoc on the Mexican columns.

The Mexican attack had turned into chaos. Men from the converging columns fired blindly after hitting their own men. Some scaling ladders had been lost. Santa Anna decided his firstline troops had no chance of success. He therefore ordered the reserves to attack. The Zapadores and grenadiers welcomed their chance. The massed bands of the battalions, standing near Santa Anna, now began to play the "Deguello," the traditional Spanish march which meant no quarter for the enemy. The grenadiers soon found hand-and-footholds among timbers used to shore up the outside of the walls, and several reached the parapet led by their general, Juan Amador.

Cos had turned his troops back toward the west and attempted the wall there next to the northwest gun parapet. The Mexicans were able to climb through new embrasures which had been built for the guns. The enemy was now in the compound on both the north and west sides. Cos's men opened the north gate and a flood of Mexicans entered the Alamo.

The gunnery captain, Dickinson, ran into the sacristy of the church and cried to his wife, "Great God, Sue, the Mexicans are inside our walls!" He embraced her and said, "If they spare you, save my child." He then returned to his guns on the top of the church. The men were resighting the cannon to fire at the plaza which was filling rapidly with Mexicans.

With the northern end now completely engulfed, the Texans either sought cover in the plaza trenches or retired into the rooms of the long barracks (the old convent), that had been prepared for a final stand. Hand-to-hand fighting went on in the plaza as the Texans dropped back, using their musket stocks, tomahawks and Bowie knives against the bayonets of the Mexican soldiery and their officers' sabers.

On the south wall, defending the palisade, the thirteen Tennesseans fought with such wrath that the enemy could scarcely believe their fury. A Mexican sergeant, Felix Nuñez, wrote of one man, who could have been Crockett himself:

> He was a tall American of rather dark complexion and had on a long buckskin coat and a round cap without any bill, made out of fox skin with the long tail hanging down his back. This man apparently had a charmed life. Of the many soldiers who took deliberate aim at him and fired, not one ever hit him. On the contrary, he never missed a shot. He killed at least eight of our men, besides wounding several others. This being observed by a lieutenant who had come in over the wall, he sprang at him and dealt him a deadly blow with his sword, just above the right eye, which felled him to the ground, and in an instant he was pierced by not less than twenty bayonets.

The men who reached the barracks had firing posts already prepared; semi-circular buttresses of hide and earth had been put up at the door of each room. The Texans raked the plaza with steady fire, and the Mexicans had no place to run for cover. General Amador, the first ranking officer over the wall, ordered the gun next to Travis's body to be turned on the barracks; Col. Morales did the same with the eighteen-pounder. In the tumult and confusion no orders had been given to spike guns when the enemy would clearly take them, so they were left operable as their crews died.

The flag of the New Orleans Greys was the only one flying that day, over the barracks. Lieutenant José Maria Torres of the Zapadores rushed to replace it. He found three color sergeants of the Jimenez Battalion dead around it.

Pulling down the flag, he put up the Mexican. He was shot dead but the flag stayed up.

One by one the barrack rooms were hit with cannon fire and then assaulted by Mexican infantry. No one expected mercy, so every Texan sold his life dearly as the enemy crashed through the door. Bowie lay on his cot, a pistol in each hand and his knife at his side. He took several Mexicans with him before the rest tossed him in the air on their bayonets.

The only cannon the Texans had left were on the church's parapets. Using nails and scrap iron, the battery shredded men of the Jimenez Battalion. Morales had the eighteen-pounder concentrate its fire on the church. Dickinson died, as did Bonham near him. The last battery was silenced.

The Mexicans entered the church. Robert Evans, wounded already, grabbed a torch and tried to get to the powder magazine to take the Mexican army with him. He was shot before he could ignite it. In the church a young boy stood up, his only weapon a blanket. The Mexicans killed him. Two other boys were killed. One man, Brigido Guerrero, managed to talk his way out by claiming he was a prisoner.

By 6:30 A.M., on the morning of March 6, 1836, it was over. One hundred eighty-three Texans had died; at least six hundred Mexicans had also died. Mexican wounded numbered as many as the dead. Santa Anna had the Texan dead piled atop pyres built by the mayor of San Antonio de Bexar and burned. According to Santa Anna, "It was but a small affair."

The United States did not take it that way. In Bonham's hometown of Charleston, South Carolina, the paper's headline read, "By the Railroad: Important from Texas! Fall of San Antonio and Massacre of the Texan Troops." The Frankfort (Kentucky) *Argus*, a conservative paper, urged that Santa Anna be taught "the virtue of American rifles and republicanism." Even a paper opposed to the Texas revolution, the Memphis (Tennessee) *Enquirer*, said, "Some of our own bosom friends have fallen in the Alamo. We would avenge their death and spill the last drop of our blood upon the altar of Liberty."

After the fall of the Alamo, Santa Anna marched north and east, intent on killing off all Texan revolutionaries. A separate column of his, under Col. Morales, headed for Goliad and Fannin. The commander of Goliad had been ordered to evacuate and sink all nonportable artillery in the river. General Urrea commanded the Mexican troops besieging Goliad.

Over time he had built up an appreciation of Fannin, but on March 24 received an order from Santa Anna reminding him that all Texan rebels should be killed, armed or not. It did not matter if they had surrendered in good faith.

On March 19, Fannin set out from Goliad with four hundred men, marching in a hollow square. By mid-afternoon Urrea's forces had overtaken the

Texans. Formed in square the accurate fire of the Texans stood off charge after charge. Finally artillery was brought up and Fannin surrendered, at "the discretion of the Mexican command."

The discretion was exercised on Palm Sunday. Nearly four hundred men were led out to the woods and shot. Those who guessed what was coming ran and sheltered in the depths of the forest. The news soon reached Sam Houston and his men.

On April 21, Houston and eight hundred men began their advance toward Mexican lines near San Jacinto at 4:30 P.M. Most of the Mexicans were still sleeping away their siesta. Santa Anna was certainly asleep, possibly with the help of opium. Houston had cavalry screening the right flank, and his two regiments formed up in column. Between the columns were his two pieces of artillery, "the Twin Sisters," and three fifes and a drum. The little band struck up the ironically romantic ballad, "Will You Come to the Bower?"

The Texans were not in a romantic mood, however. They advanced in silence until within two hundred yards of the Mexican line. They then made a frenzied charge, yelling "Remember the Alamo! Remember Goliad!" The Mexicans had no chance before the Texan rage. As one fighter wrote later it would, "have done your heart good to see them fall . . . the most delightful time that ever I heard since the world commenced. I had a first rate Rifle . . . Betsy would bore a hole in them the Claret would gush out as large as a corn stalk . . . I no that I killed four that thing I no . . ."

The battle was over in eighteen minutes; out of 783 Texans, two were killed and twenty-three wounded. At least six hundred Mexicans died and 730 taken prisoner. His Excellency Santa Anna tried to escape wearing a private's uniform, but was captured on the following day. Many Texans wanted to lynch him but Houston decided a live hostage was more useful. With Santa Anna a prisoner, Houston was able to secure the withdrawal of all remaining Mexican forces, and ultimately, the independence of Texas.

It was February 1837 before the remains of the defenders of the Alamo were properly buried. Seguin, commander of the native Mexican forces in Texas, had become military governor of San Antonio de Bexar. He gathered the ashes and bones from the three pyres and placed them in a coffin with the names Travis, Bowie and Crockett engraved on it.

On February 25, 1837, he conducted a funeral ceremony for the fallen. "These remains which we have had the honor of carrying on our shoulders are the ones of the brave heroes who died in the Alamo. Yes, my friends, they preferred a thousand deaths rather than surrender to serve the yoke of the tyrant. What a brilliant example. Worthy indeed of being recorded in the pages of history . . . The worthy remains of our venerable companions bearing witness, I ask you to tell the world: Texas shall be free and independent or we shall perish with glory in battle."

News of the results of the disastrous stand at the Alamo caused a general stampede to safety by American settlers; it came to be known as the "Runaway Scrape."

The reports of the massacre at Goliad of Fannin and his men added to the plunge in morale of the rebels of Texas. Desertions at that point ran high; but within a month of the Alamo the status of the Texas army had become viable again, ready to advance to its rendezvous with Santa Anna at San Jacinto.

The thirteen days in which the Alamo held out had given Sam Houston the time necessary to gather and organize a significant force for his offensive, culminating in the decisive battle of San Jacinto.

The Republic of Texas was established following that battle, and Houston became its first president. Nine years later, on December 29, 1845, Texas became a state. The admission of Texas to the Union marked the greatest acquisition of territory by the United States since the Louisiana Purchase in 1803.

The last stand at the Alamo, which contributed mightily to the decisive victory at San Jacinto, created the then-largest state in the Union. At the same time it altered the balance of power with finality on the North American continent, for three years later the United States army crushed Mexico and Santa Anna and took fully half of its territory from the defeated for its efforts.

# 9

# THE LITTLE BIG HORN, 1876

GENERAL J.E.B. STUART readied the six thousand cavalrymen under his command. The "Invincibles" were composed of four cavalry brigades accompanied by three horse-drawn batteries of artillery. General Robert E. Lee had given Stuart the task of circling around the Union Army's right flank and pinning it down, creating havoc for both it and the Union center.

Lee had ordered Maj. Gen. George Pickett to lead eleven brigades of infantry to break the Union center. The envelopment of the right and thrust to the center would cut the Union Army in two, leaving the panicked and disorganized halves open to destruction. The loss of Gen. Meade's Army of the Potomac would be a decisive victory for the South and possibly even lead to final Confederate victory in the Civil War.

Three brigades of cavalry were available to oppose Jeb Stuart—two understrength brigades of Gen. David Gregg's Second Cavalry Division, and the Michigan Cavalry Division under the command of the youngest general in the Union Army, twenty-three-year-old George Armstrong Custer, who had received the brevetted rank only four days earlier.

The "Boy General," as he would soon be called, had been promoted ahead of many senior officers by Gen. Alfred Pleasenton, chief of cavalry, under whom Capt. Custer had served as an aide-de-camp. When the Seventh Michigan Cavalry needed a colonel in June 1863, Custer applied for the post with strong backing from generals Burnside, Hooker, Pleasenton and Stoneman, but was rejected by Gov. Austin Blair of Michigan. A few weeks later Pleasenton himself designated Custer commander of the entire Michigan Brigade, including the First, Fifth, Sixth and Seventh Regiments.

Now, at Gettysburg, the "Boy General" had his first chance to command

158

large numbers of cavalry in battle. General Gregg placed the large and well armed yet relatively untried Michigan Brigade in the center of his position, placing weaker brigades to the left and right, who would see little action in this fight; the Michigan Brigade bore the brunt of the attack.

Stuart began the engagement by sending forward a line of 1,500 dismounted men as skirmishers. The use of cavalrymen, armed with musket or carbine along with saber and pistol as infantry skirmishers, was practiced on both sides. Custer would prove particularly effective in the mixed-arms method of fighting.

To oppose this first wave Custer ordered forward the Fifth Regiment, armed with advanced seven-shot .56 caliber Spencer repeater rifles. Colonel Alger of the Fifth posted his men behind a fence. After they had fired their first volley at 120 yards, the Confederate officers shouted, "Now for them before they can reload!" To their amazement they were met by three more rapid-fire volleys from Alger's five hundred men. The Grays broke and retreated.

The Fifth had depleted its ammunition and in turn was driven back by the next Confederate charge. Custer led the Seventh in a charge which stopped the pursuit. Stuart ordered more regiments in, and the Seventh was taken in flank by the Ninth and Thirteenth Virginia regiments. The Seventh held, but while retiring was struck again by a charge of the First Virginia. The Fifth Michigan came up in support and both sides then pulled back to reorganize.

Before the Michigan Brigade could reform, two Confederate brigades held in reserve appeared from the woods. Generals Fitzhugh Lee and Wade Hampton were leading eight regiments against the Michiganders. The Fifth had not yet remounted, the Seventh was disorganized, and the Sixth was supporting the brigade's artillery, Battery M. There remained but one regiment to stop the Grays—the "Old First," the only veterans Custer had.

General Gregg rode to the First Regiment's Col. Town and ordered him to charge Stuart's best troopers. One of Town's officers, shocked, said, "Great Heavens, we shall all be swallowed up!" Meanwhile, Battery M ripped the oncoming Confederates with canister shot, tearing holes in the line which were filled immediately. As the First Michigan drew their sabers and began their trot, Custer spurred four lengths ahead of the regiment. Brandishing his sword, he shouted, "Come on, you Wolverines!" With a wild cheer, the First broke into a gallop and drove a wedge through the Gray ranks which outnumbered them nearly eight to one.

The Fifth and three squadrons of Gregg's hit the Confederates on the flanks, and with Union troopers attacking on three sides, the Southern line broke and retreated. The Michigan Cavalry Regiment, led by Custer, had beaten the "Invincible" Jeb Stuart. It had paid heavily, suffering 219 casualties to 181 for Stuart. Yet the twenty-three-year-old Custer, a general for all of four days, had also won the respect of his men, the "Wolverines" as he had named them.

The Michigan Cavalry Brigade was composed entirely of volunteers and the men had at first been dubious about having a professional soldier from West Point made commander. Gettysburg reversed that attitude. After a few weeks of campaigning with Custer, Capt. Manning Birge of the Sixth would say, "Every man in his brigade worshipped him, and would follow him through anything. They never went back on him nor he on them."

Custer believed that a fighting formation had to have a sense of unity and pride in itself and its abilities in battle. He used every method he could devise to instill that spirit. At first, he dressed somewhat gaudily, with a broad-brimmed black hat, black jacket and trousers trimmed in gold lacing, and high boots. At his throat he wore a crimson necktie. But the outfit was not just for show. Captain James Harvey Kidd of the Sixth, who would succeed Custer, wrote, "That garb, fantastic at first sight as it appeared to be, was to be the distinguishing mark which . . . showed us where, in the thickest of the fight, we were to seek our leader." Soon all of the Wolverines wore the red necktie, and everyone knew them as such.

Custer rewarded the best turned-out and efficient companies by having them act as the brigade's escort. He also had the Seventh Regiment's band coopted as the brigade's band. His favorite song for preparing to do battle was "Yankee Doodle Dandy." "At Yankee Doodle every man's hand went to his saber. It was always the signal for a charge." When the time did come for the charge, "He never asked the boys to go ahead. He always said, 'Come.' "

To maximize the impact of his regiments' abilities, Custer designated primary uses for each. The "Old First" became his saber regiment; when a charge with steel was called for, it would lead. The Seventh Michigan and First Vermont, attached to the brigade to replace losses at Gettysburg, supported the First. The Fifth and Sixth with their repeating Spencer carbines fought as dismounted skirmishers, but would mount if a massed charge was necessary.

After Gettysburg the Michigan Brigade harried Lee's columns back to Virginia. Eleven days after the battle the Wolverines caught up with the Confederate rear guard at Falling Waters, Maryland. The entire Michigan Brigade charged four brigades of Confederate infantry situated behind earthworks. A vicious hand-to-hand fight ensued with Custer in the thick of it. Private Victor Comte wrote to his wife, "General Koster . . . commanded in person and I saw him plunge his saber into the belly of a rebel who was trying to kill him. You can guess how bravely soldiers fight for such a general." Casualties were about equal, but the Michiganders captured over 1,500 prisoners, more than an entire brigade, and three battle-flags, the standards which represent the heart of a regiment.

In the autumn of 1863 at the battle of Brandy Station, Virginia, the Michigan Brigade found five thousand Confederates in front of them. Custer stood in his stirrups and called out, "Boys of Michigan, there are some people between us and home; I'm going home. Who else goes?" "Yankee Doodle" struck up, and the ensuing charge broke the enemy line.

Following inconclusive winter incursions by both sides, cavalry Gen. Kilpatrick (nicknamed "Kill-Cavalry") decided to attempt a raid on the Confederate capital—Richmond, Virginia—where fifteen thousand Union prisoners were held. He received permission from Sheridan to try it, and he chose the best troopers from all the available cavalry divisions. Among the four thousand he picked were at least eight hundred from the Michigan Brigade. The raid occurred on February 28, 1864.

Custer had the task of leading a diversionary raid. His was successful; Kilpatrick's cost Custer 176 men of the Wolverines with no tangible gain. General Sheridan had taken command of all Union cavalry; his first objective was to destroy Stuart and his forces. One of his major strike brigades was now Custer's Michigan. Sheridan wrote that at Yellow Station, "Custer's charge was brilliantly executed. Beginning at a walk, he increased his gait to a trot, and then at fullspeed rushed at the enemy." A Wolverine shot and killed Stuart that day, the last of the knights of the Confederacy.

After the battle of Cold Harbor, Maj. James Kidd, commanding the Sixth Michigan, wrote, "For all that this Brigade had accomplished all praise is due to Gen. Custer. So brave a man I never saw and as competent as brave. Under him a man is ashamed to be cowardly. Under him our men can achieve wonders."

Not only officers praised Custer's leadership. At the level of wagondriver, David Trego wrote of the general that, "He feels Proud off his men and is always at the head of them. He has had nine horses shot from under him since this [campaign] was commenced and he is still alive and after the rebs!"

Custer and the Michigan Brigade found themselves in perhaps their worst fight of the war at the battle of Trevilian Station. While attempting to sever one of Lee's main supply lines the Wolverines were cut off from the main army. Surrounded by two Confederate cavalry divisions, the brigade had to fight for eight hours against four-to-one odds. Half of Custer's staff and escort were killed or wounded and Custer himself was wounded twice while carrying a dying trooper to cover. Sheridan and the main body of Union cavalry broke through late in the day.

Not long after Trevilian Station Custer received his second star, becoming a Maj. Gen. of Volunteers. With the new rank Sheridan appointed Custer commander of the Third Cavalry Division. He gained a brigade in numbers but lost his beloved Wolverines who were placed with the First Division.

The Michigan Brigade of Wolverines had lost 525 dead in action, and 987 dead from disease and accidents including 328 who died in Southern prisoner-of-war camps. It had the highest casualty rate of all Union cavalry brigades, yet it also had won the honor and accolades that came with those deaths. The regimental commanders of the Wolverines petitioned twice to be put under Custer's new command, to no avail.

The following month, October 1864, Maj. Gen. Custer had the pleasure of defeating his old roommate at West Point. Major General Thomas L. Rosser and Custer had chased each other up and down the Shenandoah Valley to the point of capturing each other's baggage trains and then exchanging letters over the poor fit of the tailoring. Nearly a decade later they would meet on the Yellowstone and trade stories of their battles in the war.

The morning of April 9, 1865, Custer was readying his Third Cavalry for yet another charge. A Confederate rode forward alone bearing a white flag to Custer. He accepted it and found that Lee would surrender. Custer sent the news to Gen. Sheridan who relayed it to Gen. Ulysses S. Grant. The terms were presented by Grant and accepted by Lee that afternoon at Appomattox Courthouse, Virginia.

Custer was present at the Court House surrender. Later that day he wrote a farewell to the Third Cavalry Division:

> During the past six months, although in most instances confronted by superior numbers, you have captured from the enemy in open battle, 111 pieces of artillery, sixty-five battle flags and upwards of ten thousand prisoners, including several general officers . . . You have never lost a gun, never lost a color, and have never been defeated . . .

In Washington, D.C., on May 23–24, 1865, the grand review of the victorious Union Army took place. The cavalry formed the vanguard and Custer led his Third Division down Pennsylvania Avenue to the reviewing stand. The following day he was on his way to organize a new division which was to march to Texas to help supervise Reconstruction in that state.

General Sheridan had been appointed Military Commander of the Fifth Reconstruction District which comprised the Military Division of the Southwest and Gulf, Louisiana and Texas. His orders were to maintain law and order there by disbanding and disarming recalcitrant rebels, while keeping Northern carpetbaggers in line. The major external threat came from Archduke Maximilian, planted on the throne of Mexico with French troops by Emperor Louis Napoleon III. Sheridan chose Custer, to whom he had said, "You're the only man that never failed me," to be Chief of Cavalry, Military Department of Texas.

At the city of Alexandria in western Louisiana, Custer formed a new division of four thousand cavalrymen, many of whom had been volunteers in the Civil War, and the majority of whom wanted to go home and leave the service. Grumbling from the start, troopers soon began to question orders and finally drew up a petition demanding one particular officer's resignation. This constituted mutiny and Custer acted forcefully. He demanded that those involved apologize; all did except one sergeant. After court-martial he was sentenced to be shot. A petition to pardon him, with the plea that he was a family man, was refused. Subsequent threats and plots against Custer were rumored. On the day appointed the mutineer was brought out to a field where the entire division had assembled. He was to be executed with a condemned deserter and criminal.

Though aware of the threats, Custer forbade sidearms for his officers and himself. When the men had been placed before their open graves, coffins beside them and blindfolded, a trooper took the sergeant aside. The squad fired, the deserter died, and the mutineer fainted. The sergeant was informed after he was revived that Custer had long before decided upon a pardon but would not allow himself to be seen to have been influenced.

Upon arrival in Texas immediate orders were to check the rampant lawlessness throughout the state while also hunting for Confederate Gen. Kirby Smith, who had not yet surrendered his men and arms to the Union. Custer at one point had to employ thirteen regiments of infantry and thirteen regiments of cavalry to fulfill his tasks. Less than a year after assignment to Texas he was called to Washington to testify before the Joint Committee on Reconstruction. Shortly thereafter Custer was mustered out as a Maj. Gen. of Volunteers, and reverted to his original regular army rank of captain. This happened to most brevetted high officers, for after the War there was no need for so many officers of such rank.

It cost Custer a pay cut from $8,000 a year as general to $2,000 as captain, and he returned to Michigan to consider opportunities. Political posts had been offered such as the governorship of Michigan (which he had been assured he would win), but a U.S. soldier remained his chosen career. He was offered the post of adjutant general of Mexico at a salary of $16,000 in gold a year; Grant and Sheridan both recommended him but the federal government refused Custer a year's leave.

A new appointment in July 1866 as Lt. Col. of a new formation, the Seventh Cavalry Regiment, took Custer to a new home base in Fort Riley, Kansas. The Seventh was one of four new cavalry regiments created that month bringing to ten the total for the entire regular army. Troopers were to be selected from veterans of the Union Army after an examination by a board of officers.

The Seventh's original complement of officers included many who had been reduced in rank after the war like Custer but who in addition were older than the "Boy General." Later in the year he was joined by his younger brother Lt. Thomas W. Custer, recipient of two Congressional Medals of Honor and one of the few men to seize two Confederate battle flags in the war.

Even though the enlisted men were mainly veterans, there were many recruits who simply sought employment and might easily desert under the hardships of service on the Prairie. Food was uniformly poor due to the depredations of the army contractors, and living conditions were harsh in the subzero winters and torrid summers. The only way to build a new regiment from scratch was by repeated drill instruction.

The new Seventh had its first opportunity for action in Gen. Hancock's campaign against the Cheyenne, Sioux and Arapahoes. The Indians had been raiding isolated post stations on the stage route, killing and disemboweling men and burning the posts afterward. The Seventh rode over a thousand miles on the expedition, but saw little fighting.

It was on the return march that Custer's group got into trouble. A party of ten men under Lt. Kidder had been following the Seventh's trail with dispatches from Gen. Sherman. They were guided by the Sioux chief Red Bead. When Kidder and his men didn't arrive, the Seventh traversed its trail. They found the missing men, as Custer wrote:

> Lying in irregular order, and within a very limited circle, were the mangled bodies of poor Kidder and his party, yet so brutally hacked and disfigured as to be beyond recognition save as human beings. Every individual of the party had been scalped and his skull broken—the latter done by some weapon, probably a tomahawk—except the Sioux chief Red Bead, whose scalp had simply been removed from his head and then been thrown by his side.

Each of the men had twenty to fifty arrows in him.

With cholera and the lack of decent provisions at their next destination, Fort Wallace, Custer set out to provide for supplies. He also wanted to see his wife at Fort Riley. Shortly thereafter Custer was court-martialed for leaving his command and allowing his officers, under his personal supervision, to shoot several deserters without benefit of trial.

With the Hancock campaign a costly failure, Congress wanted a scapegoat and Custer was available. The upshot was that he was found guilty in October 1867 and sentenced "to be suspended from rank and command for one year and forfeit his pay proper for the same time." Custer returned to Monroe, Michigan, to serve his sentence time "off-duty."

But the Great Plains failed to quiet down and the following summer a critical situation arose. On September 17, 1868, a company of men under Gen. Sandy Forsyth was attacked at Beecher's Island on the Republican River by nearly a thousand Sioux and Cheyenne under the chiefs Roman Nose and Medicine Man. Though greatly outnumbered Forsyth's men held out until relief arrived.

Sheridan, military commander of the Department of the Missouri, was exasperated by the number of Indian attacks and the lack of aggressive counterattacks by his commanders on the Plains. He therefore formally requested the remainder of Custer's punishment be remitted and he be reinstated in his command.

Sheridan telegraphed Custer in Michigan on September 24:

Generals Sherman, Sully, and myself, and nearly all the officers of your regiment, have asked for you, and I hope the applications will be successful. Can you come at once? Eleven companies of your regiment will move about the first of October against the hostile Indians, from Medicine Lodge Creek toward the Wichita Mountains.

Custer was in Fort Hays, Kansas, by the morning of September 30, and rejoined the Seventh almost immediately. To increase order in the regiment Custer instituted the "coloring of the horses," by which each company received horses of one color. He also formed a special unit of the forty best marksmen out of the eight hundred men to be sharpshooters.

The regiment was practically under siege in its own camp with daily raids being made against it. No retaliation had yet been made. Custer and Sheridan decided that a winter campaign should be mounted. Winter's harsh conditions were best for operations against the Indians because it was the time of year when their ponies were at their weakest due to the lack of grass for feeding. In good weather Indian ponies were faster than the heavy cavalry horses and easier to feed. Also, in winter tribes tended to congregate along streams.

A large concentration reportedly had encamped along the Washita River, south of Fort Hayes and Dodge City in Oklahoma. Its actual size came as a disagreeable surprise. Still, the troopers of the Seventh marched out in a heavy snowstorm on November 23 with a foot of snow on the ground. The total complement numbered nearly nine hundred men plus Osage Indians and scouts.

On the fourth day scouts found the trail of a war party of at least 150 warriors. They concluded that the villages were nearby. The Osage cautioned a delay until daylight to prepare an attack, but Custer did not want to lose the element of surprise. The regiment moved up after midnight.

As would become his major tactic in Plains warfare (and would fail once and utterly at the Little Big Horn), Custer divided his regiment into four detachments. He sent one each to the left and right of the village, dismounted the sharpshooters to form a line of skirmishers and himself advanced leading the center. The regimental band followed his column. Each detachment would approach as stealthily to the village as possible, and attack at dawn. As Custer advanced he wondered whether the other troops had reached their assigned positions; there was no way of knowing. Suddenly at the far side of the village a single shot rang out.

Custer signaled the band to strike up the "Garry Owen," the Seventh's attack song. Cheering from both sides of the valley let him know the other units were in their proper positions. The bugles joined in sounding the charge and the entire command rushed the village:

> The Indians were caught napping; but realizing at once the dangers of their situation, they quickly overcame their first surprise and in an instant seized their rifles, bows, and arrows, and sprang behind the nearest trees, while some leaped into the stream, nearly waist deep, and using the bank as a rifle-pit began a vigorous and determined advance. Mingled with the exultant cheers of my men could be heard the defiant war-whoops of the warriors, who from the first fought with a desperation and courage which no race of men could surpass.

The lodges of the village were secured rapidly but the warriors who had taken up firing positions held out quite a while. Teenage boys fought also. A boy of perhaps fourteen or fifteen with pistol in hand charged Maj. Benteen, who attempted to treat him as a noncombatant. The boy fired three times, missing Benteen's head and finally wounding his horse. The Major finally fired in self-defense killing the boy who turned out to be a chieftain's son.

Many of Custer's men now dismounted to fight the Indians on foot, firing from cover as the enemy likewise was. In this way pockets were gradually wiped out or driven off. At about 10 A.M., a small band of Indians was spotted downstream about a mile below the village. At first they were thought to be from the village currently under attack. Soon "California Joe," a top scout for Custer, drove in a pony herd of several hundred.

After interrogation of a village squaw, Custer had learned to his great surprise that extending down the valley for over ten miles were the winter villages of all the southern plains' tribes with which they were at war. These included the Arapahoes, Kiowas, more Cheyennes, Comanches and some Apaches.

An Indian attack was not only building, it was imminent, and obviously would come in much superior numbers. Since the village had been secured, Custer reorganized the regiment and had his casualties tended to. Twenty-one men had been killed and thirteen wounded, including Tom Custer. The quartermaster arrived with much-needed ammunition. One hundred three Cheyenne had been killed including Chief Black Kettle.

The Seventh itself was now encircled with the village at its center. Custer ordered the lodges burned and captured weapons and supplies destroyed. Though Custer disliked it, as did his men, the pony herd was shot. The herd could not be used by the cavalry, its presence would hamper the march, and most critically it was an exceptionally valuable lure to the rest of the warriors. Also the Indians (and outside observers) might interpret its capture as the taking of plunder, and thus see the Seventh's mission as marauding rather than a punitive expedition as Custer had intended.

Over fifty women and children had been taken as hostages, and an hour before nightfall the Seventh set out. Custer sent out a strong force of skirmishers and had the band playing and full colors flying—a show of force which helped convince the other tribes that their villages were threatened. After moving several miles toward the next villages, Custer about-faced the command and headed back toward the supply train and remainder of the column.

The regiment reached the destroyed village at 10 P.M., and then followed their own trail from the previous day. The next morning the column met the supply train, and horses and men were properly fed. Custer wrote a report for Sheridan, and asked the scout California Joe how many men he would need to get through. Joe decided he and one fellow scout could do the best job. Joe figured that he was safe enough, for "This thing of pumpin' 'em when the snows a foot deep, and no grass for their ponies, puts a new wrinkle in these Injuns' scalp, an' they ain't goin' to git over it in a minnit either." The two scouts made the ride in record time.

Upon receipt of Custer's report, Sheridan had wired Sherman that Custer had "wiped out Black-Kettle + his murderers + rapers of helpless women." Sherman sent his congratulations from St. Louis. Secretary of War W. W. Belknap wired to Sherman, "I congratulate you, Sheridan, and Custer on the splendid success with which your campaign is begun. Ask Sheridan to send forward the names of officers and men deserving of special mention." Custer replied that was impracticable, "for the gratifying reason that every officer and man belonging to the expedition had performed his full part in rendering the movement against the hostile tribes a complete success."

The Seventh Cavalry made its entry into Camp Supply on December 2. General Sheridan reviewed the regiment and said:

> the appearance of the troops, with the bright rays of the sun reflected from their burnished arms and equipments, as they advanced in beautiful order and precision down the slope, the band playing, and the blue soldiers' uniforms slightly relieved by the gaudy colors of the Indians, both captives and Osages, the strangely fantastic part played by the Osage guides, their shouts, chanting their war songs, and firing their guns in air, all combined to render the scene one of the most beautiful and highly interesting he remembered ever having witnessed.

Before the Seventh embarked on the Washita Expedition Custer warned that no matter how hard the regiment fought, the people in the West subject to Indian raids and depredations would find them inefficient. On the other hand, the ever-active lobbyists in Washington for crooked contractors and

Indian agents who made money off the tribes would object loudly to the campaign.

There were also "a class of persons truly good in themselves and in their intentions, but who were familiar to only a very limited degree with the dark side of the Indian question, and whose ideas were of the sentimental order." The dark side included the young white woman and her eighteen-month-old child, scalped and with their skulls crushed in, found in the abandoned Kiowa village further down the Washita Valley.

*The New York Times* agreed to some extent by suggesting, "We must come back to the old army policy of reservations—peace for the Indian on the reservation, war for his hostilities outside the reservation." Sheridan, commanding general for the region, had the final military operational word, regardless of Eastern opinion.

In a letter to Sherman from Fort Cobb, Sheridan wrote:

> I do not care one cent as far as I am concerned myself, whether they (the hostiles) come in or stay out. If they stay out, I will make war on them winter and summer as long as I live, or until they are wiped out. They cannot come here and make peace with me now, and then commence killing white people again in the spring. If I make peace with them, I want it to be a peace which will last; and if they commit robberies and murders afterwards, they must be punished.

The Cheyenne and Arapahoes still had to be dealt with and brought in to the reservations. Custer had 1,500 men under his command for the Seventh had been joined by the Nineteenth Kansas Volunteer Cavalry, assigned to help clear the Wichita Mountains. They marched on March 2, 1869.

Custer "followed the dictates of my own judgment—the judgment upon which Gen'l Sheridan said he relied for the attainment of the best results. He had authorized me to do as I pleased, fight or not." Custer believed his mission was not to kill hostiles, though he would if he had to and neither Sheridan nor Sherman would have done anything but congratulate him. Rather they were to be returned to their reservations peacefully, if possible. He therefore decided to parley when feasible.

With the Arapahoes he had no problem. After a council and a promise that there would be no punishment by the "Big Knives" (as the cavalry were called for their sabers) the Arapahoes went back to their reservation.

The Cheyennes posed much more of a problem—they were known to be holding two white women hostage. The expedition located the village which contained the entire Cheyenne nation. A parley was called and the major chief, Medicine Arrow, invited Custer to his lodge. There they smoked a peace pipe and negotiated.

It became apparent that Medicine Arrow was stalling for time; Custer ordered four of his sub-chieftains put under arrest. When the chief continued to stall, while withdrawing his people over several days, Custer gave an ultimatum: deliver the women or he would hang the chieftains. The women were surrendered the next day. The Cheyennes promised to return to their reservation.

Custer wrote to his wife Libby of the Cheyennes that, "I outmarched them, out-witted them at their own game, proved to them that they were in my power, and could and would have annihilated the entire village of over two hundred lodges . . . now, when I can review the whole matter coolly, my better judgment and my humanity tell me I have acted wisely. . . . and now my most bitter enemies cannot say that I am either blood-thirsty or possessed of an unworthy ambition.

"Had I given the signal to attack, officers and men would have hailed it with a shout of gratification. I braved their opinion and acted in opposition to their wishes; but to-day not one but says I was right, and any other course would have been disastrous."

Concerning the Cheyennes Custer said, "I think we have rendered them sick and tired of war." Sheridan sent a letter of congratulations over the success of the winter campaign. The Plains were at peace for the time being. The remainder of 1869 and the year 1870 were relatively calm. In 1871 the Seventh Cavalry was transferred to the deep South for more Reconstruction duty. Some went to South Carolina; the rest were assigned to Kentucky under Custer for a two-year tour.

By June 1873 the entire Seventh Cavalry had arrived in the Dakota Territory for service against the Sioux. The Northern Pacific Railway was going to push through the Badlands and their survey engineers would need protection. The Yellowstone Expedition consisted of the railway's engineers escorted by 1,500 men under Col. David Stanley, who commanded twenty infantry companies, accompanied by ten cavalry companies of the Seventh under Custer.

As was his custom, Custer rode ahead of the column with a small escort. In a dangerous encounter which would presage the Little Big Horn, Custer camped with ninety men at the forward campsite chosen for the main column which lagged far behind. Six Sioux rode up and stampeded some of the troop's horses. Custer mounted and pursued with part of his troop.

The six braves were decoys and upon approaching some woods Custer and his men were ambushed by several hundred braves. The troopers had to turn around and gallop for their lives. "I was up, the Indians were up, and for a little while, I thought it was 'all up' with me. It was a dash race. I'm glad it wasn't heats. I won the dash, but might have lost the second heat." The company then held out until reinforcements arrived.

Two unarmed members of the column who had been riding between the main body and Custer were later found dead, stripped and mutilated. The veterinary surgeon and a sutler were great favorites of the Seventh, who wanted revenge. Four days later the regiment got an opportunity. Scouts discovered the trail of a large village. Custer and four companies took off to follow the trail by moonlight. They covered thirty-three miles before resting the next day. After a three-day chase over broken, rocky ground Custer caught up with several hundred Hunkpapa Sioux, with the raging Yellowstone River between them. Because their hardy ponies were accustomed to fording such waters, the Sioux crossed. Custer had formed up with a company on each wing and himself leading the center with two companies. The Sioux were allowed to land. The band struck up "Garry Owen" and the whole line charged. The Sioux, unable to withstand a disciplined cavalry charge, broke into flight: at least forty braves died while the Seventh lost four dead and three wounded. Custer's horse was shot from under him again.

In his report on the fight Custer emphasized that the Sioux were mainly armed with the "latest improved patterns of breech-loading repeating rifles . . . So amply have they been supplied with breech-loading rifles and ammunition that neither bows nor arrows were employed against us." The arms were provided by a "sentimental Government manipulated and directed by corrupt combinations," alluding to rifles supposedly for buffalo hunting supplied by unscrupulous agents of the Indian Bureau at the agencies.

Custer was so embittered by the discovery of the nature of the Sioux's weapons that he wrote, "I only regret that it was impossible for my Command to effect a crossing of the river before our presence was discovered, and while the hostile village was located near at hand, as I am confident that we could have largely reduced the necessity for appropriations for Indian supplies the coming winter."

The Seventh went into its winter quarters in late September 1873. The following July, Custer commanded an expedition into the Black Hills. Militarily it was uneventful but for the future of the Native American it would be decisive—if not ultimately fatal. Sheridan and the War Department charged that the Black Hills country, sacred to the Sioux, was being used as a sanctuary from which to launch raids.

The expedition set out with over one thousand men, 110 wagons, and three Gatling guns accompanied also by a geologist, a paleontologist, and a photographer. Though shadowed occasionally by small groups of Sioux there were no hostilities.

The event that would ultimately and irrevocably change the history of the West was recorded in the August 27, 1874, issue of the Chicago *Inter-Ocean*:

Gold!

The Land of Promise—Stirring News from the Black Hills
The Glittering Treasure Found at Last—A Belt of Gold

Territory Thirty Miles Wide
The Precious Dust Found in the Grass Under the Horses' Feet—
Excitement Among the Troops

The next day the paper read, "General Sheridan Warns Miners and Prospectors to Keep Away from the Scene, As by Treaty that Section is Exempt from Settlement by the Whites, Some Doubts as to Whether all the Gold Region is Within the Reservation." The sacred Black Hills of the Sioux had become a target for exploitation because of its mineral wealth.

The Black Hills belonged to the Sioux under the terms of the Treaty of Laramie, signed in 1868. The treaty prohibited war between the United States and treaty Indians; the Sioux were given all of present-day South Dakota including the Black Hills; parts of what is now Wyoming and Montana north of the Platte River and east of the Big Horn Mountains would be "unceded Indian territory" and could not be entered without Indian consent; the Sioux would permit construction of the Union Pacific Railroad on lands "not passing through reservation."

Violations of the treaty soon occurred on both sides but no official trespass occurred until the government-ordered exploratory expedition under Custer. The army was able to maintain the integrity of the Black Hills through 1875, but Indian raids on settlers in parts of Minnesota, Nebraska, Wyoming and Montana were rapidly increasing in number.

Though it could not be proved or disproved that treaty Indians were involved, many of the younger braves of treaty signatories would leave the reservations for a summer of raiding and then return for the winter. Accordingly, one last peaceful effort was made by the Commissioner of Indian Affairs to bring in the renegades. Messengers went out in the early winter of 1875–1876 with word that the options were either peaceful settlement or the prospect of punitive campaigns. Deadline for the Sioux and Northern Cheyennes to be on their reservations was set for January 31, 1876. After that date all warriors found off-reservation would be treated as hostiles. There were now three major army commands—the Divisions of the Atlantic, the Pacific and the Missouri.

Sheridan commanded the Missouri with four departments under him—including the Platte, commanded by Gen. George Crook and the Dakota under Brig. Gen. Terry. Both would be active in the campaign against the Sioux and Cheyenne.

A massive three-pronged attack was planned against the Sioux and Cheyenne in 1876. Crook would command ten companies of the Third Cavalry, five companies of the Second Cavalry, and five companies of the Fourth and Ninth Infantry, about 1,300 men in all. The column would move north from Fort Fetterman in Wyoming toward the Rosebud River. Colonel John Gibbon was to advance east from Fort Ellis, Montana, leading four companies of the Second Cavalry and six companies of the Seventh Infantry, equipped with two Gatling guns. Terry would march west from Fort Abraham Lincoln with twelve companies of the Seventh Cavalry under Custer, three companies of the Sixth and Seventeenth Infantry, three Gatling guns, and a detachment of Arikara Indian scouts.

Custer originally had been designated to command the column from Fort Lincoln in the Dakota Territory. Unfortunately, he had been called upon to testify in Washington that spring concerning corruption in the War Department. Though he could report only hearsay, Custer managed to make for the record damaging statements about the War Secretary Belknap and—much worse—Orvil Grant, the President's brother. Custer's statements rang true for Belknap had sold the lucrative army post traderships, and Orvil Grant owned several, though that was illegal.

But the veracity of Custer's statements did not matter, for President Grant held grudges. Aside from his testimony about Orvil, Custer had also arrested Grant's son for drunkenness on the Black Hills expedition. The President issued an order to Sherman and Sheridan that Custer not be allowed to command the Dakota columns in the imminent campaign against the Sioux.

Custer was crushed. He went to Gen. Terry and begged him to forward this message to the President (who had refused to see Custer in Washington):

> I respectfully but most earnestly request that while not allowed to go in command of the expedition, I may be permitted to serve with my regiment in the field. I appeal to you as a soldier to spare me the humiliation of seeing my regiment march to meet the enemy and I not to share its dangers.

Grant relented; the old soldier could not keep the young one from meeting his destiny with his men.

Lieutenant Colonel George Armstrong Custer had approximately six hundred men in twelve companies when he left with the Dakota column from Fort Abraham Lincoln on May 17, 1876. His two ranking officers were Maj. Marcus A. Reno and Capt. Frederick W. Benteen. Neither liked Custer and with Benteen the dislike seemed to approach outright hatred.

Reno had attended West Point and served with distinction in the Civil War. Cited twice for bravery, he was brevetted to the rank of brigadier general. He graduated five classes ahead of Custer. Unlike Custer and most of his company commanders, Reno had no experience in Indian fighting and his lack of nerve eventually became apparent in battles with the Sioux and Cheyennes.

Benteen had no such excuse. Born in Virginia to a family of slave-holders, he nevertheless fought for the Union in the Civil War as a commander of Missouri volunteer cavalry. Like Reno, he was older than Custer (by six years) and not happy to be a subordinate to the "Boy General." An experienced Plains officer, he had served for a decade fighting the hostiles.

Custer did have his own men, however. Captain Tom Custer commanded C Company. He had enlisted with a Michigan volunteer regiment at the age of sixteen and joined his brother in 1864. He won the Medal of Honor twice in the war and was with the Seventh from its formation.

Lieutenant James Calhoun led L Company; he was married to Custer's younger sister, Margaret. Captain Yates of F Company had been in the Fourth Michigan Infantry and served for a while on Custer's staff. Captain Myles Moylan was Calhoun's brother-in-law and commanded Company A; he later won the Medal of Honor. Captain Thomas Weir, also from Michigan, had been with the Seventh virtually from its inception. Weir had Company D; he was the only commanding officer to try to relieve Custer when the others refused.

General Terry commanded the Dakota column in lieu of Custer, displaced by his frictions with the President. Terry had been in administrative command of the Department of the Dakota for nearly a decade. He had never commanded in the field against Indians. On May 30, Terry ordered Custer out on a scouting mission up the Little Missouri River. The river valley revealed no signs of recent occupancy and the search headed to the next valley. Soon after, Maj. Reno was sent on a scouting mission with six companies of cavalry, one Gatling gun and crew, some Arikara scouts with the top scout Mitch Bouyer, and a pack-train of seventy mules. Reno was to go up the Powder River, cross to the Tongue, and travel back to the Yellowstone, scouting minor tributaries on the way. Custer had wanted this assignment but Terry did not want to appear to be giving Custer an independent command at this time.

On June 10, Reno's reconnaissance-in-force set out. The scouting party returned on the evening of June 19. General Terry reported his findings to Gen. Sheridan on June 21:

> Traces of a large and recent camp have been discovered twenty or thirty miles up the Rosebud. Gibbon's column will move this morning . . . for the mouth of the Big Horn . . . thence it will proceed to the mouth of the Little Big Horn and so . . . Custer will go up the Rosebud tomorrow with his whole regiment and thence to the headwaters and thence down to the Little Big Horn . . . I only hope one of the two columns will find the Indians. I go personally with Gibbon.

Also that day, Terry held a council of war on the "Far West." Present were Custer and Gibbon. At the meeting it was decided that the Seventh would proceed up the Little Big Horn Valley, where Terry suspected a major Indian village to be.

No one at the conference was aware of a vital piece of information. On June

17, Gen. Crook's column of over one thousand men in twenty companies had met between 1,500 and two thousand Sioux and Cheyenne on the Rosebud River. An all-day battle ended in a virtual standoff, though with light casualties.

The Indians withdrew northward but Crook failed to follow them. Having expended much ammunition, the general simply turned his one thousand men around and marched south. This reversal destroyed the overall plan of three-pronged attack and removed the largest column from the field. The same Sioux and Cheyenne would annihilate Custer eight days later only forty miles north. Crook did not attempt to inform the other columns of this retreat until early July, more than a week too late for Custer and his men. Crook simply wanted to cover up for his lack of nerve.

On June 22, Custer was sent a message "for guidance" by Terry:

"The Brigadier-General Commanding directs that, as soon as your regiment can be made ready for the march, you will proceed up the Rosebud in pursuit of the Indians whose trail was discovered by Major Reno a few days since.

"It is, of course, impossible to give you any definite instructions in regard to this movement, and were it not impossible to do so the Department Commander places too much confidence in your zeal, energy, and ability to wish to impose upon you precise orders which might hamper your action when nearly in contact with the enemy.

"He will, however, indicate to you his own views of what your action should be, and he desires that you should conform to them unless you shall see sufficient reasons for departing from them."

Terry wanted Custer to help enclose the Indians and, in concert with Gibbon's column, keep them from escaping. Custer's cook at the time swore that Terry and the lieutenant-colonel met after the conference in his tent. Under notarized testimony, she stated that, "Terry said to General Custer: 'Custer, I don't know what to say for the last.' Custer replied, 'Say whatever you want to say.' Terry then said, 'Use your own judgement and do what you think best if you strike the trail. And whatever you do, Custer, hold on to your wounded.' "

Whether or not that testimony is accurate, Custer and the Seventh Cavalry set out at noon on Thursday, June 22. Custer ordered fifteen days of bread to be taken along with twelve days of bacon rations. He also ordered a supply of salt to be carried in case horse meat had to be eaten on the campaign. He believed that the Seventh would be out until they found the hostiles, regardless of how long it took.

Custer led 597 troopers and fifty scouts and civilians. Each trooper had one hundred rounds of ammunition for his .45 caliber Model 1873 Springfield carbine, and twenty-four rounds for his Model 1872 Colt revolver. Only two men, lieutenants de Rudio and Mathey, carried their sabers. For the purpose of silence cavalry sabers had been prohibited from the column. Custer had been offered the use of a battery of Gatling guns but their fragility in transport over rocky territory rendered them unusable in the highly mobile campaign planned by him.

After sunset on June 22, Custer held a meeting of his senior officers, one of whom was Capt. Edward S. Godfrey, commanding K Company under Benteen:

"It was not a cheerful assemblage; everyone seemed to be in a serious mood ... He took particular pains to impress upon the officers his reliance upon their judgement, discretion, and loyalty. He thought, judging from the number of lodge fires reported by Reno, that we might meet at least one thousand warriors; there might be enough men from the agencies, visiting their hostile friends, to make a total of 1,500. . . .

"This 'talk' of his, as we called it, was considered at the time as something extraordinary for General Custer, for it was not his habit to unbosom himself to his officers. In it he showed concessions and a reliance on others; there was an indefinable something that was not Custer. His manner and tone, usually brusque and aggressive, or somewhat curt, was on this occasion conciliating and subdued. There was something akin to an appeal, as if depressed, that made a deep impression on all present."

Godfrey walked back to the bivouac with two other officers. Lieutenant Wallace remarked, "Godfrey, I believe General Custer is going to be killed." Godfrey replied, "Why, Wallace, what makes you think so?" "Because, I have never heard Custer talk in that way before." (Cited from Captain Godfrey's narrative account in the January, 1892 issue of "The Century" magazine.)

Terry had also offered Custer an additional battalion from the Second Cavalry, but he had declined it because he felt the Seventh could handle anything it would face. "If it could not, no other regiment in the service could; if they could whip the regiment, they would be able to defeat a much larger force, or, in other words, the reinforcement of this battalion could not save us from defeat."

On June 23 at 5 A.M., Custer mounted and rode up the Rosebud, accompanied by two sergeants—one carrying the regiment's standard, the other his personal, headquarters flag, the same kind used by Custer in the Civil War. The day's march found three empty villages. By camping time at 5 P.M., the column had covered thirty-three miles.

The following day Godfrey reported, "We passed a great many camping-places, all appearing to be of nearly the same strength. One would naturally suppose these were the successive camping-places of the same village, when in fact they were the continuous camps of the several bands." Custer, along with his officers, did, in fact believe the villages successive camps by the same tribal group rather than a string of many bands. The trail had grown to a width of roughly three hundred yards as the Seventh followed it.

Camping on June 24, officers were summoned after sunset to a strategy-planning meeting. The command had by now marched seventy-five miles in fifty-six hours and was ahead of the schedule set aboard the "Far West." With the lead the Seventh had on the other columns, Custer still intended to push on.

The regiment would follow the trail which led over the Little Big Horn River, marching that night so as to be in as close proximity as possible to prepare for an attack the next day, June 26. That was the day that had been originally decided upon with Terry and Gibbon for a coordinated attack. While the Seventh rested on June 25, scouts would reconnoiter the village and their reports would be used to help plan the onslaught.

The first night march on June 24 began at 11 P.M., and ended at 2 A.M., having pushed through a dust storm. The troopers slept; the march would resume at 8 A.M. Before assembly that final morning Lt. Godfrey went to see Custer who was meeting with his scouts.

"The General wore a serious expression and was apparently abstracted. The scouts were doing the talking, and seemed nervous and disturbed. Finally Bloody Knife made a remark that recalled the General from his reverie, and he asked in his usual quick, brusque manner, 'What's that he says?' The interpreter replied, 'He says we'll find enough Sioux to keep us fighting two or three days.' The General smiled and remarked, 'I guess we'll get through with them in one day.' "

The march on June 25 began at 8:00 A.M., and continued until 10:30 A.M., when a halt was made. At that time the men were ordered to keep quiet, concealed, and avoid any action that would draw attention.

The plan's most important component was the attack at dawn. Custer had used it in his charge at the battle of the Washita eight years before. Godfrey (later to be a general) described this strategy for Indian campaigning (again cited from "The Century"): "When following an Indian trail the 'signs' indicate the length of time elapsed since the presence of Indians. When the 'signs' indicate a 'hot trail,' i.e., near approach, the commander judges his distance and by a forced march, usually in the night-time, tries to reach the Indian village at night and make his disposition for a surprise attack at daylight.

"At all events his attack must be made with celerity, and generally without other knowledge of the numbers of the opposing force than that discovered or conjectured while following the trail. The dispositions for the attack may be said to be 'made in the dark,' and successful surprise to depend upon luck."

The Sioux and Cheyenne had put up their villages. It was not intended as their battleground, though they knew from their own out-parties that battle was near. The vast camp was formed by band upon band simply putting up their tepees one after another, formed up only by the tribal grouping to which each warrior belonged. Ordinarily an encampment of many villages, as this was, would be widely spread, and not necessarily easily supportive of each other under attack. This time they were vast *and* in communication.

At Custer's camp the Ree scouts had gathered together with their medicine man. He anointed them and invoked the Great Spirit's protection against the Sioux. "They seemed to have become satisfied that we were going to find more Sioux than we could well take care of."

Custer's Indian scouts had been surveying the Little Big Horn valley since first light from a high point called "Crow's Nest." Some fifteen miles distant there seemed to be a dense haze, as of countless campfires, and a vast stirring movement "like worms crawling in the grass," the indication of a giant pony herd. One scout, Charley Reynolds, said, "That's the biggest pony herd any man ever saw." Another, the half-breed Mitch Bouyer, said "Biggest village. A heap too big." A courier carried the news to Custer.

The next move of the Seventh Cavalry was determined by the simple loss of a supply chest by F company. It had been dropped from the train during the night of June 24–25. A detail sent back by Capt. Yates reported that they had found an Indian breaking it open; he escaped.

Captain Tom Custer then brought news of their discovery to his brother. "Officers' Call" was sounded. All information pointed to the column having been discovered. Custer had said he wanted to attack on June 26, but with the Indian knowledge of their presence, he would attack that day.

At 8:45 A.M., on Sunday, June 25, the Seventh Cavalry mounted up. After an advance of four miles the column halted. Custer rode ahead to Crow's Nest to observe the valley. The heat of the late June day had already brought a haze that obscured the view, but scouts reiterated their impression of the immensity of the village. The total numbers can reasonably be stated at well over seven thousand. This meant that at least two thousand warriors would be able to take the field against six hundred men of the Seventh. From agency reports, however, and estimates of other transient Indians, Custer believed that the number of hostiles would be between one thousand and 1,500.

The march continued. Shortly after noon Custer divided his regiment into three fighting battalions, with one company assigned to guard the pack train. The standard tactic used by the U.S. Cavalry in attacking a village, no matter its size, had been to divide the force into units and charge from several sides, preventing dispersal of the enemy. Custer had done this with much success at the Washita and planned to do so again, whatever the numbers facing him. It would not be dawn, however, and the Sioux and Cheyenne knew he was coming.

Half-yellow-face, a Crow scout, tried to dissuade Custer from attacking, or at least from attacking piecemeal. He said that when the soldier-chief gave the order that divided his men, he had spoken to him, through an interpreter, saying, "Do not divide your men. There are too many of the enemy for us, even if we all stay together. If you must fight, keep us all together." He said Son-of-the-morning-star (Custer) had not liked these words and that he had replied, "You do the scouting, and I will attend to the fighting."

As soon as the soldiers had begun to separate into bands, as they had been ordered, Half-yellow-face had stripped and painted his face. "Why are you doing all this?" Son-of-the-morning-star had asked. "Because you and I are going home today, and by a trail that is strange to us both."

Custer designated three battalions for the attack. Captain Benteen received Companies D, H and K, numbering 115 men, with orders to search on the left flank and attack any villages he might encounter. Should the mission prove fruitless, he was to backtrack and rejoin the main column.

Major Reno was given Companies A, G and M, numbering 140 men. Since Reno was the senior officer subordinate to Custer he received the command of the first-strike force (unfortunately, his inexperience in Indian warfare showed when he faced a large number of Sioux). Custer ordered Reno to take his battalion, cross the Little Big Horn River, and charge the southern end of the village.

Custer himself would lead Companies E, C, F, I and L, a total of 212 men. The commander sent an order to Reno to, "Move forward at as rapid a gait as you deem prudent, charge the village, and the whole outfit will support you." It has often been stated that Custer did not support Reno, but it is a much more salient argument that Custer intended to support Reno by attacking the northern end of the camp, thereby splitting the opposing forces. Benteen could then bring his battalion to bear as needed.

While Benteen took off on his search away from the main body, Reno and Custer rode for about two hours in parallel columns on the banks of the Little Big Horn. Advancing at first in columns of four, Reno next deployed his battalion in line of battle, and then as skirmishers. The Sioux took advantage of Reno's variations in deployment and Reno's detachment was met in force as it neared the village.

Reno's Civil War nerve failed him. Attacked by a little over five hundred warriors, Reno had his 140 men dismount and fight on foot. A good stand of timber was available to fortify, but a determined charge had a much greater chance of carrying the field. Reno would not order it. As an order to remount was given the scout Bloody Knife was shot through the head right next to Reno. Brains splattered on the major; his ability to command rationally for the moment was gone.

In sequence Reno ordered "mount," "dismount," "mount," within the period of a minute. Reno next ordered his command to recross the river and head for the cover of trees on the bluffs above. As for the men, panicked by their own commander's wild orders and the harrying of the Sioux firing into their ranks as they crossed, they struggled up the bluffs both with and without their horses. At the top Reno found that he had forty-five dead, wounded and missing out of 140 men.

Custer had proceeded with his companies along the bluffs on the opposite side of the river. He did not want the village to disperse; by advancing north of the village he would cut off a dispersal and at the same time open a second front of attack. While on their advance north the sounds of Reno's firing was heard. With scout Mitch Bouyer, Custer rode to the edge of the bluffs. There he saw the magnitude of the Indian encampment he faced.

Custer was not planning to lose. He sent out a call for more ammunition. Sergeant Daniel Knipe was detailed by Capt. Tom Custer to rush the pack train forward—it held all the reserve ammunition. "Tell McDougall to hurry the pack train and if any of the packs get loose, cut them and let them go." Custer then added, "And if you see Benteen tell him to come on quick."

With the column steadily advancing, Custer sent another message. At 3:20 P.M., Lt. Cooke, adjutant to Custer, handed a written message to a trumpeter, Giovanni Martini. The note read, "Benteen—Come on. Big village. Be quick. Bring packs. W.W. Cooke. P.S. Bring pacs."

Benteen came on, but only to aid Reno who couldn't help himself. Benteen, a self-professed Custer-hater, had his detachment intact. With Reno's men there were six companies or slightly over two hundred able and mounted troopers available for whatever action their commander might decide upon. Reno was still not functioning well, so Benteen took acting command. Well dug-in by this point, their immediate danger had passed. Benteen declined to ride to the sound of the guns.

The danger that had passed Benteen and Reno headed north toward Custer and his 210 men. Disregarding Reno's force, all of the warriors of the Sioux and northern Cheyenne nations converged to attack Custer and his five companies.

There are only Indian accounts from this point on, each giving only a small part of the whole. The Sioux and Cheyenne, though having several great individual leaders, did not operate under one overall strategy. Each warrior fought on his own, and their wildly skewed views of the battle reflect this.

After advancing nearly three miles Custer realized he could not reach the village and would therefore have to establish a defensive perimeter to await the hoped-for arrival of Benteen and Reno's companies. If Reno could not come, at least Benteen should be free to do so.

Custer halted his five companies on a hill which he thought would be defensible until help came. Company L, the Greys, held the outflung southernmost position. L was commanded by Lt. Calhoun, Custer's brother-in-law. His position was intended to have been that of a beacon to which the rest of the Seventh would come. None did. Custer was now surrounded on a bleak

hillock by at least two thousand warriors of the Sioux and Cheyenne nations.
No effort had been made to move the supply train forward; Benteen simply
let it come at its own pace. Custer's men would have only the ammo they
carried; there was no one with the nerve or inclination to attempt to relieve
them, except one man.

He was Capt. Thomas Weir. Some time after they had joined Reno, at
around 4:50 P.M., Weir, commanding D Company under Benteen, was disturbed that neither Reno nor Benteen seemed interested in riding to the sound
of the guns in the north. Custer obviously was under heavy attack and Weir
believed it their duty to ride to his aid.

Weir took his Company and headed north. They had gone about a mile
when they reached a spot on the bluffs now known as "Weir's Point." From it
a smoke and dust cloud could be seen in the distance with Indians riding in
and out, firing at the ground. The rest of the companies soon followed Weir
but large numbers of Indians began to approach the Point, and the decision
was made to withdraw to the previous position.

Custer had formed his defensive position in the shape of a V, with himself at
the point with Capt. Yates's Company F. To the south were Capt. Keogh's
Company I, and the most outlying, Company L under Lt. Calhoun. To the
west was Custer's brother Tom and his C Company. Lieutenant Smith's E
Company was closest to the river occupying a position called "Deep Ravine,"
the banks of which they made use of as buttresses.

For most of Custer's men, however, the only cover available were their most
important companions in the field, their horses. The troopers were forced to
shoot their mounts to use them as breastworks. The troopers fired their single-
shot carbines as rapidly as possible, but the guns tended to overheat and jam.
Often a knife had to be used to pry the expended cartridge out of the breech.

The Sioux and Cheyenne had forty different types of guns, from muzzle-
loaders to repeating rifles supplied by the Indian agencies. They also fought
with bow and arrow, tomahawk and knife. Indians did not make organized
charges; they knew that the losses incurred in charging Custer's position
would be very heavy. Instead, they fought on foot, creeping closer and closer
and firing at targets of opportunity while the troopers did likewise. The much
greater volume of Indian fire, however, made the outcome inevitable.

The full force of the Indian attack on Custer could not have been brought to
bear until about 4 P.M., after Reno had dug in. Benteen was reinforcing him
and thus the warriors abandoned the attack there and rode north.

Chief Gall of the Hunkpapa Sioux, who had lost his wife and two children in
Reno's attack, hit Company L on Custer's southern flank. Calhoun and his men
were in a fairly strong defensive position and put up a fierce fight. Around some
of Calhoun's troopers' bodies as many as forty spent cartridges were found.

Custer was, as always, the center upon which many of the men formed up.

Crazy Horse and his Sioux struck at Custer and Companies F and I. Captain Tom Custer had gradually fallen back toward his brother's standard with the remnants of C Company. E Company, furthest out on the west flank, fought to a desperate end. The Cheyenne, led by Lame White Man, charged the twenty-eight men fighting from the banks of the ravine. The chief exhorted his warriors, "Come. We can kill all of them!" They did kill all the members of the "Greys," but one of the troopers managed to kill Lame White Man.

Company L had dissolved under heavy fire from the Hunkpapas. Company I next received the brunt of the attacks from the south and east. Captain Myles Keogh went down with his left leg shattered. His horse, "Comanche," was also wounded; it was the only living being found on the battlefield two days later. Keogh was surrounded by his sergeants, his trumpeter, and his guidon bearer. They all "died in a bunch" together as the Sioux rolled on toward Custer.

He stood with perhaps forty men at the center of the vortex. Custer fought with a Remington sporting rifle and two English Webley "Bulldog" pistols. The ever-faithful scout Bouyer had stayed with him, even though he had been given the option to leave with the other scouts. Tom Custer was only ten yards away, and their youngest brother Boston was there, having galloped from the pack train to join them.

The Indian warriors made one concerted charge against Custer that day. Gall gathered his warriors and hurled them at the remnant of the Seventh Cavalry on the hillock. They swept the crest . . . and it was over. An Arapaho mercenary, Waterman, said, "When I reached the top of the hill I saw Yellowhair. He was dressed in buckskin, coat and pants, and was on his hands and knees. He had been shot through the side, and there was blood coming from his mouth. He seemed to be watching the Indians moving around him. Four soldiers were sitting up around him, but they were all badly wounded. All the other soldiers were down. Then the Indians closed in around him, and I did not see any more."

Sitting Bull of the Sioux, who did not actually fight in the battle, said of his braves' accounts, "I cannot find one who saw Longhair (Custer) until just before he died. He did not wear his long hair as he used to wear it. It was short, and it was the color of the grass when the frost comes. Longhair stood like a sheaf of corn with all the ears fallen around him. He killed a man when he fell. He laughed. He had fired his last shot. He rose up on his hands and tried another shot, but his pistol would not go off. I did not see it. It was told to me. But it is true."

The body of George Armstrong Custer was found on the field above the Little Big Horn River on June 27, 1876. It had been stripped, but it was unmutilated. That was not true of his men, most of whom had been scalped and butchered. Why Custer was spared is not clear. His brother Tom had been horribly disfigured; he was identified only by a tattoo on his arm. Major Reno and Capt. Benteen held on to their fortified position a few miles from Custer's death-place, and they were relieved on the morning of June 27 by Gen. Terry and Col. Gibbon's column. Aside from Reno's first losses, they had come through quite well, as one might expect. (Benteen could have secured Reno's position and then ridden with three hundred men to the sound of the guns. He didn't. When he saw Custer's body on June 27 Benteen said, "There he is, God damn him! He'll never fight any more.")

Also on June 27, 1876, members of the U.S. Cavalry rode toward Custer Hill. Godfrey and Weir wondered what the objects were which they saw before them. Godfrey used his binoculars and exclaimed, "The dead!" Captain Weir said, "Oh, how white they look! How white!"

———

To a nation which had survived a vicious Civil War and looked with great anticipation to the celebration of the Centennial of its founding in one week, the loss of one its heroes of that war and virtually all his men was devastating.

Once over the initial shock, an outraged nation demanded retaliation. A North Dakota newspaper, the Bismarck *Tribune Extra*, asked, "Shall This Be the Beginning of the End?" The heads of the United States' army leadership were in Philadelphia attending the Centennial of Exposition entitled "A Century of Progress" when they heard the news of the last stand at the Little Big Horn. Troops poured into Indian territory, so that by the fall of 1876 fully one-third of the U.S. army had been concentrated against the Sioux and other Plains tribes. By the following spring most of the tribes had been sent back to reservations. Although the Sioux and Cheyenne had emerged victorious at Little Big Horn, in a sense, Custer's last stand had been theirs too.

The final act in the long tragedy of the Plains Wars began in the early part of 1890. Spurred on by Wovoka, a self-proclaimed prophet, various tribes took up a mystical rite, the Ghost Dance. The prophet preached that faithful Ghost Dancers would be delivered into an eternal paradise in which no white man lived. No bullets could harm the wearers of the "ghost shirts."

Sitting Bull died in a raid by Indian reservation police at Pine Ridge, South Dakota in 1890. The police had been ordered in to stop the Ghost Dance. Soon thereafter the reconstituted Seventh Cavalry commanded by Col. James Forsyth, under orders to disarm another band of perhaps five hundred Miniconjou Sioux headed for Pine Ridge, intercepted them at Wounded Knee Creek on December 29, 1890. A fight ensued, intentional or not; at least 146 Sioux and twenty-five soldiers died. The Plains Indian era had ended in the snows of Wounded Knee. The soldiers of the Seventh Cavalry had avenged the deaths of Custer and his men at the Little Big Horn. Native American tribes would not rise again.

# 10

# BERLIN: THE BUNKER, 1945

EARLY ON DECEMBER 16, 1944, a massive German force of twenty-eight divisions rolled through the heavily-wooded and snow-laden Ardennes Mountains. The attack of three armies was led by the largest SS army unit yet put together, the Sixth Panzer Army.

The Sixth consisted of four of the best Waffen SS divisions in the German army: "Liebstandarte," "Das Reich," "Hitler Jugend" and "Hohenstauffen." Five infantry divisions supported the panzers of the Sixth. These Waffen SS divisions were equipped with the best tanks available to the German armored forces. Each battalion had Mark V Panthers with ninety giant Tiger tanks in a central reserve. The tank corps was virtually unbeatable.

Supporting the Sixth was Gen. von Manteuffel's Fifth Panzer Army on the northern flank; the Seventh Army protected the southern flank of the German advance. The twenty-eight German divisions crashed onto a front occupied by four undermanned U.S. divisions. Fighting stubbornly, the U.S. divisions broke under the weight of the last great German offensive of World War II.

The surprise massive counterattack by 250,000 men and one thousand tanks from the German army's strategic reserve came to be known as the "Battle of the Bulge." Its seriousness prompted U.S. Gen. George S. Patton, Jr., to write in his diary on January 4, 1945, "We can still lose this war." Ironically, German Chancellor Adolf Hitler's final gamble of his career decided the Western Allies' own strategic course in the decisive drive of the war.

During the final campaigns on the Western front, the key question which confronted the Anglo-American armies and their Supreme Commander, Gen. Dwight D. Eisenhower, was how to win the war most rapidly and efficiently with the least loss of life. Since equipment supplies—especially gasoline

183

for tanks—was limited, a decision had to be made regarding the precise location and ultimate objective for a decisive, crippling thrust into the heart of Nazi Germany.

There were two overriding views of how to win the war on the Western front. One faction of military and political leaders believed that the American and British armies's main task was to destroy the Third Reich's ability to wage war by defeating German armed forces in the field—everywhere—while capturing or destroying industrial areas which supplied the war machine.

The second faction believed that German forces should be beaten and industrial areas taken on the way to conquering Berlin, the political and symbolic heart of Nazi Germany and capital of Hitler's self-proclaimed "Thousand Year Reich." Just as France had surrendered a week after Paris had fallen in 1940, the members of this group agreed Berlin's fall would signal the end of the Third Reich. In general, the American command favored the former approach while the British advocated the latter.

The final decision rested in large part upon the fundamental views with which the British and Americans perceived the military's role in a war that began with political ends in view. British Prime Minister Winston Churchill's main objective at this point of the war was to save as much of His Majesty's Empire and influence as possible. He therefore viewed the formulation of military strategy with a broad political perspective, one which went beyond the immediate military objectives of the moment to encompass the possible postwar political results of those judgments.

General Eisenhower and the American command, on the other hand, came from a military tradition able to sharply distinguish between military and political imperatives and act upon only those factors deemed to be in the province of the military.

This basic divergence in overall outlook would inevitably result in a major disagreement over grand strategy as the combined allied forces approached the Rhine. The British High Command's plan, as envisioned by Field Marshal Bernard Montgomery, favored one great stroke at Berlin supported by all other forces while the Americans, though not initially discounting that concept, generally leaned toward the more conservative broad front approach (with the prominent exception of Gen. Patton, among others).

Soon after D-Day (June 6, 1944) the debate began in earnest. Throughout the summer and fall Montgomery, commanding the Twenty-first Army Group, continually prodded Supreme Allied Commander Eisenhower to be permitted to launch a "full-blooded thrust" towards Berlin, an assault which he believed would require the fullest logistical support possible, and the "other Armies would do the best they could with what was left over."

Eisenhower, however, though agreeing Berlin was the ultimate goal, wished to approach it "with combined U.S.-British forces supported by other available forces moving through key centres and occupying strategic areas on the flanks, all in one coordinated, concerted operation." (September 15, 1944). Thus the narrow front approach of the British and the broad front approach of the Americans were opposite in concept to each other in the taking of Berlin, though that ultimate objective was agreed upon.

While Eisenhower was not, at this point, ruling out the possibility of a main drive through Holland and the north of Germany, Montgomery would not be put off. He continued to press Eisenhower on the issue with such vehemence that it became a source of irritation to Generals Patton and Omar N. Bradley. Montgomery also became a threat, in a sense, to Bradley and Patton in that they feared relegation of themselves and their men to a secondary role in the forthcoming campaign should the Field Marshal plead his case successfully. Patton believed that if his Third Army did not secure a bridgehead on the Rhine before the British did on his left wing, the result might be that "we lose troops to them and have to assume a defensive role. This was not at all to our liking."

By October 28, 1944, Montgomery's dogged persistence had some effect, but not that which he had intended. A directive issued after a meeting of Generals Eisenhower, Bradley, Montgomery and Air Marshal Arthur Tedder (Montgomery's deputy) was less specific and did not mention Berlin. The plan at this point remained directing a major effort in the north (Montgomery's area) to defeat the enemy west of the Rhine, and securing bridgeheads over the river. The next step would be to seize the industrial heartland of Germany, the Ruhr, and then advance deep into the Reich, final objective unnamed.

The advent of November 1944 brought even more unpleasant exchanges between Eisenhower and Montgomery with the latter stating the failure to implement the directive of October 28 had led to a "strategic reverse." Montgomery continued to be worried over what he considered to be a "fatal dispersal of strength and a disintegration of the Allied plans," and he, with the British Chiefs of Staff, judged that Eisenhower's plan for simultaneous attacks north and south of the Ardennes would leave that area vulnerable if the Germans chose to utilize any of their strategic reserve in a counteroffensive.

Hitler realized that there was strong dissension among the Western Allies over strategy, while at the same time the hordes of the Soviet Red Army continued their seemingly inexorable advance from the east. Germany still had a strategic reserve but it was the last it would be able to amass for a great offensive of its own. The Führer decided, against the advice of most of his generals, to make one last throw, its intent to split the Western armies in Belgium. The Waffen SS spearhead would be aimed at the Allied supply port of Antwerp. If successful, the American and British armies would be cut in two with the British isolated in northern Belgium where they could then be encircled and crushed. That would cause a rupture in the Western alliance and a negotiated peace might then be forced, leaving Hitler still in control of much of western Europe. The bulk of available German forces could then be turned to the east in an attempt to hold off Stalin's vast numbers.

An order to Hitler's commanders on November 25, began "This war will determine the survival or extinction of the German people. It demands the unqualified commitment of every individual. Even seemingly hopeless situations have been mastered by the blind courage and bravery of the troops, the stubborn steadfastness of all ranks, and by calm, unyielding leadership."

Eisenhower and Bradley knew of their vulnerability in the Ardennes area, of course, and Ike took complete responsibility for the weakening of the line. But it was Bradley who showed his overconfidence regarding the decision. When Gen. Walter Bedell Smith sent the SHAEF (Supreme Headquarters Allied Expeditionary Force) intelligence chief, Gen. Strong, to Bradley the first week of December with a warning that "the attack might come in the Ardennes or east of the Vosges whenever the Germans had a prediction of six days of bad weather . . . Bradley said let them come."

The men of the Waffen SS who would spearhead the attack still believed in Hitler. A young soldier in the Hitler Jugend division wrote to his sister on the morning of battle, "I write during one of the momentous hours before the attack, full of excitement and expectations of what the next days will bring. Some believe in living but life is not everything! It is enough to know that we attack and will throw the enemy from our homeland. It is a holy task. Above me is the terrific noise of V-1's and artillery, the voice of war."

The Waffen SS had become the single most potent strike force in the German army. The SS itself had begun as the bodyguard for Hitler in the late 1920s. The SchutzStaffeln, or Protection Squads, were of minor importance until an unassuming, seemingly harmless Nazi Party member named Heinrich Himmler was made their commander.

Always looking to expand his power until his death by suicide at the end of the Reich in 1945, Himmler enlarged the SS over the years until it became his personal empire within the Reich. When internal concentration camps were created the SS was reorganized into two distinct organizations: the Waffen, or Armed SS, the military arm, and the Allgemeine or General SS which controlled the camps. Himmler wanted military rank under Hitler, the Commander-in-Chief, and was able to convince the Führer that the Waffen SS would provide a loyal and brave counterweight to the Wehrmacht, the regular army which was still commanded in large part by old-line Prussian aristocrats.

The original Waffen SS division was the "First Liebstandarte Adolf Hitler" in 1933, followed as war neared by the Second, "Das Reich," and the Third, or "Totenkopf"—"Death's Head." These units came to be known as the 'classic divisions' of the Waffen SS. The Waffen divisions' numbers would increase geometrically as the war progressed, and especially after 1942, when the war worsened for Germany.

The Waffen SS first saw action in the invasion of the Lowlands in May of 1940, and then on to Dunkirk. With Western Europe secured, Himmler and the SS had to face their most immediate problem: manpower. The Wehrmacht was still in complete control of the recruitment-conscription of German citizens. Himmler did not yet have enough political power to circumvent that fact. He therefore decided to tap the populations of newly-conquered territories—Norway, Denmark, Holland, Belgium—which most approached the "Nordic" ideal he prized. These countries, in fact, already had quasi-Nazi parties in place. In Norway there was Quisling's Nasjonal Samling; in Holland, Mussert's Nationaal-Socialistiche Beweging; in Belgium there were the "Rexists" led by Leon Degrelle.

From these countries two regiments were initially raised. Danish and Norwegian volunteers formed the "Nordland" regiment, and Dutch and Flemings the "Westland" regiment. The regiments were combined with the "Standarte Germania" into a new division called "Wiking" (Viking), which became the first mainly non-Germanic born Waffen division.

By spring 1941 the Waffen SS order of battle included four divisions, two brigades and one regiment. An urgency had arisen to raise new units, for "Operation Barbarossa"—the invasion of Russia—was in the operational mode. Himmler felt this was the moment for his SS troopers to show their value as the vanguard of National Socialism.

In Barbarossa, Army Group C would attack Leningrad; Totenkopf and Polizei would accompany. Das Reich fought with Group B against Moscow. Liebstandarte and Wiking moved with Army Group A toward the Caucasus. They were to spend three horrific years in Russia, the units being transferred to the Western or Italian fronts by rail when they were needed to lead an offensive or hold a line. Mobility became the key to the Waffen panzer divisions; they could fight effectively on the Eastern front and in minimal time be available for action upon arrival in the west or south.

As of the end of 1940 six Waffen SS divisions had been formed. The following winter the German invasion of Russia was stayed by the weather, six miles short of Moscow. The Russian winter counteroffensive began in early 1942. With the fighting intensifying and casualties increasing, more divisions of high quality would be needed to help hold the two thousand mile eastern front.

During 1942 three more Waffen SS divisions were created. One was the Seventh, the "Prince Eugen," composed of racial Germans recruited in Yugoslavia. At this point Himmler needed recruits so badly to fill his ranks that the strict Waffen SS standards were relaxed to those of the Wehrmacht, the regular Army.

To expand the power of the Waffen SS divisions available, Hitler began to form "Panzer-Grenadier" divisions. Each would have tracked and half-tracked personnel vehicles. The offensive punch would be provided by a battalion of tanks or tank destroyers. The resources for the Waffen SS could thus be stretched, allowing the deployment of more divisions with more overall mobility.

In March 1943 the Norwegian, Dutch and Danish regiments were consolidated into the Nordland Panzer-Grenadier Division, with native Germans filling out the complement. The Belgian-Fleming unit, Flandern, became one formation, "Sturmbrigade Langemarck," which later was designated a division.

Politically, to foreign eyes the French volunteer regiment was most important. Originally known as the "Legion Volontaire Francaise," it was raised by French Fascists as the French Antibolshevik Legion in July 1941. It would later become the Thirty-Fourth Waffen SS Division, the Charlemagne. At the same time Degrelle's division, raised from his French-speaking Rexists in Belgium became the Twenty-Eighth Wallonien Division. In the course of the war Belgium provided approximately forty thousand men for the Waffen SS, half each from the Walloon and Flemish divisions. Holland provided the most volunteers, fifty thousand men in all over five years. France provided twenty thousand men, and Denmark and Norway each six thousand men. The greatest number of these volunteers joined toward the end of the war, and many died on the Russian front attempting to stem the Russian tide.

The legions were raised from the Volksdeutsche regions conquered by the Wehrmacht. In Czechoslovakia there were 250,000 ethnic Germans; in the Balkan states of Albania, Bulgaria and Yugoslavia, there were 750,000; Hungary had 500,000, and Rumania, 800,000. The Baltic states and Russia had a total of 250,000 ethnic Germans. The overall pool for conscripts was 2,500,000 men.

Degrelle was head of the Belgian Rexist Party and in 1941, after Germany had invaded Russia, offered to raise a volunteer battalion of Walloons. Speaking of the foreign legions who fought for the Third Reich in the Waffen SS, Degrelle said:

> Between that age-old Europe and the Soviet onslaught, its horrible leveling, the overflowing of its swarming little tribes, they made their choice at once. A new generation, all over Europe, took its stand. Blond giants from Scandinavia and the Baltic countries, Hungarian dreamers with long moustaches, stocky, swarthy Rumanians, enormous Croats with violet greatcoats; Italians, whimsical and sentimental; Spaniards with jet black eyes; bantering Frenchmen; Danes, Dutch, Swiss: all hastened to the battle for Europe. All the nations were there. We even saw some Englishmen volunteer, a dozen in all, a dozen nonetheless.

Almost all of these nationalities would fight for the capital of the Reich, Berlin. The Belgians who enlisted were grouped by language, one battalion each of Flemings and French-speaking Walloons. By 1943 the battalions had become brigades; in 1944 there were two Belgian divisions—the Wallonien and the Flemish Langemarck.

In the Belgian Ardennes the German army answered Bradley's challenge of "let them come." They did, in force, on December 16, 1944, when the spearheads of the Fifth and Sixth Panzer SS Armies led elements of twenty-eight divisions in the crushing assault on four divisions of the U.S. First Army holding a seventy-five-mile front. Under cover of fog which grounded the Allied air forces, the Fifth Panzer Army was nearly able to reach the Meuse River, the main objective before its ultimate goal of the port of Antwerp in Belgium, the major source of supplies for the Allied armies on the continent.

The subsequent disruption in communications and chain of command led Eisenhower to see the necessity of appointing one overall commander for each flank of the German salient. As a result, all U.S. forces in the north passed under Montgomery's command, and were thus reinforced by his own British reserves. At the same time, Bradley directed the southern operations and awaited Patton's counterattack with the U.S. Third Army.

The German salient in the Bulge was vulnerable simply because the operation's objectives were much too great. The German army could no longer exploit a massive breakthrough as it had three years before.

Patton force-marched the Third Army north to Bastogne (Belgium) to relieve the U.S. 101st Airborne Division there. The Fifth and Sixth Panzer Armies had not reached their objectives; the giant Tiger tanks that had accompanied the attack were not even brought to bear. The assault finally broke down completely and the Battle of the Bulge ended by January 28, 1945. Hitler's great gamble had cost Germany its last strategic reserve. The badly mauled Waffen SS divisions managed to withdraw to fight again.

The Western Allies remained torn by dissension. The idea of leaving U.S. forces north of the Ardennes under Montgomery's control was opposed not only by the commanders, but also by SHAEF and the U.S. War Department. Meanwhile the London press, extremely critical of Eisenhower, had been predicting just such a move. U.S. General George Marshall, expressing some of the nationalistic sentiment stirred up over the matter, had cabled Eisenhower on December 30, not to make any concessions whatsoever, for "You not only have our complete confidence but there would be a terrific resentment in the country following such action."

Affairs had now reached such a state that several of Eisenhower's advisors were suggesting a showdown with Montgomery, a confrontation of which SCAEF's (Supreme Commander Allied Expeditionary Force) own chief of staff warned him "someone would have to go and it would not be the Supreme Commander." Montgomery might well have sealed the fate of a Twenty-First Army Group drive on Berlin with his January 7, 1945, press conference. The Field Marshal suggested that he and the British forces under his command had "saved the day" in the Battle of the Bulge. Bradley and his Twelfth Army Group staff "were exasperated, if not outraged, by the interview." They felt the confidence of the U.S. soldiers and public in their commanders was at stake.

Bradley believed U.S. public opinion would not tolerate the battle south of the Ardennes to be neglected, while strongly reaffirming that it was politically important that the next, and last, major offensive of the Western front be given to a U.S. commander. To emphasize his point, Bradley threatened to ask to be relieved if he was placed under Montgomery's command. Eisenhower was under pressure for weeks afterward from other U.S. commanders and the press. He wrote to Bradley, "No single incident that I have ever encountered throughout my experience as an Allied commander has been so difficult to combat as this particular outburst in the papers."

Eisenhower's personal pride and Bradley's had been stung by this public display by a subordinate criticizing strategic judgements. Added to this was the feeling that Bradley and his Twelfth Army Group had not been receiving the credit they deserved for their efforts, and thus merited the directive and resources for the vital thrust into Nazi Germany.

Although factors other than military ones contributed to the decision, they did not, unfortunately, include political considerations in keeping with U.S. policy. This represented a frustrating obstacle to Churchill in his attempts to guide military planning in a direction which would materially aid the West in its postwar situation vis-a-vis the Russians. Within three years of the end of the war Stalin cut off all food, coal and other supplies to Berlin which necessitated the Berlin Airlift by the three other Western Allies (the U.S., Britain and France).

Soon after this incident the British Chiefs of Staff asked Eisenhower for a restatement of his plans. He provided one on January 20, 1945. It was essentially a very detailed elaboration of the October 28 directive, except that one very important sentence had been attached to the end, namely that in case of difficulties in securing Rhine crossings, the Supreme Commander was "therefore making logistical preparations which will enable me to switch my main effort from the North (Montgomery to Berlin) to the South (Bradley to the central industrial areas) should this be forced upon me."

By a monumental stroke of luck members of the Ninth Armored Division of the U.S. First Army found and secured intact the Ludendorff Bridge at Remagen, between Bonn and Koblenz, on March 7, 1945. This was the opportunity Bradley had hoped for but scarcely thought possible to reassert American preeminence in the final campaign. As early as February 21 in a message to Patton, Bradley was "indicating that the First and Third (Armies) were to play the major role in the next big attack" and that the time should be used to prepare to "be able to deliver a decisive blow when the proper moment came."

Whatever he thought, or knew of Eisenhower's intentions, Bradley was taking no chances. When Gen. Courtney Hodges of the First Army reported the capture of the bridge and requested permission to send a third division across to support the first two, Bradley replied, "Shove everything you can across it, Courtney." By chance, Maj. Gen. Harold Bull, Eisenhower's operations chief, was dining with Bradley that evening. Bull immediately realized that Bradley, by committing his forces across the Rhine, would now make priority claims on supplies. Bull therefore accused Bradley of trying to force Eisenhower to make a diversion of forces from Montgomery to Bradley.

In any case, Bradley and the U.S. army were across the Rhine in force. The army had to be supplied fully so that the coup would not turn into an embarrassing, abortive failure. Montgomery's British Army Group thus could not receive the absolute priority in supplies which he had demanded. And finally, U.S. public opinion had something to be quite proud of, and proportionately disappointed in, if the momentum were now taken away from their army.

Montgomery and the Twenty-First Army Group, after a long, deliberate buildup of forces, crossed the Rhine on March 23, 1945, while the breakout of the strongly reinforced Remagen bridgehead did not begin until March 26. That day Eisenhower summed up his feelings about the entire disagreement in a letter to Marshall: "I hope this does not sound boastful, but I must admit to a great satisfaction that the things that Bradley and I have believed in from the beginning and have carried out in the face of some opposition from within and without, have matured so splendidly."

The decision of whether or not to advance on Berlin with its capture the paramount objective was made solely by Eisenhower as SCAEF. During the crucial period at the end of March–beginning of April 1945, Churchill vainly attempted to sway President Franklin D. Roosevelt into sharing his concerns over ultimate Russian intentions, and thereby make him appreciate the need for an immediate drive on Berlin. The Prime Minister later wrote, "though I did not realise it the President's health was now so feeble that it was General Marshall who had to deal with these grave questions."

Marshall, chairman of the U.S. Joint Chiefs of Staff, felt that "The battle of Germany is now at a point where it is up to the Field Commander to judge the measures which should be taken." The Joint Chiefs concurred, and since the United States now had twelve million men under arms as opposed to five million for Britain, the combined chiefs of Great Britain and the U.S. were also bound to agree.

By then, the final decision had been taken. Not surprisingly, Bradley and the Twelfth Army Group were chosen to mount the decisive assault on the Third Reich. This fateful choice was transmitted on March 28, 1945, to the Western Allies through a copy "for information" of a telegram sent by Eisenhower to Marshal Josef Stalin—outside of established channels—that same day. The Supreme Commander proposed to divide the remaining enemy forces by striking through the center of Nazi Germany along an axis which would effect a juncture with the Red Army in the Erfurt-Leipzig-Dresden area, more than one hundred miles southwest of Berlin.

Prime Minister Churchill and the British Chiefs of Staff (not to mention Montgomery) were deeply disturbed over, first, the important shift in the strategic plan, and second, the method by which this shift was communicated directly to Stalin—a head of state—and not through the Combined Chiefs of Staff. Accordingly, Churchill wrote Eisenhower urging him to reconsider his plan in order "that the Ninth Army should march with the Twenty-First Army Group to the Elbe and beyond Berlin." He also wrote a mildly critical letter on April 1 to President Roosevelt, protesting the lack of consultation over the change in the overall strategic plan, and the way in which it was communicated to Stalin before the British themselves received word. In the letter Churchill also raised the political implications inherent in the capture of Berlin, especially by the Western Allies.

Eisenhower's reply to Churchill reaffirmed his own plan and assured him (in the unlikely event), "If at any moment collapse should suddenly come about everywhere along the front we would rush forward, and Lubeck (a port city controlling the Baltic sea) and Berlin would be included in our important targets."

Churchill, in turn, reiterated his position on April 2, and closed the argument by stating, "Much may happen in the West before the date of Stalin's main offensive." During this same period Marshall and Eisenhower also corresponded, and the U.S. Chiefs strongly reconfirmed their support for the Supreme Commander.

It seems quite probable that the continued and persistent criticism by the British, particularly Montgomery, led in large part to the denial of the decisive drive on Berlin—and the resultant glory accompanying it—to the Twenty-First Army Group. By the same measure it coalesced with the desire on Eisenhower's part to have Bradley, an old and valued friend, lead a total of forty-eight divisions, the largest *exclusively American* force in history, on the great drive into the heart of Nazi Germany.

Marshal Stalin was quite ready to accommodate Eisenhower's displacement of the last major Western drive to the southern American sector, with its final objective being the industrial area, Leipzig-Dresden. His reply to Eisenhower's telegram of March 28 agreed that Berlin had lost its former strategic importance, and that the Soviet High Command planned "to allot secondary forces in the direction of Berlin." These "secondary forces" equalled 750,000 men and eleven thousand artillery pieces under Marshal Georgi Zhukov, with flank support from another 500,000 men and an equal number of artillery pieces under Marshal Ivan S. Koniev.

During the first week of April 1945, Churchill nearly succeeded in getting Roosevelt to take a hard line with the Russians. After Stalin accused Churchill and Roosevelt of trying to deal with representatives of the *SS* behind his back, the President replied bitterly. Stalin backed down and apologized. This tougher policy toward the Russians did not last long, however, for sadly, within a week the President died suddenly of a cerebral hemorrhage in Warm Springs, Georgia, on April 12.

The political void left by the death of the man who had been President for over twelve years is not easily measured. In that void the new U.S. President, Harry S. Truman, would have liked to act if possible, but he felt constrained by the late President's previous agreements on postwar occupation zones at the Yalta Conference.

Meanwhile, on April 11, spearheads of Simpson's U.S. Ninth Army reached the Elbe River with Berlin fifty miles distant. The final Russian offensive had not yet begun. General William H. Simpson was notified by Bradley on April 14 to hold his position. Simpson, with fifty thousand men ready to go for Berlin, was stunned: "I could be in Berlin in twenty-four hours."

It was Patton who would have the last word: When Eisenhower informed him "it is highly inadvisable for the American Army to take Berlin," Patton replied, "Ike, I don't see how you figure that out. We had better take Berlin quick—and then on to the Oder!" The conversation was taken up again soon after, with Patton stating Simpson could take the city in forty-eight hours. "Well," Eisenhower asked, "who would want it?" Patton responded, "I think history will answer that question for you."

Stalin, at least, clearly saw eminently redeeming value in taking Berlin. So did Churchill. He realized Berlin was of immense political and psychological importance and that the capture of this symbol of the heart of the Reich would signal the emotional end of the German people. He reasoned further that the Red Armies would no doubt overrun Austria and capture Vienna. Therefore, he wrote to Roosevelt on April 1, just eleven days before the latter's death, "If they also take Berlin will not that they have been the overwhelming contributor to our common victory be duly imprinted in their minds, and may this not lead them into a mood which will raise grave and formidable difficulties in the future?" Already Churchill and Roosevelt were having problems with Stalin over the governing of Poland, and, clearly, as more territories were being continually overrun by the Red Armies only more difficulties would arise.

Stalin also knew of the divided strategic intentions of the Western Allied armies and it pleased him. He had no doubt as to where his Red Army was going: Berlin. While the Britons and Americans had been feuding over which route and which objective was most important, Stalin had been amassing more than 1,500,000 men to be aimed at one city, the capital of the Third Reich.

Marshal Zhukov would lead approximately 770,000 men in his central thrust at Berlin. He asked Stalin to support him with a minimum of 250 pieces of artillery for each square kilometer to be attacked; this amounted to one cannon for every thirteen feet of frontage. His attack would begin with eleven thousand guns.

Marshal Koniev would attack Berlin from the south with 512,000 men. He wanted the same artillery density as Zhukov would have, 250 guns for each kilometer of front. Zhukov had eight armies available for his attack; Koniev had five. Marshal Rokossovskii, in a supporting drive, was to move north of Berlin with the intent of cutting it off from the rest of Germany. He had 314,000 men. The total for the three army groups was 1,594,000 men.

Hitler, in a habitually-deluded state of mind, decided that the battle for Berlin would be the decisive engagement which would finally halt the Russian tide. He planned to concentrate all possible forces against the Russians; for the moment there was still hope that the allies on the Western front would split. There was also the belief that the Americans and the British would come around to the notion that Communist Russia was the true enemy and join with Germany against the East.

The man in charge of the German defense on the Oder River front, east of Berlin, was General Gotthard Heinrici. When the German drive into Russia stopped in the snow in 1941, Heinrici had the task of holding the position of the Fourth Army, directly opposite Moscow. Heinrici utilized a technique of defense Hitler would have had him shot for had he known. Defying the Führer's dictum to stand one's ground to the death, whenever a counterattack by the Russians was expected Heinrici would withdraw his troops several miles behind the front to a secondary position. The massive artillery barrage would then fall on empty positions. Heinrici had never been a favorite of Hitler because of his Christian religious beliefs, but after a forced leave of absence the general was brought back to hold the line of the Oder, and Berlin.

Marshal Zhukov had roughly twenty thousand assorted artillery pieces and mortars with which to attack Berlin. Heinrici had a total of 744 guns with six hundred antiaircraft guns converted for artillery use. Heinrici's defense was crippled by the stripping of several of his panzer divisions. They were to be sent to the defense of Prague in accordance with Hitler's belief that a major Russian attack would occur there. Meanwhile the greatest onslaught of the war since Germany's attack upon Russia would soon fall in the opposite direction.

On the morning of April 16, 1945, between 4–5 A.M., close to half a million shells hit the German lines which had been temporarily abandoned by Heinrici. He had his men withdraw several miles to secondary defensive positions on the Seelow Heights above the Oder River. If Marshal Zhukov's offensive was to be stopped somehow short of Berlin it would be in the valley of the Oder into which the Red Army would cross. On it all of Heinrici's guns of the Third and Ninth Armies were trained.

To ensure that the men of each division would at least have a small fighting chance Heinrici had distributed his guns all along the line. By doing so there was no chance for mounting a counterattack, and even so the defense could not hold long. The Eighth Guards Army led Zhukov's attack supported by 6,500 fighter planes and bombers. On the heights the Fifty-Sixth Panzer Army fought desperately to hold on. It did, but for only three days. On April 18, a savage hand-to-hand battle was fought with the Waffen *SS* Nederland Panzer Grenadier Division of Dutch volunteers thrown in to counterattack. They were far too few, though, and by nightfall Zhukov had the Seelow Heights and his army group had its road open to Berlin.

To the south, Koniev and his 500,000 men had already secured bridgeheads over the River Neisse on the first day. By April 17 it was obvious to everyone, even Hitler, that Berlin was the main objective and not Prague. Heinrici rued the seven more panzer divisions he would have had if Hitler had not ordered them toward Prague: "If I had them, the Russians wouldn't be having much fun now."

German counterattacks failed. The autobahn bridges heading west to the capital were blown up. All available planes, including the latest Messerschmitt jets, were sent up to try to halt the Red Army. Hitler still declared, "The Russians are in for the bloodiest defeat imaginable before they reach Berlin!"

By the afternoon of April 19, the Russians had broken through at several points into the open country before Berlin. The city that had been home to four million people at the beginning of the war had had its numbers reduced to half that, and only about ten percent were under the age of thirty. Those inhabitants who were now being exhorted to fight block-by-block to the end were either teenagers of the Hitler Youth or over fifty year-old members of the Volkssturm, the Home Guard.

The chief members of the Nazi hierarchy had built the vast Atlantic Wall to defend the European coast, the Siegfried Line to hold the Rhine, and the Gustav Line to defend Italy to the south. No serious thought or effort was given to fortifying the capital of the Reich until the Red Army approached the Oder, forty miles away. No one believed the war would come to the gates of Berlin.

After the realization of Berlin's plight set in work began at a feverish pace. Four lines of varying strengths were constructed around the city. The outermost—and weakest—consisted mainly of linked natural obstacles such as woods and marshes, lakes, rivers and waterways. The local Volkssturm units were ordered to hold their ground in the extremely weak positions on the ring which ranged between twenty and thirty miles outside Berlin. Three concentric rings constituted the main defenses of the capital.

The first ring, sixty miles in circumference, lay around the outskirts of the city. Anything available which was heavy and could be used to stop tanks or artillery or men was thrown in. The ruins of buildings destroyed in Allied raids—cinder blocks, concrete rubble, railroad cars, wagons, even abandoned air raid bunkers—were utilized in linking together Berlin's rivers and lakes.

The city's middle ring had a circumference of twenty-five miles. If manned and armed properly it would be the strongest ring. Utilizing the Berlin railway system, deep track cuttings were converted into excellent anti-tank ditches. Trapped in gullies as much as one hundred to two hundred yards wide, tanks would be prime targets for gunners on the opposite bank.

The final defensive position, called the Citadel, consisted of government buildings surrounding the Reichschancellery in the heart of Berlin. The Chancellery contained Hitler's palatial offices and reception rooms from which the Führer had held sway over most of continental Europe. The building had become a bombed-out shell by early 1945.

Fifty feet beneath the Chancellery and its garden lay the Führerbunker, a warren of some thirty rooms constructed during the war as protection against Allied bombing raids. The day after the Red Army broke out towards Berlin, April 20, was Hitler's fifty-sixth birthday. He had ruled the Third Reich for twelve years.

Hitler awoke to a rather "loud" birthday present—another heavy bombing raid on his capital. The day was spent receiving high officials and officers, many or most of whom were planning their exit from a lost cause. Hermann Goering, Josef Goebbels and Himmler accompanied Hitler to the Chancellery garden where the Führer decorated members of the Hitler Youth who had knocked out Russian tanks with their panzerfaust—bazookas.

Afterwards, the last important Hitler situation conference took place. Besides SS Reichsfuehrer Himmler, Reichsmarschall Goering and Minister of Propaganda Goebbels, most of the Reich's top officials still in office were present. These included Grand Admiral Karl Doenitz, who would become Hitler's successor, Field Marshal Wilhelm Keitel and General Alfred Jodl, Party Secretary Martin Bormann, Reich Foreign Minister Joachim von Ribbentrop, and the man Churchill had called the second most important man in Germany, if not first, the Minister of Armaments Albert Speer.

There was only one real topic of discussion: would Hitler remove himself and all army and ministerial headquarters to the south of Germany, there to make a final stand in the mountains near Munich? Hitler's mountain hideaway, the "Eagle's Nest," was on the Obersalzberg, a peak surrounded by mountains seven to nine thousand feet high. All had antiaircraft gun emplacements. Most of those present at the conference urged the Führer to leave before retreat was completely cut off. It was clear the Russian armies had already won to the north and south of Berlin; Marshal Zhukov was advancing steadily from the east.

Hitler refused to decide one way or another, but did allow his generals and ministers to leave and continue preparations to move their individual units. Himmler and Goering were beginning to think in terms of succeeding to supreme power themselves, even though it had to be obvious it would be short-lived.

On April 21, Russian artillery had advanced close enough to shell the center of Berlin. Armored spearheads pierced the northern suburbs. To save his men Heinrici was planning to withdraw to better positions south southeast of Berlin, thereby effectively abandoning the city. By the next day Hitler had resigned himself to the end, but not without one last raging outburst in conference. In a three-hour session Hitler railed against his army, deserters, and traitors. There was, he alleged, universal treason, failure, corruption and lies. "How am I supposed to direct the war in such circumstances! The war's lost! But if you imagine I'll leave Berlin now, then you've another think coming. I'd sooner put a bullet in my brains!" Some observers thought he was having a nervous breakdown.

German radio announced on April 23 that the Führer would not leave Berlin, determined to defend it to the last. Reichsmarschall Goering, Hitler's designated successor, took it upon his own initiative to elevate himself to Führer.

From the Obersalzberg he sent a wireless to the Bunker:

My Führer!—In view of your decision to remain at your post in the fortress of Berlin, do you agree that I take over, at once, the total leadership of the Reich, with full freedom of action at home and abroad, as your deputy, in accordance with your decree of 29 June 1941? If no reply is received by ten o'clock tonight, I shall take it for granted that you have lost your freedom of action, and shall consider the conditions of your decree as fulfilled, and shall act for the best interests of our country and our people. You know what I feel for you in this gravest hour of my life. Words fail me to express myself. May God protect you, and speed you quickly here in spite of all. Your loyal—Hermann Goering.

Hitler was enraged. Goering was dismissed from all offices and dropped from the succession. At the same time Goering was attempting to claim the leadership of the Reich, Himmler opened negotiations through Count Folke Bernadotte, representative of the Swedish Red Cross. Himmler told Bernadotte that, "The Führer's great life is drawing to its close." He offered to surrender through the Swedish government. Germany would continue to fight the Bolsheviks in the East until the Western Allies came to relieve her. Unlike Goering, however, Himmler did not inform the Führer of his intentions and his treachery was not discovered for several days.

Himmler remained in accord with his leader on one point—that the Western Allies would recognize Russia as their real enemy. Hitler stated on April 26 that, "The British and Americans along the Elbe are holding back . . . I think the time has now come when out of a sheer instinct for self-preservation they must act against this belated proletarian Colossus, this Bolshevik Moloch . . .

"If I can win through here and hang on to the capital, perhaps hope will spring in British and American hearts that with our Nazi Germany they may after all have some chance against this entire danger. And the only man capable of this me."

He then reiterated his decision to stay in Berlin until the end: "First I must set an example to everybody I blamed for retreating, by not retreating myself. It is possible that I will die here, but then at least I shall have died an honorable death."

Hour by hour it became more apparent that it would occur soon. Those generals who still obeyed his orders were not succeeding in repulsing the Russians, while the disobedient chose to attempt to save the remnants of their men instead of trying to relieve Berlin. SS General Steiner, ordered to attack Zhukov's northern flank to take pressure off Gen. Hasso von Manteuffel's Third Army, procrastinated his way out of it. Heinrici had already decided to withdraw beyond the capital.

The crack Russian soldiers who led the attack on Berlin were not, in the main, opposed by their counterparts in the German army. Instead Hitler Youths, some three thousand organized into "tank-killer" brigades, defended bridges with their panzerfausts. Men too old for regular military service manned makeshift barricades as the Home Guard. More often than not they lacked supplies of ammunition or had mismatched captured ammo—Czech bullets for Italian rifles, etc. But perhaps the most paradoxical, ultimate defenders of Berlin were the members of the foreign legions of the Third Reich. These were the members of the Waffen of whom Legrelle, the Walloon, wrote, "They wanted to obey right up to the end—and the last fighters, if necessary, on ground that wasn't even theirs."

Making their last stand at the heart of the Reich, defending the Führerbunker, were men of nine other nations, volunteers all. The Waffen SS Panzergrenadier Division Nederland and the Eleventh SS Panzergrenadier Nordland were made up of Dutch, Danes, Norwegians and Swedes.

The Fifteenth Waffen SS Grenadier Division Latvia I's members came from

Latvia and Estonia. French, Spanish and Swiss constituted the Thirty-Third Waffen *SS* Grenadier Division Charlemagne.

While Germans, those too young and too old, and foreign volunteers fought ferociously in the rubble above, Hitler was making his ultimate decision: to abandon them and the German people to their fate. Reports on April 27 confirmed that no German armies would get through to the besieged city.

On April 28, Hitler learned of Himmler's treasonous negotiations. "He raged like a madman, his colour rose to a heated red, and his face was almost unrecogniseable." This was the final stab in the back. During the night of April 28–29, Hitler dictated his last will and testament and then married his longtime mistress, Eva Braun. At 3:30 P.M., April 30th, Braun bit down on a cyanide capsule. Hitler shot himself through the right temple with a Walther PPK 7.65 MM pistol. Their bodies were burnt in the Chancellery garden.

Degrelle wrote, "The armies were no longer fighting, not because they lacked courage or discipline, but because there was no longer any front, any Panzers, any ammunition, or any liaison. The roads were kilometers of suffering, hunger, and blood. The death of Hitler meant the end of the struggle in Germany."

The last remnants of the Berlin garrison continued to fight. On May 1, German radio announced, "Our Führer, Adolf Hitler, fighting to the last breath against Bolshevism, fell for Germany this afternoon." The Red flag rose over the Reichstag the same day.

The street-to-street fight for Berlin ended on May 2, 1945, with the surrender to the Red Army of the Berlin garrison by its commander, Gen. Erich Weidling. The vast imperial city was a burning ruin; more than 1 million homes were no longer habitable.

The occupation of Berlin began with several weeks of rampant rape and looting by the Soviet Red Army. Official looting took the form of stripping Berlin's major industries and shipping it to the Soviet Union. Stalin, in fact, delayed the entry of Allied troops into Berlin so that his looting of the industries could be completed. On May 12, 1945, Prime Minister Churchill, in a telegram to President Truman, stated that "An iron curtain is drawn down upon their front, and we do not know what is going on behind."

At least 100,000 Russian soldiers, 100,000 German civilians and tens of thousands of German soldiers and foreign volunteers died for Berlin.

---

Berlin and Adolf Hitler were symbiotically joined forever. To take one was to take the other; the Third Reich would join the plunge into the abyss.

Hitler's last defenders in his Bunker were Germans, of course, but also Waffen *SS* volunteers from nine other countries—Dutch, Danes, Norwegians, Swedes, Latvians, Estonians, French, Spaniards, and Swiss who stood until the end. They fought for an ideal, a deep-seated antagonism to communism, and a loyalty to Hitler and the precepts of Nazism. Their leader and ideal mattered more than their country of birth or race; they died around the burning ruins of the Reichschancellery.

The defense of Berlin, the capital of Germany and the Reich, was ultimately hopeless against insuperable odds, yet it showed the unquenchable desire of the German people and others from Western Europe to preserve the country as a whole—a bulwark against Bolshevism in the East.

That desire has remained as a potent force to this day and with the reunification of the German nation-state a seeming inevitability, the other states of Western and Middle Europe now face the prospect of a giant economic and military force, the largest in the region other than European Russia. Today the Union of Soviet Socialist Republics has breakaway states wishing and working for democracy, and the specter of its former greatest enemy, with a population of over eighty million, standing once more on the horizon.

# 11

# DIEN BIEN PHU, 1954

ON DECEMBER 3, 1953, Lt. Gen. Henri-Eugène Navarre, commander-in-chief of French-allied forces in northern Vietnam, decided to commit his forces to a pitched battle with the Communist Viet-Minh at a small overgrown airfield in northwest Vietnam.

Navarre issued his orders:

> I have decided to accept the battle in the Northwest under the following conditions: 1) The defense of the Northwest shall be centered on the air-land base of Dien Bien Phu which must be held at all costs. . . .
>
> In view of the remoteness of the northwestern theater of operations and the logistical obligations of the Viet-Minh, it is probable that the battle will be fought according to the following scenario:
>
> The movement phase, characterized by the arrival of the Viet-Minh units and their supplies in the Northwest, whose duration may extend over several weeks.
>
> An approach and reconnaissance phase, in the course of which enemy intelligence units will make efforts to determine the quality and the weaknesses of our defenses and where the [enemy's] combat units will proceed with the positioning of their means of attack. That phase may last between six to ten days.
>
> An attack phase lasting several days (according to the means employed) and which must end with the failure of the Viet-Minh offensive.

The French high command was right about the first phase: the movement phase lasted several weeks. The second phase, approach and reconnaissance, lasted nearly one hundred days, until "A-Day," March 13, 1954. The attack phase did not last for several days; it went on for fifty-six bloody and unrelenting ones.

Dien Bien Phu means the "Seat of the Border County Prefecture," named for its proximity to the Laos border. Long a market town for local opium growers, it received the attentions of both the Japanese and Chinese Nationalist forces in World War II. The French finally recovered it in 1946. Six years later, three regular Communist divisions of the Viet-Minh attacked the center of French defense in the region, an airstrip called Na-San.

The garrison there was a hastily gathered collection of French paratroops, Foreign Legionnaires, Vietnamese, Moroccans, and local T'ai mountaineers. Na-San was ringed by two lines of mutually supporting automatic weapons, with central fire support from the airstrip's howitzers. General Vo Nguyen Giap, commanding the Viet-Minh, decided to implement "human wave" attacks which had been successful in Korea. Giap ordered two divisions to attack. The outer line was breached twice but the French and colonial troopers held; the Viet-Minh gave up the assault. Unfortunately, the victory at Na-San engendered French belief that well dug-in troops in an organized fire position could hold out and eventually win over numerically superior forces.

Despite a small victory at Na-San, the French were forced to retire from the northwest. On November 30, 1952, Dien Bien Phu was evacuated. An intelligence officer explained, "Dien Bien Phu is not a strategic sector. At times in the past, rebel bands have penetrated it but have let it go again. Their occupation of this hole-in-the-ground isn't yet the invasion of Laos."

Dien Bien Phu's importance grew as the French high command studied the Viet-Minh's strategy in North Vietnam. Henri Navarre was designated military commander of French Indochina on May 28, 1953. "Navarre is master of his nerves; Navarre won't stand for a job sloppily done; and Navarre never admits extenuating circumstances." (Max Olivier, "Indochina Sud Est Asiatique," Feb., 1954)

*Time* magazine published a cover story on Navarre on September 28, 1953. The commander was described to be "the hardest general I know—clever and ruthless. He believes in nothing but the army." An American comment followed: "In our opinion, Navarre is a man of courage, energy and imagination. He knows his business and has military and political guts of a high order . . . [he] is leading a new team which looks pretty good to us." *Time* concluded its profile of the general with this quote, "A year ago none of us could see victory. There wasn't a prayer. Now we can see it clearly—like light at the end of a tunnel."

On July 24, 1953, Navarre addressed the National Defense Committee of France. Present were the Joint Chiefs, the Prime Minister, the ministers of Foreign Affairs, Finance, the Interior, Defense, Overseas Affairs and Indochina Affairs, and the service secretaries. The President of the Republic presided. The meeting was indecisive; it seemed to have been left up to Navarre whether to seize and hold Dien Bien Phu, and with it the key to Laos. Since that country had been the first of the three Indochinese states to sign a treaty with France (the others were Vietnam and Cambodia), Navarre felt there was an obligation to at least attempt to hold the base which could keep that country intact.

If the French were to hang on to Dien Bien Phu it meant attempting to control seventy-five square miles of land in the bowl of the valley. The valley had a perimeter of about fifty miles, and could possibly require as many battalions as perimeter miles to defend it. Instead of fifty the French would have ten battalions at most.

Nevertheless, Navarre went ahead with the reoccupation of Dien Bien Phu. Brigadier Gen. Jean Gilles, commander of French airborne forces in Indochina, chose his two best battalions—the Sixth Colonial Parachute Battalion and the Second Battalion of the First Regiment of the Parachute Light Infantry—for the first drop. The generals were not sanguine about the operation. General Pierre Bodet, Deputy Commander-in-Chief in Indochina, said: "The way it looks, it ought to come off all right but if the situation is really too tough down there I leave you to judge as to what you have to do in order to save the maximum of personnel and to get out. In any case, if the weather is too unfavorable tomorrow, Dien Bien Phu will never take place."

Over 1,500 men, both French and Vietnamese, jumped on November 20, 1953. They were parachuting into a rest and training area for the Viet-Minh, who thought they were far from any major French operational area. Missed drop zones and delays in the arrival of support artillery hampered the assault, but by nightfall three mixed French and allied battalions had secured Dien Bien Phu.

The Paris press reported "Lightning-like Operation in Tongking—Parachuted from 150 Dakotas, Thousands of French-Vietnamese Paratroopers Conquer Dien Bien Phu . . . 'This is not a raid. We've taken the place and we shall stay there,' declares Gen. [René] Cogny."

The daily *Le Monde* got to the real center of Vietnamese concern over Dien Bien Phu. "It is not certain, however (that the enemy), will not soon react. The whole area of Dien Bien Phu, and the whole T'ai country in general, is a major opium-producing area, from which the Viet-Minh draws many of its resources and particularly the means of paying the deliveries in matériel, arms and ammunition from Communist China. Ho Chi Minh also uses clandestine sales of opium in all of Indochina to finance his intelligence services and his propaganda and to pay his troops."

French troops were not entering the valley in force but with insufficient numbers of armor, artillery and aircraft support. The Viet-Minh's high command was being offered a large prize: continued opium royalties and a major

French garrison which could be overcome if a much-superior force of fire-power and infantry was brought to bear.

It took nearly one hundred days for the Viet-Minh to organize a concerted attack on Dien Bien Phu. During the period the French command decided to make the fortress a position on which the Viet-Minh would expend their troops in massive attacks and suffer a catastrophic loss.

To fortify the position nearly twenty strongholds on the outlying hills were established. Each one would be paid for heavily in blood, both French and Viet-Minh. Fifteen thousand French and allies eventually would occupy Dien Bien Phu, outnumbered by from four to six to one at any given time.

General Cogny and his staff sent their real feelings forward to the high command: "I am persuaded that Dien Bien Phu shall become, whether we like it or not, an abyss for the battalions, with no possibility of large-scale [actions] radiating out from it as soon as it will be blocked by a single Viet-Minh regiment."

The airfield was reinforced with steel plates to counter the mud from the spring rains and the shell holes created by Viet-Minh artillery. Navarre, commander in Saigon, and Cogny, commander in Hanoi, never agreed on basic strategy. Navarre ordered the town to be turned into a "jungle fortress" which supposedly would be the rock on which the Communist tide would break. The garrison had to not only hold very long perimeters but at the same time deploy deep reconnaissance patrols which amounted to half the fort's available strength. Time for building defense works was minimal until the command in Hanoi realized that a Viet-Minh attack was imminent.

General Vo Nguyen Giap, commander of the Viet-Minh, realized that the siege—which would commit fifty percent of their forces to one battle—was an immense gamble. The preparation required one hundred days because, "we came to the conclusion that we could not secure success if we struck swiftly. In consequence, we resolutely chose the other tactics: To strike surely and advance surely. In taking this correct decision, we strictly followed this fundamental principle of the conduct of a revolutionary war: Strike to win, strike only when success is certain; if it is not, then don't strike."

By March 13, 1954, the Viet-Minh had 49,500 combatants, infantry and artillerymen surrounding Dien Bien Phu, with 31,500 logistical support troops. The French had put together a force of 13,200 men, of whom about seven thousand were top-notch fighters—paratroopers and Foreign Legionnaires. The rest were a mix of North Africans, allied Vietnamese and T'ai tribesmen.

The French were thus outnumbered by at least five to one, with reinforcements available only from the air. The Viet-Minh could march their cadres in overland through jungle cover. The French army had opted for a battle whose uneven proportions had not been experienced within nearly a century, since the Franco-Prussian War (when the proportions were ten to one at the battle of Sedan on Sept. 1, 1870, where 200,000 Prussians fought against twenty thousand French).

"A-Day": March 13, 1954. The first day of the siege of Dien Bien Phu began with tremendous Viet-Minh artillery barrages directed at the airfield. Giap had made his most intelligent tactical maneuver his first: the destruction of the airfield and aircraft based there. Two French reporters arrived at 3:10 P.M., on the last Dakota transport to land safely. In the officers mess they discussed the attack which all believed would occur that night.

"What do you think, fellows?" said Lebon. "It's going to be the great show this time."

"You can say that again," said one of the Foreign Legion officers. "The curtain-raiser already has begun. Giap's boys are already giving us their best cards: 81-mm. mortars, 120-mm. mortars, 105-mm. howitzers—the whole works."

"It's going to be like Na-San, only ten times bigger."

"Or almost Verdun! This time they'll put all their big artillery here and will show us what they have learned about big-war fighting."

The regular infantryman in the trenches and bunkers knew it was coming, too. A Sergeant Kubiak of the Foreign Legion, stationed on the northeast position, the Hill Beatrice, was visited by a lieutenant. The officer announced that "the Viet-Minh would attack at 5 P.M., and see that your machine guns would be able to fire throughout the night."

Kubiak thought, "we would have to consider as crazy the Viets who would have the idea to try and dislodge us from our Hill Beatrice, well fortified and defended by a whole Foreign Legion battalion. Believe me, it would be no simple walk in the sun for them!" The non-commissioned officer checked his guns, had a drink, and waited.

According to Kubiak, later that evening: "We are all surprised and ask ourselves how the Viets have been able to find so many guns capable of producing an artillery fire of such power. Shells rained down on us without stopping like a hailstorm on a fall evening. Bunker after bunker, trench after trench, collapsed, burying under them men and weapons."

By 6:15 P.M., the garrison on Beatrice was under heavy attack by assault regiments of the People's Army's Three Hundred Twelfth Division. Major Paul Pégot of the Legion called in final protection fire: artillery fire as near as possible to his own lines. A short time later the major and his staff died from a direct hit on the command bunker.

Companies now fought individually at their positions. At 10:30 P.M., Tenth Company was overrun. Near 11 P.M., Eleventh Company reported they were fighting around the command post—"Viets were all over the place." Then silence. The last message from the radio operator requested artillery fire on the last bunker and himself.

On March 14, the French prepared to counterattack for Hill Beatrice. Before it began, a truce to recover the wounded was offered by the Viet-Minh. Eight wounded were found along with the bodies of over three hundred Legionnaires.

The counterattack on Beatrice never occurred. If it had it would have involved the fort's strategic reserves of paratrooper battalions, its tanks and heavy artillery support. However, Gen. Christian de Castries and his staff realized that Giap would try to keep his momentum. Hill Gabrielle, the northernmost position, was the next target. Good news arrived at 2:25 P.M., with the parachuting in of the Fifth Vietnamese Parachute Battalion which immediately dug in. Hill Gabrielle's position was the best fortified of all, and was the only one with an inner, second line of defense. Ammunition and food rations for four days fighting had been issued, more than normal for any other position. The garrison was a mix of French and tough Algerians, the Fifth Battalion, Seventh Algerian Rifles.

Its commander, Maj. Roland de Mecquenem, was quite confident in his men and defenses. In his mess he had a cooler of champagne: "We're going to drink them together after the battle is over and the Viets are clobbered."

Unfortunately Giap had decided to commit elements of four regiments against Hill Gabrielle; the French were outnumbered by eight to one. Throughout the night of March 14, the Algerians and French fought at close quarters with infiltrating squads of Viet-Minh. Finally, with accurate French artillery support, the Communist attack broke off at 2:30 A.M., March 15.

An hour later the bombardment resumed. As had happened at Hill Beatrice earlier, a shell caught several of the commanding officers together. Orders had been given to keep the top officers and at least their second-in-command in separate bunkers to avoid losing both in one volley. But a meeting which was to last only a few minutes ended with all the chief officers seriously wounded and radio connection with the outposts and central command knocked out. Just before the meeting, Hill Gabrielle requested final defensive fire to the *second* line of defense. A counterattack from Dien Bien Phu with tanks and infantry was promised, if necessary. After the command post was hit young Capt. Gendre of Third Company, Foreign Legion paratroopers, took command of the Hill and from his post radioed a request for a strong counterattack. He was told to hold out at all costs; it would come.

Led by a tank platoon, the counterattack began at 5:30 A.M. Foreign Legion paratroopers followed behind the tanks in close support. But the new Fifth Vietnamese Paratroopers froze at 7:30 A.M., failing to support the Legionnaires, who pressed on anyway. On top of Hill Gabrielle handfuls of

Legionnaires were trying to hold out. The Third Company, toward which the counterattack was pressing, had waves of Viet-Minh continually hitting them. Legionnaires Zimmerman and Pusch of the Third each grabbed abandoned automatic rifles. The two of them cut down two assault waves but nothing could stop their numbers. With an Algerian sergeant they broke out using hand grenades. Any troopers able to get down the slopes toward Dien Bien Phu now did so. At the same time the tanks and Legionnaires of the relief force came into sight, too late.

Hill Gabrielle had fallen and would not be retaken. The loss of the strongest hill, along with Beatrice, cast a pall over the garrison. Hill Gabrielle had cost the French approximately one thousand combined casualties (killed and wounded). The Viet-Minh had lost that many dead plus and two–three thousand wounded. The losses had been some of Giap's best troops but he had ample reserves; if not quality, then quantity.

The commander of the French artillery had promised that his guns would keep Hill Gabrielle and the other positions unscathed. Colonel Charles Piroth said to his friend Col. Trancart, "I am completely dishonored. I have guaranteed de Castries that enemy artillery couldn't touch us—but now we are going to lose the battle. I'm leaving." Around dawn on March 15 the veteran Piroth, who was one-armed, lay down on his cot and pulled the pin of a grenade with his teeth.

No one else had given up, however. Seven hundred paratroopers dropped in the following day. De Castries's order of the day ended, "Everything rides on us here. A few more days, and we shall have won and the sacrifices made by our comrades shall not have been made in vain."

An impartial observer, the French photographer Jean Péraud (a survivor of Nazi camps) wrote from Dien Bien Phu that, "Our artillery smashed up by Viet-Minh—Attempt at embarkation of wounded under fire of Viet-Minh 105's—Tragic—Many wounded.—Gloomy atmosphere reminds of German concentration camps—Catastrophic."

Nevertheless, the French dug in deeper. The two overriding problems for the defense were, and would remain to the end, the vulnerability of air supply and reinforcement, and the exposed and enfiladed artillery.

The week following the loss of Beatrice and Hill Gabrielle was one of regrouping and consolidation of positions on both sides. Giap then initiated his next move: digging trenches to encircle and strangle each of the French strong points individually. To the oldest of the French officers memories of World War I became vivid again.

The first success for the French came on March 22. The furthest outpost of Dien Bien Phu was Isabelle, six miles to the south. It held 1,800 men and had eleven 105-mm. howitzers and three tanks. A Viet-Minh regiment had cut the road between the outpost and the main base.

The First Foreign Legion Parachute Battalion led by a tank platoon under Sgt. Ney, fought its way south while the tanks of Isabelle with Algerian riflemen drove north. The Communist regiment in-between was nearly annihilated and the road opened. The predominance of the paratroops, both French and Foreign Legion, led one of their own, Lt. Col. Pierre Charles Langlais, to take de facto command at Dien Bien Phu from de Castries on March 24. De Castries seems to have become more and more detached from the complex overall operations, and Langlais, in a fait accompli, simply took over responsibility: "Though I was only a simple paratroop lieutenant colonel at the beginning of the battle, I had directly under my orders ten thousand men; but nobody in Hanoi or elsewhere sought to deprive me of that handsome command. It would nonetheless have been easy to get to Dien Bien Phu with a parachute on one's back; or up to March 29 even by landing there. I was in the damned valley up to my neck and I stayed in it to the bitter end."

Langlais wanted to keep on the offensive constantly; de Castries, though relinquishing much authority, still had his hand in planning and believed the garrison should remain on the defensive until a relief force would be sent by Hanoi.

Enemy flak batteries continued to proliferate daily with Red China the major logistical source. De Castries realized that some of those batteries had to be eliminated to protect incoming men and supplies. Major Marcel Bigeard of the Sixth Colonial Parachute Battalion was given carte blanche to eliminate batteries to the southwest.

On March 28, the Sixth and Eighth Battalions set off behind a rolling barrage from the 105 and 155-mm. howitzers and 120-mm. mortars. A battalion of the Legion followed with another in reserve. A tank platoon rolled in support of the paratroopers. The sortie was completely successful. The batteries were captured, 350 Viet-Minh were killed, and cannon, anti-aircraft machine guns, automatic weapons and hundreds of small arms seized.

But the conquered ground simply could not be held. It was again time to return to the defensive. Giap had been preparing his next big offensive—the "Battle for the Five Hills."

The battle had become a siege of attrition and simultaneous attacks on five hills, Dominique One and Two, and Eliane One, Two and Four, would ensure heavy losses in men and ammunition on both sides. The five hills were directly to the south of hills Gabrielle and Beatrice, and Giap intended to acquire the whole eastern flank of Dien Bien Phu.

Langlais, however, deduced Giap's intentions. He therefore reinforced all positions east of the Nam Yum River, which basically consisted of the five hills. The Dominiques were lost; the Elianes held through successive attack and counterattack over two days of vicious close-in combat.

Repulsed on the east side of Dien Bien Phu, Giap turned his attention to the large northwestern sector, the strong points called the Huguette. Control of Huguette would completely eliminate the airstrip as a landing field or drop zone. Massive reinforcements by air drop was the only possible hope to save Dien Bien Phu. A top-level conference in Hanoi decided, however, that parachuting in complete battalions would not be ordered. The possibility of heavy losses and the diversion of needed space for ammunition and supplies argued definitively against it.

Of course, as Langlais and others pointed out, ammunition without men to fire it was not quite the answer either. Cogny agreed with those opposing massive reinforcement. Instead, he believed a major drive from the Red River Delta would free the besieged garrison. Colonel Sauvagnac, the officer in charge of paratroop replacements, said, "the only possible solution: the night-time dropping of personnel by single planes coming in at irregular intervals."

And so Dien Bien Phu would receive reinforcements a drop at a time, while Giap would have a flood. The attack on Huguette began in the night of April 1–2 and continued for four days.

Just as Huguette Seven, a hill on the northwest tip, was about to go under, French tanks and Legionnaires saved the hill and drove the Viet-Minh out. A heavy bombardment rained on the French for the rest of April 2. That night fifty paratroopers dropped. It was not nearly enough to replace losses. De Castries's staff estimated that even with a successful drop of one hundred men each night Dien Bien Phu could hold out for only fifteen more days.

Infiltration parties now began to use Bangalore torpedoes to blow gaps through the French barbed wire. Huguette Six was in desperate shape until Ney with his three tanks and the last reserve company were committed by Langlais. The Viet-Minh were again driven out. The most successful drop for some days that night brought in 305 men. Over the course of the fifty-five day siege, 4,277 soldiers jumped into Dien Bien Phu. Of those, 3,596 were qualified parachutists; 681 were not. The non-qualified jumpers, many first-timers, were chosen from a pool of 2,594 volunteers. They were volunteers who would jump blindly through flak, anti-aircraft machine gun and small arms fire into a valley of death and destruction. Of the 2,594 volunteers, 2,048 were Europeans, 451 were North Africans, and ninety-five were Vietnamese.

The first four days of the battle for the Huguettes cost at least 1,500 Viet-Minh and three hundred French dead. On April 15, Bigeard put together a mop-up operation to clear the final remnants of the Minh offensive from the Huguettes. By 10:15 A.M., the second major offensive against Dien Bien Phu was over. Five hundred more Viet-Minh dead were found.

While the battle for the Huguettes raged, an extremely important debate took place in Washington, D.C. "Operation Vulture" had been proposed. "Vulture" would be a massive air strike carried out by United States forces. U.S. Secretary of State John Foster Dulles had warned that the fall of Indochina might lead to the communization of all of Southeast Asia, and that "the United States might eventually be forced back to Hawaii." U.S. Air Forces estimated that a simple strike aimed at destroying Viet-Minh flak guns and artillery would require ninety-eight B-29 Superfortresses each carrying fourteen tons. Two wings would fly from Okinawa and one from Clark Field in the Philippines. Four hundred fifty U.S. Navy and Air Force jet fighters would be available to fly support. They would be particularly needed if Chinese MIG fighter planes entered the battle.

U.S. Congressional leaders, asked for support by President Dwight D. Eisenhower, stipulated their assent contingent upon three points: U.S. intervention must be part of a coalition to include other southeast Asian countries, the Philippines and the British Commonwealth; second, the French should hasten the independence program for Indochina so the U.S. would not appear to support colonialism; and third, the French must agree to stay in the war.

The requirement for a coalition served to make the possibility of U.S. air support academic because one could not be coordinated in time for the strike to help save Dien Bien Phu. Dulles is believed to have offered the French Foreign Minister, Georges Bidault, the use of two atomic bombs. Bidault politely declined, pointing out that the bombs would also annihilate the garrison along with the Viet-Minh.

Giap, meanwhile, had lost several thousand men in this failed attempt on the Huguettes but he had a reserve pool of 25,000 men in camps throughout the jungles of the north. The French had only the sky. By April 5, Giap had lost approximately ten thousand men in both massive frontal assaults and small, though numerous, infiltration attacks. He therefore decided, "To advance our attack and encirclement lines, improve our positions and occupy new ones; progressively tighten further our stranglehold so as to completely intercept reinforcements and supplies . . . utilizing trenches which have been driven forward until they touch the enemy lines, the tactic of gnawing away at the enemy piecemeal."

The French prepared another counterattack for April 10, aimed at retaking Eliane One. Bigeard planned a heavy barrage by all of Dien Bien Phu's 105s; 1,800 rounds would be fired in ten minutes. Mortars would open up and lead Bigeard's Sixth Battalion's advance by twenty meters. The artillery would continue its fire forty to one hundred meters ahead of the infantry. The last four tanks would direct their fire at the hilltop of Eliane One.

The Sixth Battalion numbered slightly over three hundred men. With so few men, Bigeard decided to use commando tactics, with small units advancing as fast as possible. The first wave could destroy enemy pockets; they did. Others were left for the second and third waves.

The Viet-Minh artillery commander could not bring his guns to bear because the French were intermingled with his forces. Two of Bigeard's companies took the crest; they were relieved at 4 P.M., by two fresh companies. Giap put a full regiment, with three battalions, against the French on sector Eliane Two, attacking at 6:45 P.M. The French company commanders were both wounded, and sector Eliane One was leaderless. Bigeard refused to relinquish his paratroopers' gains.

All counterattack companies were alerted; the First Foreign Legion Paratroopers supplied two small companies of fifty men each. Giap now threw another battalion into the fray. The French faced odds of ten to one.

The one hundred men of the reinforcing companies advanced on Eliane One. Someone began to sing. The French paratroops' songs, often from the original German, were taken up by the German Foreign Legionnaires. Both sides ceased firing momentarily. Then the relief companies were swallowed up on the top of Eliane Two. Bigeard decided to throw in everything he had left. The Fifth Vietnamese Paratroopers, who had faltered once before in relieving Hill Gabrielle, now had their chance to redeem themselves. Following the example of the paratroopers who had already been thrown into the caldron, the Fifth Vietnamese mounted the slope singing. They did not know the French paratroop songs, nor their German equivalent. In their stead, they sang what every schoolchild in French Indochina had learned: La Marseillaise was sung by Vietnamese advancing to fight Vietnamese in France's last great colonial battle there.

The First Foreign Legion Battalion and Fifth Vietnamese took and held the hill for the next twenty days.

Giap turned all his attention to seizing and destroying all air approaches, the landing strip and drop zones. Eliminating them would finally seal Dien Bien Phu's fate, barring a large scale outside intervention. On April 14, Giap had available 35,000 front-line infantry and twelve thousand artillerymen and engineers to throw at the airfield and its surrounding positions, especially the Huguettes. Langlais and de Castries had five thousand effective infantrymen, though most were top-notch French and Foreign Legion paratroopers.

De Castries sent a prophetic message to Hanoi command regarding their insistence on not dropping in unqualified parachutists:

> The fate of [Dien Bien Phu] . . . will be sealed by May 10 regardless of parachute training regulations . . . Evolution of [enemy] works threatens Huguette One and Huguette Six. Attempt at clearing Huguette One this morning fell upon numerous mined zones between Huguette One, Huguette Three and Huguette Five and mortar and artillery fire. Will be attempted again at nightfall at the same time as repairs on landing strip . . .

> Insist once more upon dropping each night five aircraft of personnel.

On April 15, C-119's (piloted by contracted-for American crews) and C-46's and C-47's (piloted by French civilian and military crews) dropped 250 tons of supplies. This represented two days' supply of food and nearly six days of artillery ammunition. Air supply in mid-April reached its peak, but as ever, supplies precluded reinforcements. Giap launched assault after assault on sector Huguette Six, commanding the northern end of the runway. The cost of holding and resupplying Huguette Six was deemed too costly, and Langlais and de Castries ordered it abandoned on April 18, Easter Sunday.

The garrison on Huguette Six was, however, given the option of surrendering or attempting to break out. For the French, Vietnamese and Foreign Legion paratroopers there would be no surrender. A breakout was planned using grenades as the main weapon.

The Viet-Minh expected an attempt from the south to relieve Huguette Six, not an attack from the north. At 8 A.M., on Easter Sunday, Foreign Legion Sgt. Ganzer opened up with the last automatic rifle the company had. He was wounded already and stayed to cover the breakout; he died within a few minutes. By that time, however, the French had blown a hole through the surprised Viet-Minh and raced to the outer lines of the main positions.

Huguette One became the new goal for Giap. Duplicating the envelopment of Huguette Six, the Viet-Minh infiltrated by means of at least thirty small trenches which had been worked up to the French perimeter. They then attacked in small squads of from five to eight men, not in human wave assaults. Huguette One fell.

At 7 A.M., on April 23, a few Legionnaires from Huguette One crawled through to Huguette Two. They said that the last thing they saw was their Capt. Chevalier making his last stand on top of his command post with a square of ten Legionnaires.

With the acquisition of Huguette One, Giap had virtual control of ninety percent of the airfield. Reinforcements via parachute became virtually impossible. Langlais and de Castries had to decide whether to attempt to retake Huguette One, guaranteeing devastating losses, or accepting losses and conserving the elite troops which remained for the attacks yet to come.

The decision was made to retake Huguette One, but only a half-hearted attempt was made. The fighters were so exhausted by this point that even Bigeard took a rest, leaving the operational command to a subordinate. Unfortunately, the officer in charge sat in his bunker, radio on the wrong wave length, and assumed the counterattack was going well.

Bigeard, summoned to check on the assault's progress by de Castries, saw the debacle in the making and halted the attack. A Lt. Geurin, deputy commander of the Indochinese Company, had his legs shattered by a shell during the retreat. His comrades began to crawl to him; he drew his pistol and shot himself in the head to save useless losses over retrieving him.

The three northern Huguettes had fallen and the airfield's drop zone was virtually closed. The victory cost Giap most of three regiments in dead and wounded, or over five thousand men. He acknowledged what the losses had done to the morale of the Viet-Minh:

> Our forces have not been able to avoid decimation, which requires rapid reorganization and reinforcement . . . among our cadres and combatants there appear negative rightist tendencies, whose manifestations are the fear of having many killed, the fear of suffering casualties, of facing up to fatigue, difficulties, privations . . .

Not until May 1 did Viet-Minh forces replenish their supplies and troops in order to be able to launch the final overwhelming offensive.

With the loss of the three Huguettes the drop zone for allied pilots had diminished so much that the transports had to fly ever lower into the flak. American pilots realized that in most cases they were taking even greater risks than the French Air Force pilots were taking. After their runs on April 24, American pilots refused to fly the often suicidal Dien Bien Phu corridor anymore. Supplies thus dropped radically, and on a clear April 28, with the monsoon relenting, no supplies whatsoever arrived. While Dien Bien Phu made do with what it had, Giap had called in reinforcements again. Raw recruits were assigned to veterans for training: two new men were placed with two veterans to form a "cell." By this means Giap was able to build his force to at least 35,000 men once more. At this point it meant the French were outnumbered by ten to one.

Four percent of the French military in Vietnam were holding sixty percent of the Viet-Minh to one area of operations, but whatever strategic gain accrued to the French meant nothing to the starving, wet and wounded men in the bunkers and trenches of Dien Bien Phu.

The most knowledgeable and hardened of the French veterans had even now not yet given up. They knew that a relief force was advancing east from Laos to their relief. With the suspension of "Operation Vulture," "Operation Condor" was enacted.

Three thousand men, slightly over half Laotian troops, with the Second Battalion of the Second Foreign Legion along with a commando group, had moved out by April 21, intent on drawing Communist forces away from the siege of Dien Bien Phu. By picking up reinforcements on the way, the force hoped to reach Isabelle by May 25. The inability of the French high command to deliver an airborne group to reinforce Condor forced the advance to stop. It never got close to Dien Bien Phu. In the fortress on April 29, an unusual ceremony took place. Lieutenant Genevieve de Galard, the only woman nurse in the garrison, was invited to the command post. There the chief officers, Langlais, de Castries, Bigeard and several others, decorated her for unstinting devotion in the care of thousands of wounded in the month she had been there.

She was given the croix de guerre with palms, donated by Langlais, and the white enamel cross with blood-red ribbon of the Knight's Cross of the Legion of Honor, given by an officer who had just won it himself. The French were making preparations for the end.

There was time for yet one more celebration, however. The following day, April 30, was "Camerone Day" for the Legion. On that day in 1863, sixty-five men of the Foreign Legion serving in Mexico for the Archduke Maximilian held off two thousand Mexicans at the walled hacienda of Camerone. Nearly all died; at the end of a day-long fight five Legionnaires who could still stand fixed their bayonets, and with one round in each rifle, charged.

It was the Legion's day, and in the middle of the jungle, surrounded by many thousands of the enemy, the garrison, both Legion and non-, celebrated. The American transport plane crews decided to help again considering the desperate situation, and dropped over two hundred tons of supplies. Due to the height from which drops were made plus the smaller target zones, losses occurred as usual. One loss would not be borne, however. Two crates of vinogel, which mixed with water made an awful wine, fell into Viet-Minh positions. A volunteer commando platoon of Legionnaires was immediately formed to rescue the wine needed for a proper Camerone celebration. The platoon proceeded to completely destroy one Viet-Minh blockhouse with plastic charges and heavily damage two others. They then secured the wine.

On Camerone Day the Foreign Legion could make a few non-Legionnaires into honorary members with low ranks, no matter how high they might be. De Castries and Langlais were made honorary corporals; Bigeard and nurse de Galard privates.

With May 1 came the gathering storm. The French now had about three thousand capable infantrymen in the trenches awaiting over thirty thousand of the enemy. Langlais was near the edge emotionally in trying to get Hanoi command to airdrop full battalions, entire and at one time, no matter the losses involved. The colonel was so worked up that he closed his message, "We will win the battle without you and in spite of you. This message, copy of which I shall transmit to all airborne battalion commanders here, will be the last I shall address to you."

Shortly after the message was transmitted Gen. Giap's artillery opened up along all fronts. The final attack was on. French and allied companies began to decide that all of Dien Bien Phu depended on their one small unit to survive, and acted accordingly.

On Dominique Three one company of paratroops, of the Sixth Colonial, with some T'ai tribesmen and Algerians stayed and fought it out until the end at 2 A.M., on May 2. Sector Huguette Five had thirty men left when the Communist wave hit. It went under at 10 P.M.

Another message went out to Hanoi:

No more reserves left. Fatigue and wear and tear on the units terrible. Supplies and ammunition insufficient. Quite difficult to resist one more such push by Communists, at least without bringing in one brand-new bathroom of excellent quality.

General Cogny in Hanoi finally decided, too late, to send in the last battalion of his Airborne Reserve, the First Colonial Parachute. At the same time in France, U.S. Air Force Globemaster transports were preparing to airlift 450 French paratroops, about one battalion, directly from their training schools to Indochina. They arrived there the day the fortress fell.

Eliane One was lost at 2:07 A.M., on May 2. Having lost about 420 men, nearly a battalion, the garrison received 107 men via parachute. Walking wounded were now being assembled from underground hospitals. A common remark was, if we've got to croak, we might as well croak with our buddies. Commanding Huguette Four was Capt. Jean Lucciani. He had been wounded three times already, and wore a heavy bandage over where one of his eyes had been.

Incessant monsoon rains flooded the trenches and hindered the already lessening supply drops. The question of a breakout by all able-bodied members of the garrison came to the fore. Cogny felt that an attempt to break out, given the condition of the men, would result in annihilation. A badly-defeated attempt would reflect poorly on the French also. "There will be neither capitulation nor rout under the pretext of a sortie. On the other hand those units whose leaders would still think them capable of it, would be given a chance to slip through." Nothing came of it.

At 12:20 A.M., on May 4, over three thousand men from four regiments of the People's Army struck an eighty-man company under the one-eyed Lucciani on Huguette Four. It was probably the most preponderant in numbers advantage that any Viet-Minh attack had during the siege. Two hours later Huguette Four still held, and there were hundreds of Minh dead on the barbed wire. At 3:35 A.M., the command post heard from a young lieutenant from the Moroccan platoon on Huguette Four: there were ten men left. A moment later the officers heard him die.

Also on May 4, de Castries began to come to himself again as the end neared. He wished to decorate all the seriously wounded but he had no medals to give out. Instead he visited the wounded in every bunker in the whole of Dien Bien Phu, touching every man's shoulder as if decorating him and saying his citation would be noted in the record books of the command. The decoration ritual took all day. It may be that some died the better for it.

A large, successful supply drop shortly after midnight began May 6. At 4:12 A.M., men of the First Colonial Parachute Battalion began to jump. Ninety-one men made it before the flight was aborted with the onset of dawn. Those ninety-one were the last to join the garrison before its fall at sunset the following day.

Langlais and de Castries still hoped that just one complete veteran fighting battalion would drop in—all together, equipped and experienced in fighting as a cohesive unit. With them perhaps Dien Bien Phu could hold off the numbers as they had held before when Hill Beatrice had fallen or Hill Gabrielle; the Huguettes and Dominique were under intense attacks. If they could get twelve quiet hours the drop would be made.

Intelligence was then informed by Hanoi that Giap's last attack would commence on the evening of May 6. The dozen hours would not be available. Everyone began to make arrangements as to how they would meet the final Communist assault. Captain Yves Hervouët, who had commanded the seven-tank squadron until both his arms were broken, went to the doctor and his casts were taken off. He wanted to fight in the last operational tank. Langlais and Bigeard personally placed their best remaining men and commanders on the Elianes. About 750 paratroopers were told not to expect infantry reinforcements, that ammunition would be short and artillery support minimal. "Adieuxs" were exchanged all around.

On Hill Claudine, a counterattack by members of the platoon of sappers of the Second Foreign Legion simply overawed the Viet-Minh. The sappers retook the hill but they and the men there could hold only until 2 A.M., on May 7.

At 3 A.M., Eliane Two blew up. Viet-Minh miners had tunneled beneath the position and one-and-a-half tons of TNT were placed under the strong point. The French sensed something of the kind was underway, but had not the means to definitively detect and stop it.

By 4 A.M., Capt. Jean Pouget, commanding Eliane Two, had thirty-five men who could fight effectively. Pouget saw how hopeless it was and requested permission to break out to Eliane Three. He was told, "After all, you are a paratrooper and you must resist to the death—or at least until morning."

Morning brought no respite. The clinging monsoon rain squalls continued to hamper further drops. Though some troops on Eliane Four attempted a breakout, the commander, Capt. Andre Botella, radioed, "Dede calling Bruno. It's all over. They're at the CP. Goodby. Tell that guy Pierre [Langlais] that we liked him a lot."

His last staff officer was a young Monaco-born lieutenant named Jean Armandi. He would not leave his chief or the wounded. When the Viet-Minh had closed in on the command post Armandi said to HQ, "I'm going to blow up the set," and then he yelled the French paratroop war cry, the simple "Hip-hip-hip-hurray . . ."

A breakout was still planned. Misgivings spread through the ranks when it became known that only those in the best shape who comported themselves well in the fighting would go. Even then, the choice was enmeshed; when the time came the two columns comprising the breakout would split up. A coin toss would decide the sacrifice—the winner would head into the jungles and on into the highlands. The loser would be bait for an eventual Communist mass attack.

In Dien Bien Phu the officers gathered to decide their course. A unanimous agreement was reached under which a cease-fire would take place at 5:30 P.M., on May 7, 1954. At that time the French, colonial and allied forces would surrender to the forces of the People's Republic of Vietnam.

In Dien Bien Phu itself the commanders prepared for the end. De Castries sent one last message to Hanoi high command, "I'm blowing up all the installations. The ammunition depots are already exploding. Au revoir." The reply was, "Well then, au revoir, old boy."

This was not the final communication, however, for fittingly, an unknown engineer spoke the last words from Dien Bien Phu: "We're blowing up everything. Adieu."

———

After the fall of Dien Bien Phu the government in Paris quickly followed suit. The collapse of the government, in turn, led to the demise of the constitution of the Fourth Republic. This first post World War II attempt at democracy in France failed four years after the debacle at Dien Bien Phu. France summoned Gen. Charles DeGaulle to head the Fifth Republic.

The battle has been compared by a contemporary French general with Waterloo. As at Waterloo, the outcome signaled the beginning of the end of empire. In this case France had effectively lost its Asian empire. The former imperial capital of Paris now held in its tenuous grasp its important Departemente (roughly equivalent to a second-level province of France itself) Algeria, along with numerous client-states and dependencies in Africa.

Within two months of Dien Bien Phu, on November 1, 1954, the Algerian National Liberation Front initiated an open offensive against French forces and civilians. Attacks later spread to mainland France itself, with anti-Gaullist officers becoming involved. Assassination plots against DeGaulle were attempted, and failed. By the time Algeria had been granted its independence by DeGaulle in 1962, other African dependencies had already achieved a quasi-independent status in the French Community (much like the British Commonwealth). Dien Bien Phu ended France's imperial progress, quite possibly forever.

After the fall of Dien Bien Phu the United States was forced to realize that Red China was not the only communist power to be reckoned with in

Southeast Asia—the forces of the Viet Nam People's Army had achieved a telling victory over the French empire. Had the U.S. committed the Air Force to support strikes against the besiegers of Dien Bien Phu it may well not have been necessary to fight a second war in Indochina, a war with American and not French dead.

# CONCLUSION

THOUGH NO ONE CAN SAY with certainty what a soldier faced with imminent death actually believes in at his last battle, there are certain values one can reasonably infer that bolster a warrior's will to stand and die. Most often, as might be expected, the individual soldier owes an allegiance to his state. Whether he belongs to a city or an empire, the soldier dies for the protection of the state.

Though he represents the state, more immediately the individual is part of a fighting unit, most often an elite. The soldier then is bonded to a group, whether small or large, which fights and dies for its own honor.

The men willingly die for their unit, their fellow soldiers, but when they have a leader they can trust, they fight to the end believing that somehow he will deliver them from death, or die with them. The leader can, through his charisma, instill in his men the will to stand and hold an extremely vulnerable position, or die in the attempt.

Finally, there are those who fight for their religion or an ideal. The idea, the symbol, is often more potent than the political fact. The idea can kill its believers who fight for it, yet still produce an effect much stronger historically than could be expected without the stand.

In considering the key factors, it becomes apparent that loyalty is the common denominator to all last stands, from Thermopylae to Dien Bien Phu, and beyond.

## LOYALTY TO STATE

In every battle all units fought for their state. All the soldiers were motivated, at least in part, to make their sacrifices out of loyalty to the country, state or political system to which they owed allegiance, by birth or belief.

The Spartans gave everything for their city-state even though it was not in immediate danger from the vast Persian army. In the Sicilian Expedition the

| | Loyalty to State | Elite/Pride in Unit | Loyalty to Leader | Ideology |
|---|---|---|---|---|
| I.) Thermopylae | Sparta | King Leonidas's Personal Bodyguard | King Leonidas | Greece versus "the barbarian" |
| II.) The Sicilian Expedition | Athens | Athenian Knights and Hoplites | | |
| III.) Chaeronea | Thebes | The Sacred Band | | "Platonic Friendship—Warrior Bond" |
| IV.) Aduatuca and Teutoberger Wald | Roman Empire | Legions of Rome | | |
| V.) Jerusalem and Masada | Judea<br>Judea | Zealots<br>Zealots | Eleazar | Judaism (in part)<br>Judaism |
| VI.) Stamford Bridge and Hastings | England | Viking Housecarles<br>King Harold's Housecarles | Harald Hardraada<br>King Harold | |
| VII.) Waterloo | French Empire (1st) | The Guard | Napoleon | The Revolution |
| VIII.) The Alamo | Texas | Individual Regional Units | Travis, Bowie and Crockett | (Freedom) |
| IX.) The Little Big Horn | United States | Seventh Cavalry | General George Armstrong Custer | |
| X.) Berlin | Third Reich | Waffen SS | Adolf Hitler | Nazism |
| XI.) Dien Bien Phu | France | Paratroops, Foreign Legionnaires | | |

knights and hoplites of Athens took the battle to their hated Spartan enemy's bread-basket, Sicily. The Sacred Band of Thebes died for their city-state, as did the Zealots for Jerusalem, Masada, and Judaea.

The legions of Rome died in the forests of the north to protect the Roman Empire from what they considered barbarian encroachment. At Hastings the king's housecarles and men of the fyrd were killed defending an Anglo-Saxon England against the Norman state. The three days of Waterloo saw the last of the French Revolution's Guard and many of its common citizen-soldiers fall for the First Empire.

At the Alamo soldiers from different regions of the United States joined themselves in death for the promise of an independent state of Texas and land for all its settlers. The Seventh Cavalry at the Little Big Horn fought for the United States and thereby its western expansion toward the Pacific. In Berlin the Waffen *SS* and the Home Forces attempted to hold the capital of Germany—soon to be divided. At Dien Bien Phu the French Legionnaires and Paratroops defended the last outposts of France.

## ELITE/PRIDE IN UNIT

In every last stand presented here we find elite troops. For example, the Spartans were the bodyguard of their king; the Imperial Guard of the French were veterans of two decades of conquest throughout continental Europe; and the Waffen *SS* were in the vanguard of the fighting from the English Channel to the gates of Moscow. The Athenian knights and hoplites, the most powerful forces of the city-state, lost their lives as members of proud divisions. And while the legions of Rome fighting in the forests of northern Europe represented the imperial state, each legion also had the pride of its divisional record to uphold and thus willingly died under the Eagle it bore.

At Chaeronea the hoplite Sacred Band died en masse, fighting to the death, every man with his companion. The Zealots and the Sicarii, though bands of market and street terrorists (who might have been motivated by religious ideals), were a special type of partisan fighter, both in Jerusalem and Masada.

Stamford Bridge saw the last of the Viking conquerors who had ravaged Europe, threatened Russia and repeatedly held the British Isles to the sword. At Hastings the housecarles of Harold and the fyrd of England fought for their king and their state. The members of the household formed the elite bodyguard of the leader, as at Thermopylae and Waterloo. The Seventh Cavalry, under the command of a man believed to be the best cavalryman of the Plains, considered itself a special unit, engaged in the country's expansion west.

Even at the Alamo, which involved a number of disparate regional units, the men held allegiances as volunteers—Crockett's Tennesseans, the New Orleans Greys, the Texans under Travis and Bowie, and other local companies. The Foreign Legionnaires and paratroop regiments who held the fort at Dien Bien Phu for fifty-five days took pride in their tradition of being among the best soldiers of the modern French Army.

## LOYALTY TO LEADER

The royal bodyguard of King Leonidas at the end fought out of personal loyalty to their commander. The Old Guard of Napoleon covered his retreat from his final defeat on the field of Waterloo. The wide array of citizen volunteers at the Alamo retained their individual loyalties, particularly to Colonels Crockett, Bowie, and Travis. The Waffen SS divisions that defended the Führer Bunker in Berlin also fought first for their commander.

Harold Hardraada's housecarles died in a shield ring around their chief; soon after King Harold and his brothers fell in the shieldwall of Hastings. Though the defenders of Jerusalem were led by leaders of rival factions, at Masada the besieged committed suicide at the command and request of their leader, Eleazar. Custer's men, the ordinary dogsoldiers who believed in him, died around him on a lonely hilltop.

## IDEOLOGY

The idea of freedom and democracy in Greece and the West kept the Spartans at their post in the pass. The French Revolution's egalitarian goals held Napoleon's veterans in a battle in which they were badly outnumbered. The Texicans were bonded together by their hopes for a union with the democratic promise of the United States. German defenders of Berlin fought for the idea of the Reich, however unsound that may have been, and for the territorial integrity of Germany, against the threat of Bolshevism from the East.

The Sacred Band at Chaeronea died in a bond of true warrior Platonic friendship in its original sense, man with man, fighting to the end. At Jerusalem and Masada the besieged Jews defended their strongholds partly for their religion.

A last stand is thus a time and a place when an end is made. The individuals and the causes for which they fought and died reflect the entire political and social spectrum, from the imperialist to the democrat, the religious fanatic to the atheistic fascist, the citizen-soldier to the mercenary, the conscript to the professional soldier, the serf to the king.

Even in cases where trapped with escape or surrender barely possible some men will still band together on a hillock, or behind their dead mounts, in a muddy ditch or the ruin of a fort and, in Kipling's words, "go to their God like a soldier."

As the previous chart shows, five of the battles considered here, Thermopylae, Masada, Waterloo, the Alamo, and Berlin, shared all the motivational characteristics of the last stand. On the other hand we find only two prime motivations—loyalty to the State and pride in an elite unit—were involved in battles at Aduatuca, the Sicilian Expedition and Dien Bien Phu. From this observation one might pose this question: Could an analysis of the number of loyalties shared by a particular group of defenders produce a model that will, if not *predict* the occurrence of a last stand, at least help determine when these soldiers will fight with unusual determination? This is not an easy question to answer, for the *intensity* of the loyalties felt is a factor as well as the number (and these human emotions are difficult to measure). Thus, a stand with the fewest galvanizing forces does not mean that the warriors necessarily fought with less spirit or intent, for as we have seen, the men at Aduatuca and Dien Bien Phu all fought to the last.

And yet, I believe that contemporary and future military planners should take into account, as much as possible, the motivational forces that guide the enemy forces. For example, at Dien Bien Phu the troops of the Vietnamese People's Army, in addition to their greater numbers, also shared more motivating loyalties than their French counterparts. They fought to free their country from a colonial power, for General Giap to whom they owed great loyalty, and lastly to a Communist ideology which promised the largely peasant conscripts a different future.

As I mentioned, an analysis of last stands throughout history should play a part in current military planning for, contrary to general opinion, last stands are not necessarily events of the past. As long as mankind wages war, last stands will be present as a phenomenon in history, regardless of the method of warfare. Even in the nuclear age, perhaps more so than previously, conventional warfare that is tactically designed to deny, absolutely, certain essential objectives to the attacking enemy (precluding the use of battlefield nuclear weapons), will call for the most determined, total effort of resistance by the defenders.

Last stands of the future will most likely involve the defense of bases housing nuclear weapons, both air and ground, strategic and tactical. If they have not yet been eliminated in an earlier strike they will be in danger of seizure by land attack. Similarly, armor marshaling points, especially in central Germany, will remain focal points of attack. Soviet and Warsaw Pact forces, regardless of possible impending political changes, still retain an overwhelming advantage in armor, over five to two, with reinforcements in troops and weaponry available by land from the U.S.S.R., while United States forces (and NATO principal reserve) must cover four thousand miles to the front.

In any case the confluences of the four loyalties—to the state, the elite unit, the leader, and the ideology—should remain the primary factor in the last stand.

Friedrich Wilhelm Nietzsche wrote in *Thus Sprach Zarathustra*, "We do not want to be spared by our best enemies. . . . What matters long life? What warrior wants to be spared?" The active death is chosen over the passive, the why and how of death known and accepted in advance of the irresistible fact of the impending event."

From Thermopylae to Dien Bien Phu, to this day and beyond, the code of death and sacrifice remains; it always will.

# SELECTED BIBLIOGRAPHY

## THERMOPYLAE

Burn, A. R. *Persia and the Greeks*. London: Edward Arnold Ltd., 1962.
Herodotus. *The Histories*. Tr. A. D. Godley. The Loeb Classical Library, London: William Heinemann Ltd., 1982.
Bradford, Ernle. *The Year of Thermopylae*. London: MacMillan London Limited, 1980.
Forrest, W. G. *A History of Sparta, 950–192 B.C.* New York: W. W. Norton & Company, 1969.
Grote, George. *History of Greece*. New York: Harper and Brothers, 1853.
Adcock, F. E. *The Greek and Macedonian Art of War*. Berkeley: University of California Press, 1957.

## SICILIAN EXPEDITION

Thucydides. *History of the Peloponnesian War*. Tr. by Charles F. Smith. London: Loeb Classical Library, 1928.
Diodorus Siculus. *History*. Tr. by C. H. Oldfather. London: Loeb Classical Library, 1946.
Grundy, G. B. *Thucydides and the History of His Age*. Oxford: Basil Blackwell, 1961.
Kagan, Donald. *The Peace of Nicias and the Sicilian Expedition*. Ithaca: Cornell University Press, 1981.
Westlake, H. D. *Individuals in Thucydides*. Cambridge: University Press, 1968.
Green, P. *Armada from Athens*. New York, 1970.

## CHAERONEA

*Plutarch's Lives*. Tr. Dryden, rev. A. H. Clough. Boston: Little, Brown & Co., 1881.
Ellis, J. R. *Philip II and Macedonian Imperialism*. London: Thames and Hudson, 1976.
Cawkwell, George. *Philip of Macedon*. London: Faber and Faber, 1970.
Arrian. *Anabasis Alexandri*. Tr. by E. I. Robinson. London: Loeb Classical Library, 1933.
Tarn, W. W. *Alexander the Great*. Cambridge: University Press, 1948.

## FORESTS OF THE NORTH

Julius Caesar. *The Gallic Wars*. Tr. by Rex Warner. New York: Mentor Books, 1960.

Dio Cassius. *Dio's Roman History*. Tr. by Earnest Cary. Cambridge: Harvard University Press, 1961.

Tacitus. *The Annals of Imperial Rome*. Tr. by Michael Grant. Harmondsworth, England: Penguin Books, 1973.

Tacitus. *The Agricola and the Germania*. Tr. by H. Mattingly, rev. by S. A. Handford. Harmondsworth, England: Penguin Books, 1976.

Velleius Paterculus. *Compendium of Roman History*. Tr. by Frederick W. Shipley. Cambridge: Harvard University Press, 1955.

Sextus Frontinus. *The Stratagems*. Tr. by C. E. Bennett. Cambridge: Harvard University Press, 1969.

Grant, Michael. *The Twelve Caesars*. New York: Charles Scribner's Sons, 1975.


## JERUSALEM AND MASADA

Josephus. *The Jewish War*. Tr. by G. A. Williamson. Harmondsworth, England: Penguin Books, 1976.

Grant, Michael. *Herod the Great*. London: Weidenfeld and Nicolson, 1971.

Grant, Michael. *The Jews in the Roman World*. London: Weidenfeld and Nicolson, 1973.

Webster, Graham. *The Roman Imperial Army of the First and Second Centuries A.D.* New York: Funk & Wagnalls, 1969.

Yadin, Yigael. *Masada: Herod's Fortress and The Zealots Last Stand.*


## STAMFORD BRIDGE AND HASTINGS

*The Anglo-Saxon Chronicle*. Ed. D. Whitelock. Rutgers, N.J.: 1961.

Furneaux, Rupert. *Conquest 1066*. London: Secker & Warburg, 1966.

Wace, Robert. *The Conquest of England*. Tr. by Sir Alexander Malet. London: Bell and Daldy, 1860.

Sturluson, Snorri. *Heimskringla—Sagas of the Norse Kings*. Tr. by Samuel Laing. New York: E. P. Dutton & Co., 1961.

Hollister, C. Warren. *Anglo-Saxon Military Institutions on the Eve of the Norman Conquest*. Oxford: Clarendon Press, 1962.

Oman, C. W. C. *Art of War in the Middle Ages*. Cornell, N.Y.: Cornell University Press, 1960.

*William of Malmesbury's Chronicle of the Kings of England*. Ed. J. A. Giles. London: Henry G. Bohn, 1847.

## WATERLOO

Lachouque, Henry. *The Anatomy of Glory, Napoleon and the Guard, A Study in Leadership*. Tr. by Anne S. K. Brown. Providence: Brown University Press, 1962.

Champagne, J., Kaulbach, Col. E., and Seymour, W. *Waterloo: Battle of the Three Armies*. Ed. Lord Chalfont. London: Sidwich & Jackson, 1979.

Chandler, D. G. *Waterloo: The Hundred Days*. London: Osprey Publishers Ltd., 1980.

Griess, T. E., ed. *The Wars of Napoleon*. Wayne, N.J.: Avery Publishing Group, 1985.

Sutherland, John. *Men of Waterloo*. Englewood, N.J.: Prentice-Hall, 1966.

Napoleon I. *A Selection from the Letters and Dispatches of the First Napoleon*. Ed. Capt. D.A. Bingham. London: Chapman and Hall, 1884.

Chandler, D. G. *The Campaigns of Napoleon*. New York: MacMillan Publishing Co., 1966.

Mercer, Capt. Cavalié. *Journal of the Waterloo Campaign*. London: Peter Davies, 1969.


## THE ALAMO

Lord, Walter. *A Time to Stand*. New York: Harper and Brothers, 1961.

Santos, Richard G. *Santa Anna's Campaign Against Texas, 1835–1836*. Salisbury, North Carolina: Texian Press, 1968.

Tinkle, Lon. *13 Days to Glory*. New York: McGraw-Hill, 1958.

De la Peña, Jose. *With Santa Anna in Texas: A Personal Narrative of the Revolution*. College Station, Texas: Texas A&M University Press, 1975.

Schoelwer, Susan P. *Alamo Images: Changing Perceptions of a Texas Experience*. Dallas: De Golyer Library and Southern Methodist University Press, 1985.


## THE LITTLE BIG HORN

Custer, Gen. George Armstrong. *My Life on the Plains*. Norman, Oklahoma: University of Oklahoma Press, 1978.

Godfrey, Lt. Edward S. *Diary of the Little Big Horn*. Portland: The Champoeg Press, 1957.

Hofling, Charles K. *Custer and the Little Big Horn: A Psychobiological Inquiry*. Detroit: Wayne State University, 1981.

Frost, Lawrence A. *The Custer Album*. New York: Bonanza Books, 1984.

Kinsley, D. A. *Favor the Bold: Custer, the Indian Fighter*. New York: Promontory Press, 1967.

Camp, Walter. *Custer in '76*. Ed. Kenneth Hammer. Provo, Utah: Brigham University Press, 1976.

Taunton, Francis B. "Sufficient Reason?" London: The English Westerners' Society, 1977.

## BERLIN: THE BUNKER

Trevor-Roper, Hugh R. *The Last Days of Hitler*. New York: The MacMillan Co., 1947.

Churchill, Winston S. *Triumph and Tragedy*. Cambridge, Mass.: Houghton Mifflin Co., 1953.

Keegan, John. *Waffen SS: The Asphalt Soldiers*. New York: Ballantine Books, 1978.

Irving, David. *Hitler's War*. New York: Viking Press, 1977.

Ryan, Cornelius. *The Last Battle*. New York: Popular Library, 1966.

Degrelle, Leon. *Campaign in Russia: The Waffen SS on the Eastern Front*. Torrance, California: Institute for Historical Review, 1985.

Guderian, Heinz. *Panzer Leader*. New York: Ballantine Books, 1980.

Patton, General George S. Jr. *War As I Knew It*. Boston: Houghton Mifflin Co., 1947.

Ambrose, Stephen E. *Eisenhower and Berlin, 1945*. New York: W. W. Norton, 1967.


## DIEN BIEN PHU

Fall, Bernard B. *Hell in a Very Small Place: The Siege of Dien Bien Phu*. New York: Da Capo Press, 1986.

Langlais, Gen. Pierre. *Dien Bien Phu*. Paris: France-Empire, 1963.

Roy, Col. Jules. *La Bataille de Dien Bien Phu*. Paris: Julliard, 1963. U.S. edition, New York: Harper & Row, 1964.

Giap, Gen. Vo Nguyen. *People's War, People's Army*. New York: Frederick A. Praeger, Inc., 1962.

Geraghty, Tony. *March or Die: A New History of the French Foreign Legion*. New York: Facts on File, 1987.

# INDEX